Your Official
America Online® Guide
to Personal Computing

D1419668

Your Official America Online® Guide to Personal Computing

Keith Underdahl

AOLPress®

Dulles, VA

Your Official America Online® Guide to Personal Computing

Published by

AOL Press

An imprint of IDG Books Worldwide, Inc.

An International Data Group Company

919 E. Hillsdale Blvd., Suite 300

Foster City, CA 94404

www.aol.com (America Online Web site)

Library of Congress Control Number: 00-110868

ISBN: 0-7645-0837-7

Printed in the United States of America

10 9 8 7 6 5 4 3 2 1

1B/SY/QS/QR/IN

Distributed in the United States by IDG Books Worldwide, Inc. and America Online, Inc.

For general information on IDG Books Worldwide's books in the U.S., please call our Consumer Customer Service department at 800-762-2974. For reseller information, including discounts and premium sales, please call our Reseller Customer Service department at 800-434-3422.

is a trademark
of America Online, Inc.

is a registered trademark or trademark under exclusive license to IDG Books Worldwide, Inc. from International Data Group, Inc. in the United States and/or other countries.

Welcome to AOL Press™

AOL Press books provide timely guides to getting the most out of your online life. AOL Press was formed as part of the AOL family to create a complete series of official references for using America Online as well as the entire Internet — all designed to help you enjoy a fun, easy, and rewarding online experience.

AOL Press is an exciting partnership between two companies at the forefront of the knowledge and communications revolution — AOL and IDG Books Worldwide, Inc. AOL is committed to quality, ease of use, and value, and IDG Books excels at helping people understand technology.

To meet these high standards, all our books are authored by experts with the full participation of and exhaustive review by AOL's own development, technical, managerial, and marketing staff. Together, AOL and IDG Books have implemented an ambitious publishing program to develop new publications that serve every aspect of your online life.

We hope you enjoy reading this AOL Press title and find it useful. We welcome your feedback at AOL Keyword: **Contact Shop Direct** so we can keep providing information the way you want it.

AOLPress®

About the Authors

Keith Underdahl is an electronic publishing specialist, programmer, network administrator, and graphic artist for Ages Software (which specializes in publishing classic Christian literature in electronic format). Keith's diverse experience makes him an expert, not only in graphic arts, but also in hardware configuration of Windows environments. He has authored or co-authored several books for IDGB, including *Windows Movie Maker For Dummies*, *Teach Yourself Microsoft Word 2000*, *Internet Bible*, and *Teach Yourself Microsoft Office 97*.

Brian Underdahl is the well-known, best selling author of over 50 computer books, including several current titles from IDG Books Worldwide: *Pocket PCs For Dummies*, *Opera Web Browser For Dummies*, *Windows 98 One Step at a Time*, *Internet Bible*, 2nd Edition, *Teach Yourself Office 2000*, *Teach Yourself Windows 2000 Professional*, and *Teach Yourself Windows Me*. Brian spends most of his time at the keyboard writing about personal computing. When he finds the time, he enjoys taking in the view from the home he and his wife Darlene built in the mountains 2,000 feet above Reno, NV. He tries to find the time to attend Mensa meetings whenever possible, and has become a fairly decent gourmet cook in recent years, too.

Credits

America Online

Technical Editors:
Joseph Coughlan
Sandra Jackson

Cover Design:
DKG Design, Inc.

IDG Books Worldwide

Senior Project Editor:
Nicole Haims

Acquisitions Editor:
Carol Sheehan

Senior Copy Editor:
Kim Darosett

Copy Editor:
Rebecca Huehls

Proof Editor:
Seth Kerney

Technical Editor:
Kathy Gill

Senior Permissions Editor:
Carmen Krikorian

Publishing Director:
Andrew Cummings

Editorial Manager:
Leah Cameron

Media Development Manager:
Laura Carpenter

Project Coordinator:
Dale White

Layout and Graphics:
LeAndra Johnson
Kristin Pickett
Brian Torwelle
Erin Zeltner

Proofreaders:
David Faust
Susan Moritz
Carl Pierce
Christine Pingleton
Marianne Santy

Indexer:
Maro Riofrancos

Author's Acknowledgments

First and foremost, I wish to thank my wife, Christa. She has tirelessly supported and encouraged me as I follow two careers, and I truly couldn't do this without her. My sons, Soren and Cole, have also been quite patient with me and always provide inspiration.

Speaking of family, I also wish to thank my father, Brian, for filling in on several chapters at the last minute, allowing me to help IDG Books with another project. Thanks, Dad.

Thanks also to my friend Kathy Gill for once again providing great input as technical editor. Her diverse experience has helped us ensure that this book will be helpful to anyone who is new to PCs.

And, of course, this book's success owes greatly to the hard-working editorial staff at IDG Books. Nicole Haims worked especially hard keeping the project focused and ensured that we met our goals for the book. Her input was invaluable. And of course, I also wish to thank Carol Sheehan for giving me the chance to write this book.

Dedication

To my friend and shipmate, Kevin Rux, and all of the men and women who perished aboard the USS Cole.

Contents at a Glance

Table of Contents

Introduction

Welcome to *Your Official America Online Guide to Personal Computing!* If you've just bought your first computer and want to put it to use quickly and easily, you've come to the right place. As the 21st century dawns, personal computers (PCs) have become an essential part of daily life. PCs aren't just for work anymore; you can use your PC for entertainment, to plan your day, or to communicate easily with other people using the Internet. This book helps you start off right by showing you the basics of using a PC, and then you find out how America Online connects you to the modern online world.

About This Book

Not so long ago, PCs were used almost exclusively by professionals and hobbyists who didn't mind spending months or even years learning how to program and use their computers. Today's PCs are much easier to use, and in just a few minutes, you can boot up your computer and go online.

Still, if this is your first computer, some parts of it can seem a little daunting. *Your Official America Online Guide to Personal Computing* introduces you to the basics of using a PC by covering everything from recognizing basic PC components to surfing the Web. Topics covered include

- ▶ Understanding PC components and terminology
- ▶ Using Microsoft Windows, the software that controls your PC
- ▶ Getting online with AOL and using its most popular features
- ▶ Finding and using other programs on your PC
- ▶ Maintaining your PC and basic troubleshooting
- ▶ Upgrading your PC to make it more powerful

With this book, you can learn PC basics in a way that is easy to understand. But even though this book concentrates on the basics, it does so by showing you how to perform specific tasks and giving you knowledge that you can put to use right away.

Who This Book Is For

If you have just bought your first PC, *Your Official America Online Guide to Personal Computing* is for you. Maybe you just spent hundreds or even thousands of dollars on a new PC, or maybe a friend or relative has given you an older PC. You have a PC, but you're not exactly sure how to use it or take care of it. You'd like to access the Internet, but you want your online experience to be safe and hassle free. Because you want an Internet service that is easy to use, you're interested in AOL.

This book also assumes that you have a PC running Microsoft Windows instead of a Macintosh. Specifically, this book assumes that you have Windows Me, which is also called Windows Millennium Edition. If a feature is available only in Windows Me or if a Windows Me feature is significantly different from earlier versions of Microsoft Windows, I indicate that in the book. If you have a Macintosh, check out *Macs For Dummies,* 7th Edition, by David Pogue, and published by IDG Books.

Who I Am

It was over 20 years ago when I put my hands on the keyboard of my first computer, a TRS-80 that my father bought at the local Radio Shack store. Back then, computers were not easy to figure out and use, and if I wanted to use a program, I pretty much had to create it myself. I read a few books, learned the ropes, and before long I was having my first "online" chat with a friend who lived across town and had an Apple IIe computer. In the years since, I've learned how to use four or five different kinds of computers, and each time I've felt like I was starting over from scratch.

Today I work as a product developer and technical support specialist for Ages Software (www.ageslibrary.com), a company that publishes classic Christian books on CD-ROM and DVD-ROM. I've also written or contributed to a few other books, including *Internet Bible, Teach Yourself Microsoft Word 2000,* and *Microsoft Windows Movie Maker For Dummies,* all from IDG Books Worldwide.

By the way, remember my father, the guy who bought that TRS-80 at Radio Shack? He has contributed to *Your Official America Online Guide to Personal Computing* as well. Brian Underdahl wrote several chapters and has authored over 50 computer books in his career.

How This Book Is Organized

This book is organized by providing the information you need first, first. You can read this book cover-to-cover if you like, but if you have specific questions about something like computer viruses or downloading software from AOL, you can jump to the information you need. The book is organized as follows:

▶ **Quick Start.** Start here to take a quick tour of your PC's features and see how your PC and AOL can help you throughout your day.

▶ **Part I: Understanding Computer Basics.** The chapters in this section describe the basic parts of a PC, and help you choose a new PC and connect to AOL.

▶ **Part II: Getting Around on Your PC.** Here you can find chapters that introduce you to the basics of using Microsoft Windows and AOL. You can also find out how to customize AOL to make it safer for your whole family to use.

▶ **Part III: Understanding PC Hardware.** Even if you never take apart your PC, understanding each component and what it does is important. You can also learn about working with extras like digital cameras, printers, and more.

▶ **Part IV: Finding and Using the Right PC Software.** A lot of cool programs are available for your PC. Here you can learn how to install and use a variety of programs and learn how to download software from AOL.

▶ **Part V: Maintaining and Enhancing Your PC.** Like any mechanical or electronic device, your PC needs some basic care to stay in top condition. The chapters in this part show you how to keep your PC running strong, how to protect against computer viruses, how to enhance the capabilities of your PC, and how to get PC help from AOL.

▶ **Part VI: Appendixes.** If you run across a PC term that you don't recognize, check the glossary in Appendix A. Appendix B helps you troubleshoot connection problems to AOL, and Appendix C helps you take inventory of your PC and recognize connectors and other components.

What AOL Provides

A lot of Internet services are happy to take your money and give you nothing more than a few cryptic instructions for connecting to the Internet. But AOL offers much more:

▶ Connecting to the Internet is fast and easy.

▶ Customer service and technical support are available for virtually all your PC-related questions.

▶ AOL Anywhere lets you access AOL services and features from a telephone, a cell phone, or any computer that has Internet access.

▶ A huge online community, which is available only through your AOL account, is easily accessible.

Throughout this book, you'll see how AOL makes your PC easier to use. Pointers on where to get more information online from AOL can help you — especially specific AOL keywords that you can visit to learn more or access a specific feature.

Conventions

Throughout this book, you'll find references to online information and features. Usually you'll see a specific AOL keyword. That keyword appears in boldface, like this: AOL Keyword: **Computing**. Just type the boldfaced word into AOL's keyword box and click Go.

Whenever I give you instructions that require you to type something on your PC, the text you need to type is in boldface. For example, instructions might look like this: To visit the AOL Anywhere Web site, type **www.aol.com**.

Sometimes you have to choose features from program menus. Most PC programs, including AOL, have a row of menus listed across the top of the screen. The first menu on the left is almost always called File. If I give you instructions to choose the Open item in the File menu, the command will look like this: Choose File⇨Open.

To make finding Web sites easier, I've removed all the extra stuff you don't need, such as the `http://`. Also, Web addresses appear in a slightly different font so that they stand out. The address for AOL Hometown looks like this: `hometown.aol.com`.

To make this book easier to navigate, I use several icons to point out useful information or resources:

I use the Tip icon to call your attention to shortcuts, useful resources, and smart ways to work.

Note icons point out pieces of information worthy of further mention.

When I have additional online resources that I think you'll want to use, I highlight them with this icon and include a specific AOL keyword.

Whenever I introduce a new term, I provide a definition with this icon.

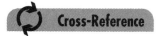 **Cross-Reference**

I use this icon to let you know what other sections in this book you can visit to find more information. Sometimes I might use this icon to let you know about other books you may want to check out.

 **Caution**

I use this icon to advise of something you *shouldn't* do or to help you prevent a potential problem with your PC.

 **Troubleshooting**

I created this icon especially for this book so that you can quickly apply information and better use your PC. Sometimes, I use this icon to let readers with an earlier version of Windows know that a tool may be unavailable or look different.

Quick Start

Why have personal computers (PCs) become so popular? They've been popular in the workplace for a while now, but their recent success in the home is due in large part to the Internet boom of the 1990s. Having access to the online world gives millions of people many great reasons to own a PC at home and at work. With America Online, you have access to the world's most powerful information network. And best of all, AOL is easy and quick to use.

Believe it or not, getting your computer to work for you isn't that difficult. The hardest part is getting used to the way things work. In this Quick Start, you find out just how easy your PC is to use and how it can help you get through your busy day. After you get your PC up and running, AOL can help you plan your day and get through it hassle-free. Then, when your day's over, AOL can help you enjoy the fun stuff the Internet has to offer, such as e-mail and instant messaging. AOL also helps you sift through and organize files, download software, get your digital pictures online, do research, and more.

Learning about Your PC

As you read this book, you'll discover that your PC isn't as complicated as you once thought. Operating systems like Microsoft Windows make your computer simple to use, and America Online makes being a part of the online world even easier.

If you're brand-new to computers and AOL, you don't need to be skeptical that your PC can simplify your life. Because software is so easy to use, the main thing you need is a good lay of the land. In the following sections, I give you the basics to get you up and running so that you can get the most out of your PC — and your AOL experience.

Getting to Know Your Hardware

PCs come in many shapes and sizes. Some are big and have many attached parts, whereas others (like laptops) are compact enough that you can fold them in half to fit in a briefcase. But some basic components are common to most PCs, as shown in Figure QS-1.

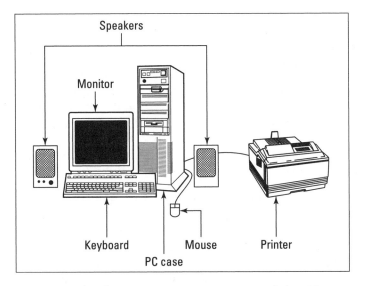

Figure QS-1. These basic components are common to many desktop PCs.

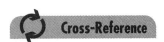 **Cross-Reference**

See the chapters in Part III of this book for more on PC hardware.

Each component serves an important purpose. The monitor displays what the PC is doing, and the speakers play sounds that some programs make. The keyboard lets you type words and numbers, and the mouse lets you move a pointer around on the monitor screen so that the PC is easier to use. The PC case is the brains of the operation (so to speak), and peripheral components make your PC more useful.

Most PCs come with pretty clear instructions on how to connect everything and get started. Each component plugs into a corresponding connector on the back of the PC case. Here are a few more things you should keep in mind when you hook up your PC:

▶ Connect all the components before you plug in your PC to an electrical outlet and turn it on.

▶ Buy a surge protector to plug your PC into. These are available at electronics stores, and they safeguard your PC against electrical damage caused by lightning strikes and other power surges in your power line.

▶ Place your PC in an area that does not experience extreme hot or cold temperatures. Also avoid setting the PC in direct sunlight.

Starting Your PC

After you connect all the components of your PC, you're ready to turn it on and get started. Simply turn on the power switch. Windows takes between 30 seconds and two minutes to fully load. If you see a screen that asks for a password, just click OK. After Windows loads, you see a screen called the Windows desktop with various program icons. Double-click a program icon to open it.

Before you turn on the power to your PC, make sure that the monitor and other components are plugged in and turned on.

Turning Off Your PC

Turning off your PC involves more than just turning off the power switch. Windows must be shut down properly, or your programs could be damaged. To shut down Windows, follow these steps:

1. Click the Start button in the lower-left corner of the screen. The Windows Start menu appears.

2. Choose Shut Down from the menu. A dialog box similar to Figure QS-2 appears.

The dialog box shown in Figure QS-2 is from Windows Me. If you have a different version of Windows, your Shut Down Windows dialog box may differ slightly.

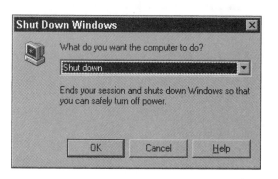

Figure QS-2. To turn off your PC, choose Shut Down from the Start menu and use this dialog box to shut down Windows.

3. If you want to shut down Windows, make sure that Shut Down is selected. If you want Windows to shut down and then immediately restart, choose Restart from the drop-down list.

4. Click OK. If you chose to shut down the computer, wait until you see a screen that says It is now safe to turn off your computer before you turn the power switch off.

Using My Computer

Your PC stores information on disk drives. Your PC has a *hard drive* — a large disk drive permanently installed inside the case — and, most likely, drives that use removable disks. The two most common types of removable disk drives are floppy disks and CD-ROMs (compact disc-read only memory), which look exactly like music CDs.

Cross-Reference

See Chapter 4 for more on exploring your PC with My Computer.

My Computer is a great tool for looking at your PC's disk drives. Start up Windows and double-click the My Computer icon that you see on the Windows desktop, which is the main screen that you see before you open any software. You then see a window that looks similar to Figure QS-3.

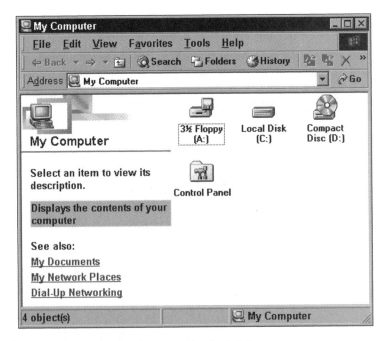

Figure QS-3. My Computer lets you explore the disk drives on your computer.

To close the My Computer window, click the Close (X) button in the upper-right corner of the window.

Letting Your PC Simplify Your Day

After you know how to maneuver around your PC, open and close files, and run programs, you're ready to let AOL and your PC help you throughout the day. You won't believe all the things your PC can do for you.

Checking the News and Weather Before You Go to Work

When your PC becomes a part of your daily routine, you'll discover that you use it do things you've always used "real-world" tools to do. For example, checking the morning's news and weather no longer necessitates you running out to the curb to pick up the paper or paying for a copy at the newsstand. Just fire up your PC first thing in the morning, and you'll see a list of the morning's headlines right on the Welcome Screen when you first launch and log on to AOL. Along the top of the Welcome Screen, you should see a clickable weather link that leads you to the current weather conditions and temperature. Click the link for a more detailed weather report, as shown in Figure QS-4.

Find It Online

If you don't see a weather icon on the Welcome Screen, just visit AOL Keyword: **Weather** and look for the link to local weather.

Note

If you don't see your local weather, you may need to type in the name of your city on the weather page.

Figure QS-4. AOL Weather gives you up-to-the-minute local forecasts.

Downloading Files When You're Away

Your PC can help you even when you're not at home. Computers were designed to automate many tasks, and that means you can have them do many things for you automatically, including downloading big files that you don't have time to download when you're home.

Cross-Reference

See Chapter 17 to find out everything you ever wanted to know about downloading software.

AOL has a lot of cool software online that you can download to your own PC, but many of these downloads can take a long time. Besides that, they hog up your online connection, making it difficult to send messages or browse AOL channels at the same time. Thus, it makes sense to do large downloads when you're not actually using your PC. AOL's Download Center makes this process easy. Choose software that you want to schedule for automatic download. To do so, choose AOL Services⊅Download Center (AOL Keyword: **Download Center**), identify the file you want to download, and then click the Download Later button. The Download Manager, shown in Figure QS-5, appears.

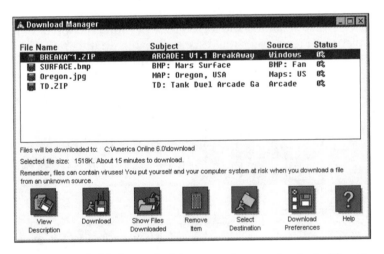

Figure QS-5. Schedule the Download Center to perform your downloads while you're away.

Caution

Because downloadable files may contain viruses, be sure to use antivirus software on your PC (see Chapter 20).

Schedule Automatic AOL sessions to download files for when you're away from your PC. You can set up and run Automatic AOL sessions by choosing Mail⊅Automatic AOL.

What About High-Speed Access?

If your PC is like most, it connects to AOL by using a standard dial-up modem connected to your telephone line. Have you noticed that software downloads take a long time? If so, you may want to consider getting high-speed access to AOL.

AOL PLUS is AOL's high-speed service. AOL PLUS provides you with a special type of high-speed modem that allows you to access AOL up to nine times faster than your current connection. Downloads happen quicker, Web pages and AOL Channels load faster, and you can watch high-quality video online. To find out more about AOL PLUS, visit AOL Keyword: **AOL PLUS**.

When You Return Home

Your day isn't over when you get home from work. Whether you want to spend your evening catching up with friends, watching TV, or getting some homework done, AOL and your computer can help.

Checking Messages

Probably one of the first things you'll want to do when you get home is check your e-mail messages and have information about the topics that interest you delivered directly to your PC. Depending on which AOL tools you use to communicate with friends, family, and coworkers, you may want to check the following:

▶ **Mail:** E-mail may be waiting for you in your Online Mailbox, shown in Figure QS-6.

▶ **Newsgroups:** Newsgroups are online discussion forums where you can read messages on a topic or post your own. If you participate in any newsgroups, you'll want to check out new postings.

▶ **Buddy List:** Your Buddy List tells you when your friends or family are online so that you can send them quick messages or chat. Check your Buddy List to see whether anyone is online.

Cross-Reference

Find out more about reading and sending e-mail in Chapter 8.

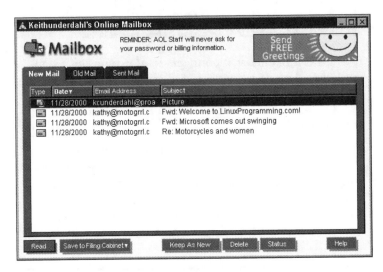

Figure QS-6. Check e-mail in your Online Mailbox.

Cross-Reference

Confused about AOL key-
words? See Chapter 8 for
details.

Looking Up Recipes for Dinner

Coming up with new dinner ideas every night isn't easy. Why
not let AOL help? Visit AOL's House & Home Channel (AOL
Keyword: **Food**), shown in Figure QS-7. Here you can search
for specific recipes for dinners, snacks, desserts, and more. You
can also browse recipes by ethnicity, or check out some quick
and healthy meals. Just click one of the links you see here to
find your next culinary delight!

Figure QS-7. Find a recipe for dinner online.

Browsing TV Listings

Sometimes, after a really long day, the best way to unwind is to sit down in your favorite chair and watch some television. What's on? You don't need to dig out the TV listing from last Sunday's newspaper because you can quickly check the day's broadcast schedule online! AOL Keyword: **Television** (see Figure QS-8) offers a searchable list of programming for the most popular broadcast and cable channels.

Find It Online

AOLTV lets you access AOL right from your television. You can read e-mail, shop online, or chat with buddies all while watching TV. Visit AOL Keyword: **AOLTV** to learn more.

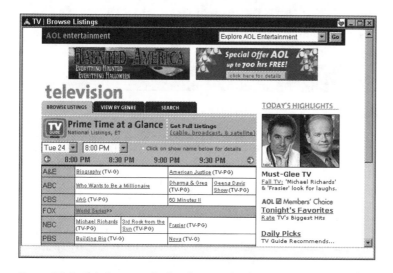

Figure QS-8. Click the name of a show for more details.

Having Fun and Chatting with Buddies Online

Using your PC doesn't always have to be work. It can also be a great way to have fun or keep in touch with friends and family. Some AOL keywords and channels you may find entertaining include

- ▶ AOL Keyword: **People Connection** — This keyword is your doorway into hundreds of chat rooms at AOL. People Connection, shown in Figure QS-9, offers chats on a wide variety of topics.

- ▶ AOL Keyword: **Games** — Here you can play a number of different games online, including sports games, casino games, card games, arcade games, and more. You can also access this area by visiting the Games Channel.

Figure QS-9. Connect with online buddies at People Connection.

▶ AOL Keyword: **Music** — Want to keep up with your favorite bands? Visit AOL Music (or click the Music Channel) to find music news and reviews, listen to online radio stations, or find great deals on CDs and MP3 music.

▶ AOL Keyword: **Sports** — AOL Sports (also accessible as the Sports Channel) is a great destination for any sports fan, with up-to-the-minute coverage, interviews, and more on all your favorite teams and athletes.

Researching and Doing Homework

Even if you're not using your PC for work or school, you can find a wealth of information about the topics that interest you. The Internet has been described as the world's largest library, and you don't have to browse too long before you see why. AOL is ready to help you research just about any subject you can imagine; AOL Search is a feature that's sure to be useful when you're researching that big report, planning a trip, researching your family history, looking for a gift, or just messing around.

To begin any type of online research, visit AOL Keyword: **Research**. AOL Research & Learn, shown in Figure QS-10, provides instant access to almanacs, online encyclopedias, maps and geographic profiles, and schooling information.

Cross-Reference

If you'd like to learn more about searching for information online, see Chapter 8.

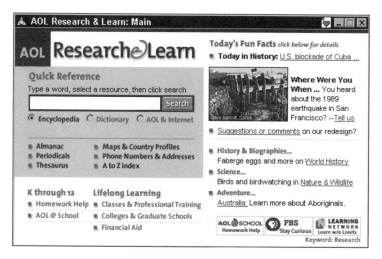

Figure QS-10. Research any topic online with AOL Research & Learn.

Summary

Your PC will soon become one of the most important tools in your life — if it isn't already. Not only can you use it to type reports and memos, but you can also use it gather information online about news, weather, and just about any other subject you can imagine. The PC can also help you manage your busy day by maintaining your personal schedule and automating various tasks. And don't forget that you can use your PC to have fun and keep in touch with contacts, friends, and family. In the chapters ahead, you delve deeper into your PC, finding out how the computer and AOL work and how to put them to work for you.

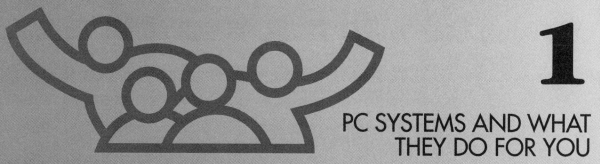

Quick Look

Chapter 1

PC Systems and What They Do for You

Not so long ago, computers were the stuff of science fiction — they helped movie heroes fly spaceships and search for intelligent life. But today computers are an important part of intelligent life here on this planet. Millions of people just like you use computers (and an Internet connection) to write letters, organize recipes, play games, check the weather, and chat with friends.

Maybe you've just bought and unpacked that shiny new computer sitting in front of you. But how does it *work?* By the end of this chapter, you'll have a better understanding of just exactly what it is you've bought and how you can put it to work for you.

Looking at a Basic Computer System

Your computer is made up of *hardware* and *software*. The *hardware* is made up of the physical components of the computer, such as the keyboard, monitor screen, disk drives, printer, and mouse. To be of any use to you, your PC's hardware must be programmed using a language of codes that only a computer can understand. These programs are the *software* of your computer.

You don't need to be a programmer to use a PC. Companies like Microsoft and America Online have programmers who create programs that are easy for you to use. All you have to do is start and use those programs, which is something you'll learn to do throughout this book.

Definition

A computer that runs Microsoft Windows is usually referred to as a **PC,** or **personal computer.** An Apple Macintosh is another type of personal computer, but in industry jargon it's usually referred to as a **Mac.**

An Overview of System Components

Your computer is actually a collection of systems and components that all work together. In some cases, a component's function is clear; for example, you probably already know what the monitor and keyboard do. Other components, like the CPU (or *central processing unit,* the computer's brain) and operating system (software that runs your PC), aren't so obvious.

Find It Online

If you ever hear a computer-related term that you don't understand, visit AOL's online dictionary at AOL Keyword: **Get Help Now**.

Your Computer Hardware

Whether you have a laptop PC or a desktop PC with a box that the monitor, keyboard, and mouse plug into, the most important components are inside where you can't see them. Your PC contains the following key components:

▶ **CPU:** The *central processing unit* is the main computer chip that runs your computer. The CPU is kind of like the PC's brain.

▶ **Memory:** Also called RAM, which stands for *random access memory,* memory provides working space for the CPU.

▶ **Hard drive:** Different from memory, your hard drive provides storage space for files and programs, including Windows and AOL.

Cross-Reference

For a more detailed description of your PC's components, see Chapter 9.

▶ **Removable disk drives:** Floppy and CD-ROM drives give you additional storage and make installing new programs easy. Although these drives are called removable disk drives, usually only the actual disk can be removed.

▶ **Modem:** Your modem connects you to the America Online service and the Internet. Most (but not all) modems are inside the main PC case.

Peripheral Hardware

All the components that plug into your computer are considered *peripherals*. Peripherals are devices that your computer runs but that are separate from the main case. Common peripherals include:

▶ **Monitor:** The monitor lets you see what is happening on your computer. If you have a laptop PC, the monitor is permanently attached to the case.

▶ **Keyboard and mouse:** These essential items let you control the PC and provide input. As with the monitor, a keyboard and a mouse (or some other kind of point-and-click device) are usually part of the case if you have a laptop.

▶ **Printer:** With a printer, you can print letters, e-mail messages, reports, pictures, and anything else you want — including information you see online and files you download from the Internet. You usually have to purchase printers separately, but they are pretty essential, even in our so-called paperless society.

▶ **Speakers:** Most PCs come with speakers that allow you to listen to music on your PC and hear other sounds. On a laptop, the speakers are usually built-in.

▶ **Other accessories:** New digital technology allows you to hook an accessory such as a digital camera, camcorder, or scanner to your computer so that you can share pictures with others online.

The Operating System and Interface Software

The *operating system* (or OS) is a software package that takes care of all the basic running functions of your PC. Think of the operating system as the manager of your computer. The most

Cross-Reference

Your PC has many different types of connectors for peripherals. See Appendix C for help on recognizing those connectors.

Cross-Reference

Chapter 12 gives you the scoop on cameras and scanners.

popular OS — and the one you probably have — is *Microsoft Windows.* Microsoft Windows was first introduced in 1985 and has come to dominate the PC world.

An important function of a modern operating system is to make your PC easy to use. Windows incorporates a *graphical user interface.* (The acronym, GUI, is pronounced like the word *gooey.*) A GUI allows you to access all the resources on your computer by pointing at and clicking icons, pictures, menus, and other graphical elements with the mouse. Not so long ago, using a PC meant that you had to memorize a bunch of cryptic commands that had to be typed on a bleak screen like the screen shown in Figure 1-1. Compare this to Microsoft Windows, shown in Figure 1-2, and you can see how the GUI truly does make the PC easier to use.

Find It Online

Other popular operating systems include the Macintosh OS and Linux. You can learn more about Linux from the Linux Journal at AOL Keyword: **Linux** (www. linuxjournal.com) and get Macintosh information at AOL Keyword: **Apple**.

Figure 1-1. Not long ago, using a computer meant typing confusing commands on a screen like this.

Application Software

If you want to do something with your computer, such as type a report, do online research for your homework, or just play a game, you have to launch an *application*, or *program*. An application is a kind of software designed to perform a specific function, and many useful applications are already on your computer right now. You may have to install additional application software, just as you installed the AOL software.

Cross-Reference

For a more complete overview of programs that come with Windows, see Chapter 15.

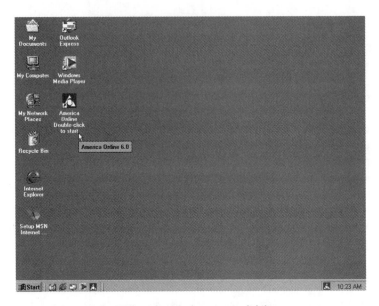

Figure 1-2. In Windows, all you have to do is point and click.

Troubleshooting

Movie Maker is the only application that isn't available to Windows 95 and 98 users.

When you buy a new PC, the Microsoft Windows operating system, which includes many useful applications, is usually already installed. Some applications that come with Windows Me include the following:

▶ **WordPad:** A simple word processor for typing letters and memos

▶ **Paint:** A graphics program for the artist in you

▶ **Movie Maker:** Create your own movies with this program

▶ **ScanDisk:** A utility that checks for errors on your disk drives

AOL and the Online Connection

When you connect to the AOL service, you're connecting to the largest network of computers in the world. The modem in your computer uses your phone or cable TV line to transfer data to and from AOL. Every time you visit an AOL Keyword, check the weather online (in Figure 1-3, I'm checking out the national weather forecast), or chat with an AOL buddy, you're actually connecting to AOL's computers.

Figure 1-3. This weather information was downloaded from AOL using the online connection.

America Online gives you access to much more than just AOL's resources. You can also access the World Wide Web, a global network of which AOL is a part. Whenever you see a Web address, you can use AOL's browser to visit it. For example, you can visit NASA's Web site (www.nasa.gov), shown in Figure 1-4, with the AOL browser.

Find It Online

For more information about parts of the Internet that you can visit, click the Exploring the Internet link at AOL Keyword: **AOL Help**.

Figure 1-4. You can use AOL to access the Internet, including NASA's Web site.

Matching a PC with Your Needs

Cross-Reference

See Chapter 2 for more on choosing a PC that matches your own needs.

Like your telephone, car, and microwave oven, your PC is a tool designed to make your life easier. But this tool is only useful if it meets the needs of your lifestyle and the requirements of your budget. When you choose a PC, you need to ask yourself several important questions:

▶ **How much can you afford?** Computers can range in price from many thousands of dollars to almost free. You probably want the best deal you can find, but you need to make sure that you buy something that meets your needs.

▶ **What do you plan to use it for?** If all you want to do is communicate with online friends and type a few letters, then you don't need a very expensive system. But if you want to take advantage of the new technology by editing home movies, playing games with complex graphics, or setting up a home network, then you need a more powerful PC.

▶ **How much space do you have?** Computer cases come in many shapes and sizes, so you should choose one that fits your life. If you want to take your PC with you when you're on the go, you may want to consider a laptop.

Using Your PC to Communicate

Find It Online

Want to build your own home page? It's easy! Visit AOL Hometown at AOL Keyword: **Hometown** to learn how. Your Internet friends can access Hometown at hometown.aol.com.

Your PC can do many things, but perhaps its most important function in modern life is as a communication tool. You can exchange e-mail with friends and coworkers, keep track of friends online with the Buddy List, chat online with people who share your hobbies and interests, and share pictures with "You've Got Pictures." In addition, you can create your own home page at AOL Hometown to share photos, news, gossip, and more with family and friends.

America Online has many communication tools built right in. Figure 1-5 shows the Buddy List, a tool that lets you see when your buddies are online and allows you to quickly send them messages or chat.

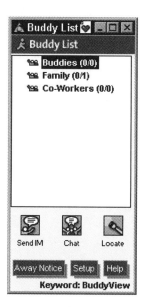

Figure 1-5. The Buddy List keeps you in touch with your online friends and family.

Taking Care of Your PC

Just like most of the machines you use, your PC needs regular care and maintenance. It is an expensive piece of technology, and you should do some important things to keep it in tip-top working condition. Thankfully, Microsoft Windows and AOL make PC maintenance easy. Here are some simple things you can do:

▶ Optimize your disk drives for best performance.

▶ Perform regular virus scans.

▶ Clean the keyboard and mouse.

▶ Keep your printer full of ink and clean the print heads.

▶ Periodically update Windows, AOL, and your other software.

Summary

American Online and your PC can be useful tools for enhancing your daily life. You can use them to communicate, get work

Cross-Reference

Learn more about using the Buddy List and other AOL services to communicate in Chapter 8.

Cross-Reference

PC maintenance is covered in greater detail in Chapter 18. You can learn more about virus protection in Chapter 20.

1

PC Systems and What They Do for You

done, research homework, or just have some fun. But first you need a basic understanding of PC systems. You should know what all the hardware does (which includes your printer and disk drives) and understand the different types of software on your PC. With a basic understanding of your PC's hardware and software, you're ready to set up your dream system and explore the online world.

Quick Look

Chapter 2

Setting Up Your
Dream System

IN THIS CHAPTER

Pricing and purchasing the perfect PC

Making your PC more useful with a printer, a digital camera, or a handheld computer

Installing and using the software that comes with your new PC

E ven if you already have a PC, you may be thinking about buying a new one. This is especially true if your current PC is an older model that a friend or relative gave you. A visit to the computer department at your local electronics superstore can be a little daunting. With so many different PCs available, how do you know which one is right for you? Which features are most important to you? Do you really need a $2,000 mega-system, or will a more affordable unit suit your needs? You may be wondering if some cut-rate deals are too good to be true or have questions about peripherals and software. This chapter helps you find and use the PC that is just right for you.

Planning the Perfect PC

Choosing the best PC is no small matter. You can expect to pay hundreds or even thousands of dollars to get a computer that fits your life, so a bit of planning will help you get the one that's right for you. But first, you need to know what you're looking at when you go shopping. You'll want to find the best deal, and decide which kind of computer best meets your needs.

Reading Specifications Charts

Every new PC — whether Compaq, Dell, Gateway, Hewlett-Packard, or another manufacturer makes the PC — has a chart listing its *specifications* (or *specs*), or everything that comes with the computer. Specification charts can seem intimidating if you're new to PCs, but the charts contain important information that you need to check before you decide to buy a computer. You certainly wouldn't ignore the list of features that come with a new car. The specs tell you whether a computer is fast enough and powerful enough to suit your needs, and whether it has the kinds of features you want. Some basic specs are common to all charts:

▶ **CPU:** The *central processing unit* is the brain of your PC. Its speed is measured in megahertz (MHz) or gigahertz (GHz, 1 GHz = 1,000 MHz). Faster is better, but speed also costs more money.

▶ **RAM:** Lots of *random access memory* helps your PC run efficiently and lets you use more programs at once. Video editing programs and some games require at least 128MB (megabytes) of RAM, but 64MB is sufficient for most other uses.

▶ **HDD:** The *hard disk drive* is where your programs and files are stored. The size of a hard drive is measured in GB (gigabytes). You need at least a 10GB hard drive, and note that bigger is better.

▶ **Video:** You may see lots of different brand names and terms used to describe the video capabilities of a PC. Most PCs come with a *video card* (the component that generates the video image displayed on the monitor) that has at least 8MB of RAM. If you play a lot of graphics-rich games or watch DVD movies, you'll want 16MB of RAM or more.

Find It Online

To get help on using AOL with a Macintosh, visit AOL Keyword: **Mac Community**.

Find It Online

Unsure about a term you see on a spec chart? Visit AOL Keyword: **Get Help Now** and search for it using the online dictionary.

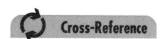

Cross-Reference

For more information on what each component of a PC does, see Chapter 9.

Choosing a PC or a Macintosh

One of the most important choices you will make when buying a new computer is whether to get a PC that runs Windows or a Macintosh (Mac for short). Although only Apple Computer (AOL Keyword: **Apple**) makes Macs, literally hundreds of companies are building and selling Windows PCs. Macs use different software than Windows PCs, even though you can usually share pictures, word processing documents, and many other files between the two.

The differences between Macs and PCs are not as great as some people might tell you. Both are easy to use, both are reasonably reliable, and both can access AOL. Macs tend to be a bit more expensive than PCs, but they often come with nice features like built-in FireWire ports (great for editing video), DVD players, and a more attractive design.

If you decide to switch to a Macintosh, you can keep your AOL account and access the same great online features. And installing AOL on a Mac is easy, because your AOL installation CD has Mac software on it.

> ▶ **Modem:** The modem is the component that connects your PC to AOL. The differences among the modems included with new PCs are minimal, so don't worry about the type of modem listed. You just make sure a modem is included with the PC.

> ▶ **Drives:** All PCs come with at least a CD-ROM drive and a 3½-inch floppy drive. The speed of a CD-ROM drive is measured as a multiple of how fast the first CD-ROM drives operated. Most PCs have at least a 30x CD-ROM drive. (30x means that the drive works 30 times faster than an older 1x drive.) Faster drives are nice because they help programs load quicker. Some computers come with handy CD recorders (CD-R or CD-RW drives), and many now come with DVD-ROM drives. DVD-ROM drives let you watch DVD movies on your PC.

Table 2-1 shows sample spec charts for two new PCs.

Table 2-1. *Sample PC Spec Charts*

Spec	PC Number 1	PC Number 2	Explanation
CPU	Intel Pentium III 900 MHz	AMD Athlon 900 MHz	Intel and AMD are two popular CPU manufacturers. A Pentium III-900 and an Athlon-900 are roughly the same speed.
RAM	64MB SDRAM	128MB PC133 SDRAM	PC Number 2 has more RAM, making it better for video editing, graphics-rich games, and other memory-sapping programs. SDRAM is a newer, faster type of RAM, and PC133 SDRAM works even faster.
HDD	16GB	40GB	PC Number 2 has a bigger hard drive, although 16GB provides plenty of storage space for most needs.
Video	8MB AGP	32MB AGP	PC Number 2 provides better video quality for advanced games and watching movies on your PC. PC Number 1's video capabilities are more than adequate for using AOL and most other programs.
Modem	56k V.90 modem	56k modem	These modems offer the same performance. V.90 is a standard that all modern modems now meet, so some times manufacturers leave *V.90* out of the spec chart.
Monitor	17 inches	19 inches	Monitor screens are measured diagonally, just like televisions. Bigger monitors are really nice, but they also add a lot to the PC's price.
Drives	40x CD-ROM, 8x CD-RW	12x DVD-ROM	PC Number 2 will let you watch DVD movies on your PC and use DVD-ROM software CDs (of which there are still few). You may find the CD-RW *(Compact Disc-Recordable/Rewritable)* drive of PC Number 1 handier because you can use a CD-RW to record (or *burn*) music to blank CDs.
Price	$799	$1,399	Overall, PC Number 2 is more powerful, and that power is reflected in the price. You may be able to save $100 or more on PC Number 2 by substituting a 17-inch monitor.

Both PCs in Table 2-1 have more than enough power to access AOL and use programs like word processors and picture editors. The added expense of PC Number 2 is probably worthwhile only if you want to use your computer to play graphics-rich games, watch DVD movies, or edit videos that you've filmed with a digital camcorder.

 Cross-Reference

There's more to choosing a monitor than just the size. See Chapter 10 for more on selecting a good monitor.

Choosing Systems for Home and Travel

Another choice you have to make when buying a new PC is whether to get a desktop PC that stays in your home or office or a laptop PC that you can take with you when you are on the go. If you're buying a second PC and plan to keep the desktop PC you already have, a laptop makes a lot of sense. Laptops have distinct advantages:

> ▶ **Portability:** Laptops are easy to take with you when you travel.

> ▶ **Communications:** Staying in touch with friends, family, coworkers, and associates via e-mail is easy because you can connect to AOL using almost any phone line.

> ▶ **Convenience:** Battery power lets you work even when an electric socket isn't available. This level of convenience means you can use your PC to work and play virtually anytime, anywhere.

> ▶ **Size:** A laptop takes up very little space in your home or office.

Not surprisingly, laptops also have a few disadvantages:

> ▶ **Value:** Laptops are more expensive and usually offer lower performance than desktop PCs. Upgrading a laptop is also usually expensive, and sometimes upgrading isn't even possible.

> ▶ **Reliability:** Laptops tend to get banged around a bit as they are moved, making them prone to failure.

> ▶ **Size:** Laptops have smaller keyboards and monitors, which may make them less comfortable to use than desktop PCs.

A laptop offers a great deal of flexibility, especially if you're looking for a PC that you can take with you when you're on the go. But it offers some disadvantages as well, especially if it will be your only computer.

Caution

Keep in mind that a laptop is a lot easier to steal than a desktop PC, too.

Find It Online

You can always find a good deal or two online by shopping for a PC with Shop@AOL (AOL Keyword: **Computer Shop**).

Finding the Best Deal

Everyone likes a bargain. If you shop around online at a site such as Shop@AOL (shown in Figure 2-1), you're almost sure to find some great deals, but you may prefer to buy your computer at a local store. Each method of shopping has advantages and disadvantages.

Figure 2-1. Shop@AOL links you to a variety of reliable online retailers.

Here are the main pros and cons of purchasing a PC online:

▶ **Pros:** Prices are often cheaper, you can usually avoid sales tax, and you'll probably find a better selection than if you shopped in a real-world retail store. You can take advantage of the customer service department of the online vendor, ask questions, and compare prices in the privacy of your own home. Browsing different retailers is as easy as a few mouse clicks. You may even find an online distributor willing to ship the PC to you for free. Some good places to start looking for PCs online include the computers department at Shop@AOL and CNET.com (`www.cnet.com`). CNET.com helps you directly compare online retailers' prices, and you can read CNET.com's customer feedback to see whether or not other people have had positive experiences with a specific retailer.

▶ **Cons:** Online retailers that advertise really low purchase prices often charge much more for shipping and handling. If you have a problem with a PC that you've bought online, you can't return it as easily. Some unscrupulous retailers may illegally charge your credit card without actually shipping the product. To avoid being defrauded, buy from a reliable retailer such as one of the stores listed on Shop@AOL.

Find It Online

Some retailers offer a free year of service with America Online when you buy a PC. One such retailer is Dell (AOL Keyword: **Dell**).

2

Setting Up Your Dream System

Tip

You can find out about AOL's Certified Merchants program and total satisfaction guarantee when you use AOL Keyword: **Shopping**. Click the Customer Service link at the top of the main Shopping Channel window.

What About Rebates?

Many retailers offer huge rebates on new computers. Sometimes the rebate is so big that the PC appears to be free! But read the fine print on any big discount. Usually, you need to sign a three- or four-year contract with another Internet service before you can receive the rebate.

If you cancel the service at any time during the contract period, you must repay the rebate. Because you already have service with AOL, you're better off paying the regular price for a new computer rather than taking a rebate that will cost you more in the long term.

Even if you prefer to buy from a local real-world store, online shopping sites can be a great place to do research. The pros and cons of purchasing a PC at a local retailer include the following:

▶ **Pros:** If you have a problem, you can easily return to the store and get a refund or a replacement PC. You can also obtain customer support, advice on installation, and all the other good stuff that comes with a real-life transaction. And of course, you don't have to pay shipping charges.

▶ **Cons:** Even though you don't pay shipping charges, you probably have to pay sales tax, and the selection is often limited to what you see in the store. Prices are usually higher than the prices that online stores offer. Also, when you shop online, you can browse for as long as you like, but in a retail store, you may feel pressured to make a decision before you're ready.

Choosing the Right Peripherals

Cross-Reference

To use a peripheral, it must be attached to a proper connector on your PC. See Appendix C to identify connector types on your computer.

A basic PC (monitor, keyboard, mouse, and computer case) is all you need to access the online world of AOL. But if you want to do more with your PC, like printing reports or sharing your pictures online, you'll need to buy some extra components called peripherals. *Peripherals* are devices — such as printers and digital cameras — that attach to your PC and make it more useful. In this section, we'll look at some of the most popular peripherals for your PC.

Choosing a Printer

A printer is probably the single most important peripheral you can own. You'll frequently use it to print out things from AOL such as Web pages, recipes, e-mail, and your calendar, and you will need a printer to print other documents such as letters and reports. If you have a color printer and special photo paper, you can even print pictures with a quality that approaches print photos.

The most common types of printers available today are

> ▶ **Inkjet:** These printers are common and affordable. Many inkjets print in color.
> ▶ **Laser:** These printers offer higher print quality than inkjets but tend to be more expensive.

When choosing a printer, keep two points in mind:

> ▶ Make sure that replacement ink or toner cartridges are available and affordable. You will run out of ink fast (especially if you print a lot of graphics), and cartridges can be very expensive to replace.
> ▶ Make sure the printer's connector is compatible with your PC (see Appendix C). Most printers can use a parallel port, a USB port, or a FireWire (IEEE-1394) port.

Selecting a Digital Camera

Digital cameras don't need film, and they make sharing pictures online easy. But which camera is right for you? What level of quality do you need, and what type of PC connection is best?

First consider resolution, which is measured in pixels. Higher resolution delivers better picture quality. The digital cameras with the lowest resolution shoot pictures at 640 x 480 pixels. Higher resolution cameras can have millions of pixels in a picture. Table 2-2 helps you determine how much resolution you need.

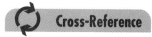

See Chapter 13 for more on choosing and working with a printer.

Definition

Inkjet printers use replaceable ink cartridges, while laser printers use replaceable toner cartridges. The difference is that laser printers actually imprint text onto the paper — the toner makes the imprint visible.

Want to share pictures online? See Chapter 8.

One million pixels equal a *megapixel*. Most digital cameras measure picture quality in megapixels.

Table 2-2. Digital Camera Resolutions

Camera Resolution	Recommended Uses
640 x 480 (307,200 pixels) through 1024 x 768 (786,432 pixels)	Sharing pictures online
1 megapixel	Sharing pictures online, printing small- to medium-sized pictures (up to 5 x 7 inches); in most cases, the picture quality is easily as good as with your standard film camera
2 megapixel	Larger printed pictures (8 x 10 inches or more)
3+ megapixel	Professional-quality pictures

Keep in mind that higher resolution pictures have much larger file sizes. This means that the pictures take up more space on your hard drive and are more difficult to share online. You'll probably have to shrink high-resolution pictures before you e-mail them to friends and family, so don't bother with an expensive, high-resolution camera unless you plan to print a lot of the pictures.

Check to see how a camera connects to your PC. This is how you get pictures from the camera into your computer. Some cameras, such as Sony Mavicas, store pictures on floppy disks. To get the pictures in your PC, all you have to do is remove the disk from the camera and place it in the PC's floppy drive. But most cameras connect directly to your computer using a cable. Common cable types that digital cameras use include the following:

▶ **USB:** This is the most desirable type because pictures transfer fast and setting up the camera is easy. Most modern PCs have USB ports.

▶ **FireWire (IEEE-1394):** Cameras that use a FireWire port are also easy to configure, and the pictures transfer even faster than with USB. However, most PCs don't have built-in FireWire ports.

▶ **Serial:** All PCs have a serial port, but chances are your mouse is already using your serial port. Serial cameras

Cross-Reference

If you're interested in sharing pictures with family and friends, *Your Official America Online Guide to Pictures Online* by David Peal (IDG Books Worldwide, Inc.) is available exclusively to AOL members. At AOL Keyword: **AOL Store**, click the Interactive Learning tab and then click the AOL Press link to find the full line of AOL Press titles.

can be difficult to configure, and serial ports are a lot
slower than USB and FireWire ports.

Using a Handheld Computer with Your PC

Computers keep getting smaller and smaller, so it was only a
matter of time before companies started offering computers
that fit in the palm of your hand. These small devices can help
you keep track of your personal schedule, take notes, check
e-mail using "AOL Anywhere"ˢᴹ, and more.

Cross-Reference

For more information on
using a handheld computer
with your PC, see
Chapter 13.

Basically, you can choose between two different kinds of hand-
held computers: Palmtops (Palms for short) and Pocket PCs.
Palms run using software called *Palm OS* developed by Palm.
Pocket PCs run a scaled-down version of Windows called
Windows CE. Palms tend to be less expensive than Pocket
PCs, but Pocket PCs usually have more capabilities than Palms.
For instance, most Pocket PCs can also be used to play MP3
music through headphones, and a lens attachment can turn
one into a digital camera!

Find It Online

A great source of information on handheld computers
can be found at AOL
Keyword: **PDA**.

Handheld computers usually come with a cradle that allows
them to synchronize with your desktop PC. The cradle plugs
into a USB port, and software on your PC helps you share files
and e-mail between the two.

Locating and Loading Software

Another important part of setting up your computer is making
sure that the software you want to use is installed. Of course,
after you install the software, you need to be able to find it so
that you can launch and use different programs.

Find It Online

Find free software down-
loads online at AOL
Keyword: **Download Center**.

Finding Software on Your PC

Your PC probably already has a lot of software installed when
you buy it. But how do you find and launch all those great programs? What about the program you just installed? Programs
are usually launched in one of two ways:

Tip

If you can't find a program
anywhere on your PC, try
choosing Start⇨Search⇨
For Files or Folders. If you're
using an older version of
Windows, choose Start⇨
Find⇨Files or Folders.

► Double-click the icon for the program on your
Windows desktop. This is usually the easiest way.

► If there is no desktop icon, choose Start⇨Programs and
search through the Programs menu, as shown in Figure
2-2. Sometimes, a program appears in a submenu that is

2

Setting Up Your Dream System

named for the software publisher rather than the program itself.

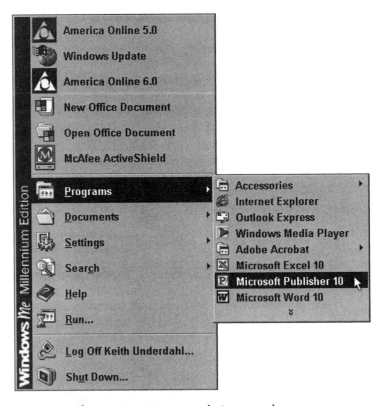

Figure 2-2. Software on your PC appears in the Programs submenu.

Installing New Software

Cross-Reference

See Chapter 17 for more on downloading and installing software from AOL.

Cross-Reference

If you're not sure which drive is your CD-ROM drive, see Chapter 4.

Most software sold today is pretty easy to install. To install software from a CD-ROM:

1. Place the CD in your CD-ROM drive. Wait a few seconds, because many CDs automatically launch the setup program when you first insert them.

2. If the setup doesn't start automatically, double-click the My Computer icon on the Windows desktop. Then double-click the icon for your CD-ROM drive. The icon may look like a CD and be labeled *Compact Disc*, or the icon may have a label for the CD-ROM disc that is in the drive. In Figure 2-3, the D: drive is the CD-ROM drive, which contains an AOL CD-ROM.

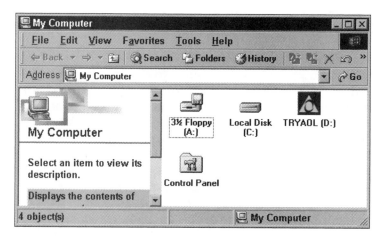

Figure 2-3. The CD-ROM icon is usually labeled with the letter *D*. Here you can see that an AOL CD is in the CD-ROM drive.

   3. Look for a file called Setup or Install, as shown in
       Figure 2-4, and double-click it.

   4. Follow the on-screen instructions to complete
       installation.

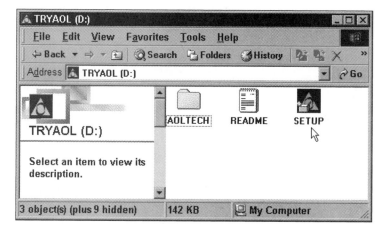

Figure 2-4. Double-click the Setup icon to begin installation.

Summary

To choose a PC that fits your needs and lifestyle, you must first know what you're looking at when you go into the local computer store. This chapter helped you decipher PC spec charts and helped you determine which features are important to you and which ones aren't. You also looked at some of the peripherals you may want to use with your PC, including digital cameras and printers. Finally, you found out how to install and launch new software on your dream system. In the next chapter, you'll find out how AOL can help answer your tough questions about using your PC.

3

THE AOL CONNECTION: GATEWAY TO THE ONLINE WORLD

Quick Look

Chapter 3

The AOL Connection:
Gateway to the Online World

The world is full of things to do, places to see, knowledge to gain, and people to meet. Thankfully, you have a tool called America Online that helps you do all these things and get more out of your world. Like AOL 5.0, the newest version of AOL, version 6.0, is your portal to the Internet and serves up a wealth of information, services, and online resources. In this chapter, you'll see what's new in AOL 6.0 and learn more about the services that AOL has always provided. If you're new to AOL, you can find some handy tips that help get you started using AOL 6.0.

Upgrading to AOL 6.0

What is the *online world*, exactly? It's a meeting place, like an old central square in the heart of town. It's a place to get news and weather, chat with friends and family about your latest news, and even find fun things to see and do. More specifically, the online world is the Internet, where people exchange e-mail, browse Web pages, converse in chat rooms, upload and download files, and more. AOL gives you access to the Internet, as well as an extensive online community and features that are available only to AOL users.

New features are always being added to AOL. The latest version of AOL is version 6.0. If you've been using an older version of AOL, you'll find a variety of new or enhanced features in AOL 6.0, including these:

▶ **The** "**My Calendar**"ᔆᴹ **service.** Plan your schedule for the days, weeks, and months ahead with My Calendar. And take your calendar with you because, with AOL Anywhere, My Calendar is accessible anytime, anywhere you access AOL.

▶ **The** "**You've Got Pictures**" **service.** You don't need a digital camera or a scanner to share pictures with online buddies. Just have your film developed at a participating "You've Got Pictures" developer, and AOL takes care of putting your pictures online and offers members unlimited, free picture storage (provided they visit the "You've Got Pictures" area once in a six-month period).

▶ **The built-in AOL Media Player.** A program that can play music and movies online is built in to AOL 6.0, meaning you don't have to download any special software when you want to enjoy multimedia online.

▶ **High-speed access.** AOL 6.0 offers enhanced support for broadband access to the Internet via DSL, ISDN, and cable modems.

If you haven't yet upgraded to AOL 6.0, you have several ways to do it:

▶ Use an upgrade CD that you receive in the mail. AOL routinely mails upgrade CDs to customers. Simply place the CD in your CD-ROM drive and wait for the setup program to run.

▶ Go to AOL Keyword: **Upgrade** and download the latest version.

▶ Visit a local electronics store that distributes AOL upgrades. Participating stores include Blockbuster, Circuit City, and Office Depot. AOL Keyword: **Upgrade** maintains an up-to-date list of stores that offer AOL upgrade disks.

Definition

The *Internet,* sometimes referred to as the online world, is a network of millions of computers spanning the globe. You gain access to the Internet by being an AOL member.

Cross-Reference

See Chapter 8 for more information about using features of AOL 6.0.

Find It Online

See AOL Keyword: **AOL PLUS** to find out whether you can access AOL up to 50 times faster.

Cross-Reference

For more details on upgrading AOL on your PC, see Chapter 7.

3

The AOL Connection: Gateway to the Online World

For a guided online tour of all that AOL has to offer, click the Quick Tour link on the Welcome Screen when you first launch AOL.

Navigating AOL

For your added convenience, AOL now offers *AOL In Home Support*. Upon request, an AOL technician can come to your house to set up, register, and demonstrate AOL services. Use AOL Keyword: **IHS** for more information.

Computer programs don't get much easier to use than AOL 6.0. It has features in common with many other Microsoft Windows programs, including menus, toolbars, scroll bars, close buttons, and other window controls. AOL also offers unique features, such as the Welcome Screen that appears when you first sign on to AOL. The Welcome Screen contains important features that you'll want to take advantage of.

AOL's Menu Bar, Toolbar, Navigation Bar, and Search Box

Like most programs that you use in Windows, AOL has a variety of menus and toolbars to help you use the features of the program. Figure 3-1 illustrates the bars at the top of the AOL window.

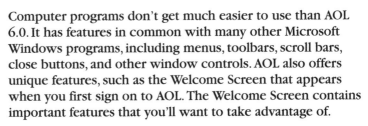

Figure 3-1. The bars at the top of the AOL window let you control the AOL program and access its features.

Each bar along the top of the AOL window serves a unique purpose. The following list tells you a bit about how to use them:

> ▶ **Menu bar:** Click a menu name to display the menu items and then click an item to access that feature. For instance, to set up Parental Controls that safeguard your kids' online experience, choose Help⇨Parental Controls.

▶ **Toolbar:** Click a button on the toolbar to access key AOL features, including e-mail, instant messaging (IM), AOL services, stock quotes, and more. You can click the Read button, for instance, to read e-mail. You can also click the down arrow next to a toolbar heading and choose an option from the resulting menu. For example, to search for people in the AOL People Directory, choose People⇨People Directory.

▶ **Navigation bar:** To return to the last Web page or AOL keyword you visited, click the Back button — the one that resembles an arrowhead. Click Forward to move forward again. Click Stop to stop loading a page; click Reload to refresh it. To visit an AOL keyword (such as **Get Help Now**), type it in the Address box (refer to Figure 3-1) and click Go. You can also use the Address box to type in the URL, or online address, of a Web page that you want to access.

▶ **Search box:** To search for something on AOL and the Internet, type a word or phrase in the Search box and click Search.

Using AOL's Windows

AOL uses a system of *windows* to help you navigate. These windows will be familiar to you if you've used the Microsoft Windows operating system (see Chapter 15). Notice that other windows have the same three buttons that the Buddy List window has in its upper-right corner (see Figure 3-2). These buttons are called the Minimize, Maximize/Restore, and Close buttons, and here's how they work:

▶ **Minimize:** Click this button to temporarily hide the window near the bottom of the AOL screen.

▶ **Maximize/Restore:** To enlarge a window to fill the entire AOL screen, click the Maximize button, which is just to the right of the Minimize button. When you want to return the window to its original size, click the button again.

▶ **Close:** To close a window completely, click Close. The AOL Welcome Screen cannot be closed as long as you are online.

Tip

You can move windows around in AOL by clicking the title bar (which is the bar that contains the Minimize and other buttons) and holding the mouse button down as you drag the window to a new location. Release the mouse button to relocate the window.

Maximize/Restore

Minimize   Close

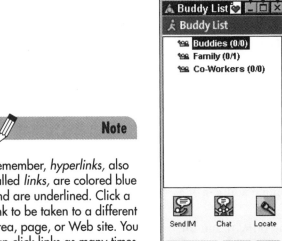

Note

Remember, *hyperlinks,* also called *links,* are colored blue and are underlined. Click a link to be taken to a different area, page, or Web site. You can click links as many times as you like, but if you come across a link you've already clicked since you signed on to AOL, the link is pink or red instead of blue.

Tip

Whenever you sign on to AOL and you've got unread mail, you hear that familiar voice saying, "You've got mail!"

Cross-Reference

For more on using AOL's on-line features, see Chapter 8 of this book and *Your Official America Online Tour Guide* by Jennifer Watson and Dave Marx (IDG Books Worldwide, Inc.).

Figure 3-2. These buttons help you control windows in AOL. Click the Maximize button, and it changes to the Restore button.

Now that you are familiar with some of the basic techniques for working with windows in AOL, you can take a tour.

Maneuvering around AOL's Welcome Screen

Whenever you sign on to AOL, you're given instant access to the Welcome Screen, shown in the center of Figure 3-3.

Here's a list of just a few of the resources at your fingertips on the Welcome Screen:

- ▶ **Weather:** Get a detailed weather forecast by clicking the weather icon at the top of the AOL Welcome Screen window.

- ▶ **Top News:** Find out what's going on in the news by clicking the Top News link near the bottom of the screen.

- ▶ **E-mail:** Click the You've Got Mail icon to check your e-mail.

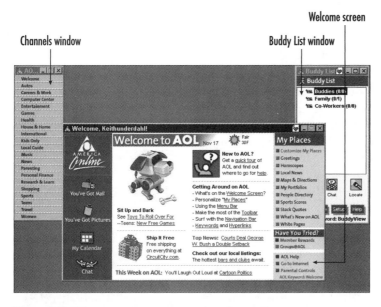

Welcome screen

Channels window   Buddy List window

Figure 3-3. AOL gives you instant access to the online world.

▶ **My Calendar:** Check your schedule for the day by clicking the My Calendar icon.

▶ **You've Got Pictures:** You can have pictures developed at a participating "You've Got Pictures" film developer and then access them online by clicking here.

▶ **Chat:** If you feel like conversing with people online, click the Chat icon to visit People Connection (AOL Keyword: **People Connection**).

▶ **My Places:** Access your favorite online features here. You can customize My Places by clicking the Customize My Places link.

▶ **AOL Help:** You can quickly access AOL Help and Parental Controls using the links in the lower-right corner of the AOL Welcome Screen.

In addition to the Welcome Screen, you also see the Channels window and the Buddy List window when you first sign on to AOL:

▶ **AOL Channels window:** AOL's 20 channels cover just about every special interest, providing you information about things like buying a new car, using your computer, parenting, and sports. Click a channel to check it out.

3

The AOL Connection: Gateway
to the Online World

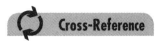

Cross-Reference

See Chapter 8 for more on using the Buddy List.

Tip

You can temporarily hide the Channels window by clicking Hide Channels on the navigation bar. Click Show Channels to show them again.

▶ **Buddy List window:** Look at the Buddy List® to see whether any of your buddies are online and available to chat.

Exploring AOL's Channels

One of the easiest and most enjoyable ways to explore AOL is through AOL's Channels window. Just as many television cable channels cater to special interests, AOL's channels are tailored to specific interests. When you first log on to AOL, a list of channels appears on the left side of the screen. Click any channel to open it. Figure 3-4 shows the main window of the Shopping Channel.

Figure 3-4. Shop@AOL is just one of AOL's specialized channels.

To help you use the channels to explore your interests and gather information, every channel has the following common features:

Cross-Reference

For more information about using AOL keywords, see Chapter 8.

▶ **Keywords:** Every channel also has an AOL keyword associated with it. The keyword is a useful tool if you're not on the Welcome Screen and want to visit a channel.

▶ **Categories:** Channels are usually broken into categories and subcategories of interest that allow you to zero in on exactly what you want. Click a category or subcategory to find out what information and special features it offers.

▶ **Search:** You can conduct a search of most channels to quickly find the information you want. Click once in the search box inside the channel window to place the cursor there, type a word or words that you want to search for, and then click Search. This search system is very accurate, because AOL searches for information only in the channel you're exploring.

Getting Basic Computer Help from AOL

The more you learn about your PC, the more questions you're likely to have. Most online services leave you in the cold when it comes to basic computer help, but AOL offers a cornucopia of online assistance, whether you need help using AOL or just have some questions about your PC in general.

To begin using Help, choose Help⇨AOL Help. The AOL Help window appears, as shown in Figure 3-5.

Figure 3-5. Choose a help category or search for a word you're interested in.

You can use AOL Help in several ways:

▶ A list of categories appears on the left side of the AOL Help window. Click a category to find more information on a topic.

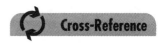

Cross-Reference

For more on getting help from AOL, see Chapter 22.

Tip

You can quickly access AOL Help anytime AOL is open by pressing the F1 key on your keyboard. Or type AOL Keyword: **Help**.

Find It Online

If you ever have billing questions, you can always visit AOL Keyword: **Billing**.

3

The AOL Connection: Gateway to the Online World

▶ A search box appears in the top-right corner of the window. Type a word in the search box and click Search. A list of results appears. Double-click a topic that interests you.

▶ A list of important links appears in the bottom-right corner of the AOL Help window. Click the Begin Exploring link to get general help with AOL. To obtain 24-hour customer service, click the Customer Service link.

Learning Online with AOL

Find It Online

You can also find online classes and tutorials at AOL Keyword: **Online Learning**.

If you're new to using a PC, you may be thinking about taking a class to help you learn more about these exciting devices. AOL is ready to help you go back to school with online classes and tutorials. You may find that AOL's online learning options fit your schedule, lifestyle, and budget better because you don't have to work around the class schedule and pay expensive tuition like you may have to at the local community college.

AOL offers several types of online learning options. Tutorials and how-to guides are available all the time, and online classes follow a specific schedule. Just like a real-world class, live instructors present material, and you can ask questions and receive answers.

Cross-Reference

For more information about attending computer classes online, see Chapter 22.

To begin an online tutorial:

1. Launch AOL and sign on if you haven't done so already.
2. Click Computer Center in the Channels window.
3. The Computer Center Channel opens. In the Computer Center, click the Get Help Now link.
4. Under the Preventative Maintenance section of Get Help Now, click the blue arrow next to Online Learning. The Online Learning window appears, as shown in Figure 3-6.
5. The Online Learning window has four tabs that you can click for more information. By default, the Welcome tab is selected. Click any of the links in this tab for more general information about online tutorials, classes, and how-to guides. Click one of the following tabs to find out more about specific learning opportunities:

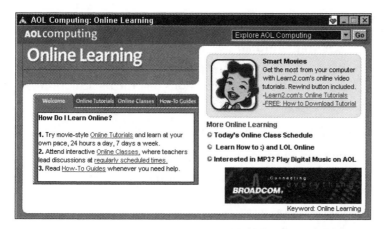

Figure 3-6. Online Learning is your virtual guidance counselor for online tutorials and classes.

- **Online Tutorials:** Hosted by AOL partner Learn2. com, online tutorials are very much like live, professionally taught classes, but you attend them online. Topics include Windows Me, home networking, and even motorist safety. You usually have to pay a tuition fee for online tutorials, but AOL members get a discount.

- **Online Classes:** AOL's online classrooms work similar to chat rooms, where a live instructor fields questions and provides feedback and tips on PC-related subjects. Online classes are free but adhere to a schedule, which you can find on the Online Classes tab of AOL Keyword: **Online Learning**.

- **How-To Guides:** These guides provide quick, easy-to-follow instructions to help you accomplish various tasks, such as building your own Web page or playing music.

Calling AOL Telephone Support

AOL's online help covers a wide range of subjects, but at times, only a human voice on a telephone can help you, especially if you're having trouble starting your computer or signing on to AOL. Before you call telephone support:

▶ Gather as much specific information about your problem as possible. Take notes and write down the exact text of any error messages you see.

Cross-Reference

See Appendix C for more on gathering information about your PC.

3

The AOL Connection: Gateway to the Online World

▶ Be prepared to answer questions about your PC, such as the brand, type of modem you use, and version of AOL you are using.

▶ Call support while you are actually at the PC so that you can follow any instructions that the tech support person gives you.

AOL telephone support can be reached at:

▶ 800-827-3338 (Technical support)

▶ 703-264-1184 (Technical support outside the United States and Canada)

▶ 800-759-3323 (TTY — or teletypewriter — support for hearing-impaired users)

▶ 800-827-6364 (Billing and account information)

Summary

America Online is your gateway to an online world full of information. AOL 6.0 is the program that you use to access AOL, and it's easy to use. You can use it to communicate through e-mail and instant messages, access AOL channels, and much more. And if you have questions, AOL offers help in many different ways. Now that you've gotten to know AOL a bit, the next section shows you the basics about using your PC and helps you delve into some more of AOL's features.

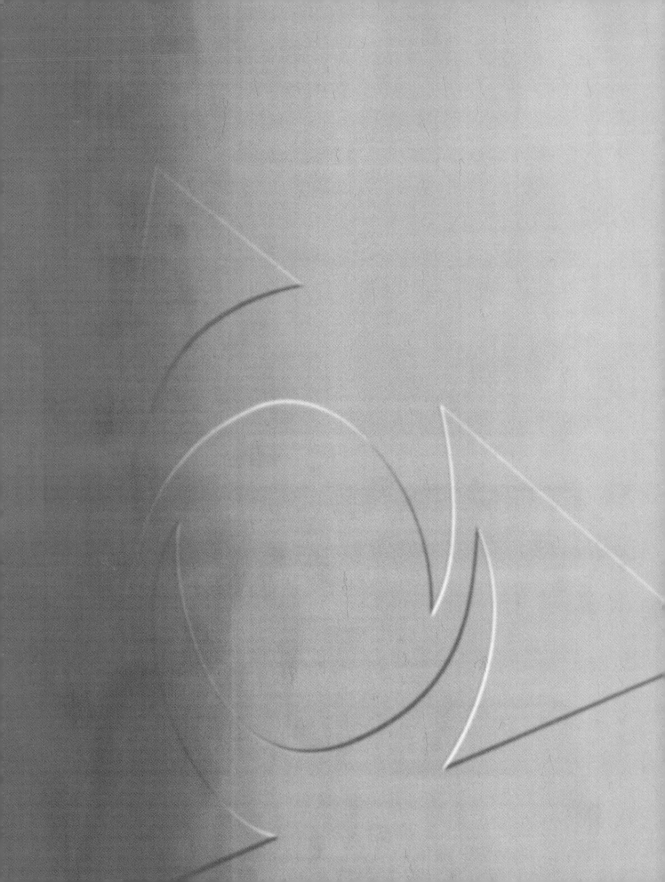

DISCOVERING THE MICROSOFT WINDOWS DESKTOP

Quick Look

Chapter 4

Discovering the Microsoft Windows Desktop

Personal computers (PCs) have come a long way in the last 20 years. Once upon a time, using a computer meant that you had to master an encyclopedia of cryptic commands and codes, and you had to type everything at a blinking command line. But thanks to Microsoft Windows, using your PC is easier than ever.

Windows controls all the functions of your computer and organizes them around a simple screen called the desktop. This chapter introduces you to the Windows desktop and helps you begin to find your way around.

Introducing the Microsoft Windows Desktop

The Windows desktop is the screen you see when you first start up your computer. It looks something like Figure 4-1. The basic layout is common to all versions of Windows since Windows 95. Pay special attention to the Start button, My Computer, and the system tray. I refer to these items throughout this book.

Definition

The word *windows* has two common uses in the PC world. *Microsoft Windows* is the software that runs your PC; the on-screen boxes that many programs use to display information are also called *windows*.

Troubleshooting

If you have Windows 95, you might not have the Quick Launch bar shown in Figure 4-1.

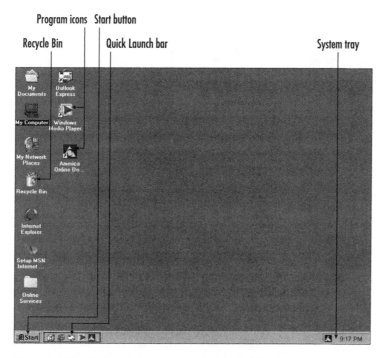

Figure 4-1. The Windows desktop is your entry into the PC world.

Reviewing the Desktop Icons

In the previous section, Figure 4-1 identifies a few icons that you'll find on the Microsoft Windows desktop. You'll use these icons frequently as you use your PC, and each one has an important purpose:

4

Discovering the Microsoft
Windows Desktop

See the section, "Exploring Your PC with My Computer," later in this chapter, for more information on using My Computer to browse your PC.

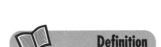

The term *double-click* means to click the left mouse button twice quickly.

▶ **My Computer:** Double-click this icon to see the disk drives on your computer. In My Computer, you'll see icons for your floppy drive (A:), hard drive (C:), CD-ROM drive (usually D:), and any other disk drives your PC may have.

▶ **My Documents:** Double-click this icon to open the My Documents folder. My Documents enables you to store files (such as word processor documents, memos, or pictures) that you create by using your computer's programs.

▶ **My Network Places:** If you have a network of computers in your home or office, this icon gives you access to those other PCs. Older versions of Windows called this Network Neighborhood.

▶ **Recycle Bin:** When you delete files from your hard drive, they end up here. If you accidentally delete something that you meant to keep, you can usually (but not always) recover it from the Recycle Bin.

When you install a new program, Microsoft Windows usually places an icon on the desktop. Figure 4-2 shows the icon that appears when you install America Online. To launch AOL, all you have to do is point at it with your mouse and double-click.

Figure 4-2. Double-click a desktop icon to open your favorite program.

Understanding the Taskbar

Windows can perform many tasks at once. If you're working on your family budget in a program that manages finances, you can leave the document open and the program running while you quickly check your e-mail using your AOL browser. Meanwhile, you may be using AOL to download some files in the background. The taskbar, which is located along the bottom of the Windows desktop, helps you keep track of all the programs that are running in Windows. Every open program or folder has a button on the taskbar, as shown in Figure 4-3.

You'll also find the following on the taskbar:

> ▶ **Start button:** Click this button, located on the bottom-left side of the computer screen to access the Start menu, which gives you access to most of the programs and documents on your computer.

> ▶ **Quick Launch bar:** In Windows 98 and later versions, this bar is customizable so that you can have quick access to your favorite programs, including AOL.

> ▶ **System tray:** Your computer has some programs that run all the time, such as antivirus software and the system clock. Windows keeps icons that represent these programs in the lower-right corner of the screen so you can easily access them.

Double-click the digital clock in the lower-right corner of the screen to easily adjust the time.

Figure 4-3. The taskbar shows that America Online, My Documents, and Solitaire are open right now.

Navigating through the Windows Environment

Windows makes it easy to see the programs and documents on your computer, but you have to know where to look. You can access most programs on your PC either by double-clicking an icon on your desktop or by finding the program on a menu. The following sections give you a walking tour of Microsoft Windows.

Getting Started with the Windows Start Button

If you're looking for a good place to start navigating around your PC, the Windows Start button is the right choice. When you click it, you see the Windows Start menu, shown in Figure 4-4, which organizes all the major tools and programs you'll use. Some of the key tools you can find include these:

Many PC keyboards have a key on the bottom row with a Microsoft "flying window" icon on it. Press that key to open the Windows Start menu.

4

Discovering the Microsoft
Windows Desktop

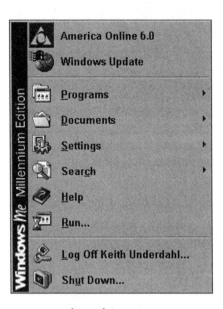

Figure 4-4. The Windows Start menu.

Manually turning your computer off without first properly shutting it down can be very hard on your computer and can even cause permanent damage. Always shut down your PC properly.

If you have Windows 95, you'll see Find in the Start menu instead of Search.

▶ **Shut Down:** Before you turn the power off on your PC, shut down Windows by choosing Start⇨Shut Down. A window appears asking if you want to shut down, restart, or just log off for a while.

▶ **Run:** Choose Start⇨Run when you want to install a new program. You'll see the Run feature referred to in many software instructions.

▶ **Help:** Choose Start⇨Help if you need help using the Windows operating system.

▶ **Search:** If you don't know where you saved that great letter you were writing last week, you can choose Start⇨Search to locate the file for you. Keep in mind that you have the best luck using this function if you can remember at least part of the filename.

▶ **Settings:** Choose Start⇨Settings to access some system tools, such as the Windows Control Panel and your printers. Chapter 5 describes many of the tools that you'll find in the Control Panel.

▶ **Documents:** Windows saves files you've worked on recently in a handy location. To find recently modified documents, choose Start⇨Documents.

▶ **Programs:** Choose Start⇨Programs to find just about every program on your PC. Some programs are actually in submenus in the Programs menu. For example, choose Start⇨Programs⇨America Online and review the items located in the AOL submenu.

▶ **Program shortcuts:** Some programs, like AOL, place handy icons here where you can find them easily.

Exploring Your PC with My Computer

My Computer helps you take inventory of your PC. Double-click the My Computer icon on your desktop to see a Window similar to Figure 4-5. Your My Computer window may differ slightly depending on which version of Windows you have, but whether you use Windows 95, 98, 2000, or Me, one of the first things you'll notice is a list of all the disk drives on your computer. Again, your PC may have more disk drives, but at a minimum, you'll see drives similar to the ones shown in Figure 4-5, which include the following:

▶ **3½-inch floppy (A:):** This is your floppy drive, located on the front of the computer. The floppy drive is always identified by the letter A:.

▶ **Hard drive (C:):** In Figure 4-5, the hard drive is named "Local Disk" but yours may have a different name. The main hard drive is always letter C:, and is located inside the PC.

▶ **Compact Disc (D:):** Your CD-ROM or DVD-ROM drive is usually (but not always) letter D:. If there is a disc in the drive, the name and icon shown in My Computer may be different.

You can use My Computer to explore the disk drives on your computer. When you double-click the icon for the C: drive, you see a window similar to the one in Figure 4-6. If you have Windows Me, your window will look similar to the figure. If you have a different version of Windows, the exact appearance of your window will vary somewhat.

Opening a Folder

You can open a folder by double-clicking it. If you want to go back to the previous folder or window you were looking at, click the Back button, shown in Figure 4-6. The Back and Forward buttons in My Computer work a lot like the Back and Forward buttons in AOL.

Tip

A black arrow to the right of a menu item means that the item has submenus. For example, when you choose Start⇨Programs⇨Accessories, you see all the different accessory programs from which you can choose. Roll your mouse over an item with an arrow to see the submenu's contents.

Cross-Reference

To learn more about working with disk drives, see Chapter 11.

Definition

Folders — like folders in a filing cabinet — hold related files and subfolders. Such a logical folder structure makes files more organized and easier to track down.

Figure 4-5. My Computer helps you take inventory of your PC.

Hiding and Closing Windows

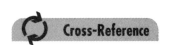

Cross-Reference

See Chapter 6 for more information on working with folders and files on your PC.

You can temporarily hide a window without closing it by clicking the Minimize button (refer to Figure 4-6). The window disappears, but it still has a button on the taskbar. Click that button to see the folder window again.

Next to the Minimize button is the Maximize/Restore button. Click this button to make the window take up the whole screen. Click it again to shrink it back to its former self.

Closing a window is easy. Just click the Close button (it's the *X* in the upper-right corner of the window).

Moving and Resizing Windows

Folders and other Windows programs open in frames called *windows*. Unlike the windows in your home, however, these windows can easily be moved around or resized to fit your tasks and preferences.

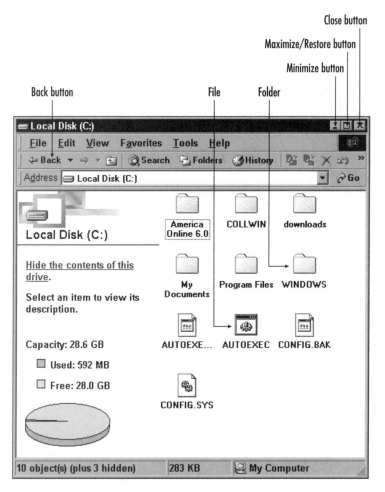

Figure 4-6. The folders and files in this window are located on the C: drive.

You move windows by clicking and dragging them around the screen with your mouse. To move a window:

1. Hold the mouse pointer over the title bar of the window, as shown in Figure 4-7.

2. Click the left mouse button and hold it down.

3. Move the mouse. Notice that an outline of the window moves with the mouse.

4. Release the mouse button when the window is where you want to leave it.

Note

Depending on how your version of Windows is set up, you may see the actual window move rather than just an outline.

Title bar

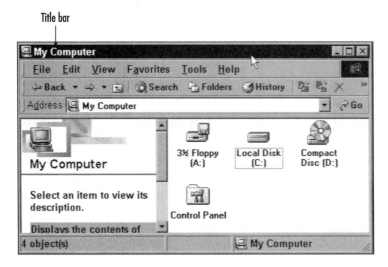

Figure 4-7. Drag a window around by the title bar.

Changing the size of a window is just as easy as moving a window. Move the mouse pointer over an edge or corner of a window. When the pointer becomes a double-headed arrow, click and hold the mouse button and drag the border to change its size.

Using the Right Mouse Button

You've probably noticed that your mouse has more than one button. Every PC mouse has at least two buttons. Some mice even have three buttons.

Use the left button to click items to select them, and double-click files and programs you want to open and use.

When you click an item with the right mouse button (commonly called *right-clicking*), you usually see a menu of options called a *shortcut menu* or *context menu*. To choose an item in a shortcut menu, click it once with the left mouse button.

Switching between Open Programs and Microsoft Windows

You can have many programs and windows open at once in Microsoft Windows. This means you don't have to close your word processing program just because you want to check e-mail or a stock quote on AOL. But after you've opened AOL,

Tip

If your keyboard has a special Windows logo button, you can press it to open the Start menu. Use arrow keys to move around the menu, press Enter to select an item, or press the Esc key to close a menu.

how do you get back to the word processor you left open?
Easy: Just click the program's button on the taskbar.

Here's another trick: Hold down the Alt key on your keyboard,
and then press the Tab key. Don't let go of the Alt key yet.
Notice that as soon as you press Tab, a menu similar to the
one in Figure 4-8 appears. The menu has a separate icon for
each program that is currently open on your computer. Keep
pressing Tab until the program you want to use is selected.
Release the Alt key and that program will open.

Figure 4-8. Choose a program by pressing Tab.

Navigating Windows without a Mouse

The design of Windows assumes that you'll use a mouse
for most actions. But if you don't have a mouse (or if you
are using a laptop and the pointing device doesn't work
very well), you might have a tough time navigating in
Windows.

Fortunately, you can still use your PC even if you only have
a keyboard. Underlined letters indicate *hot keys* (keyboard
shortcuts) in Windows and many other programs.

To use a hot key, press the Alt key on your keyboard, and
then press the corresponding letter. The File menu, for instance, is almost always opened by pressing Alt+F. Use arrow keys to move around in menus, and press Enter to
choose an item. Press Esc to close a menu.

Getting Information about Your PC

Cross-Reference

See Appendix C for more on identifying system resources.

When you install a new program on your PC, that program probably comes with some basic system requirements. The program probably needs to use some free space on your hard drive, and running the program requires a minimum amount of RAM and processor speed.

As you've probably seen, My Computer can tell you how much free space is on your hard drive (refer to Figure 4-6). You can also learn a lot about your computer by right-clicking on the My Computer icon on your desktop and choosing Properties. The Properties window that appears contains a lot of information about your PC, such as what kind of processor you have and how much RAM is installed. Use My Computer to see whether your computer meets the system requirements of some new software you want to buy, or to answer questions asked by a technical support representative.

Summary

Windows is easy to navigate, as long as you know what to look for and how to find your way around the desktop. The many desktop elements — such as My Computer, the Start menu, and the taskbar — all help you manage your programs. In the next chapter, you'll learn even more about working with Microsoft Windows on your PC, including how to customize it to fit your own needs and preferences.

CUSTOMIZING THE WINDOWS INTERFACE

Quick Look

▶ **Adjusting Microsoft Windows to Your Monitor**   **page 74**
Every PC monitor is a little different, and you may need to customize the Windows display to best suit your monitor. You'll find out how to adjust basic display settings here to make best use of your hardware.

▶ **Custom Backgrounds**   **page 76**
One way to spiff up the appearance of Microsoft Windows is to place a custom graphic on the desktop. Find out how here.

▶ **Free Screen Savers**   **page 81**
AOL offers a lot of really cool screen savers that you can download for free. Here's how.

▶ **Accessibility Features**   **page 82**
If you or someone you know has a disability that makes using Microsoft Windows difficult, you can take advantage of the accessibility features that Windows has to offer. Find out how in this section.

Chapter 5

Customizing the Windows Interface

A great feature of Microsoft Windows is the ability to customize the screen design, which is called the *interface,* by changing the colors and the size of words and icons. You can show your personality and interests by adding pictures and custom designs to the Microsoft Windows desktop and by setting up custom screen savers. Accessibility features allow you to customize Microsoft Windows to meet your needs. This chapter helps you tailor Windows to your own preferences and needs.

Using the Display Properties Dialog Box

One of the first things you probably want to customize about your PC is the way the screen looks. The beauty of customizing your screen is that no one perfect setting exists; your perfect display depends on the type of monitor you have and your own tastes. And your taste will probably change over time. That's no problem, either, because you can customize your display as often as you want.

Before you adjust your PC's settings, make sure you've closed all open programs. Windows may prompt you to restart your computer, so you should make sure that all your documents have been saved.

You can use the Display Properties dialog box in Windows to adjust most of the settings. To access the Display Properties dialog box:

1. Choose Start⇨Settings⇨Control Panel. The Control Panel appears.
2. Double-click the Display icon. The Display Properties dialog box appears.

The dialog box organizes the areas that you can modify into several categories, including the following:

▶ **Settings:** Click this tab if you want to adjust the number of colors that your monitor displays. You can also adjust the number and size of objects on your screen.

▶ **Appearance:** Click this tab to change a color scheme for every window that appears on-screen.

▶ **Background:** Click this tab if you want to modify the appearance of the background, which is also called the *desktop*. The background is what you see immediately after starting your PC, before you open any programs.

▶ **Screen Saver:** Click this tab to set up your screen saver and to decide how long you want your PC to be idle before the screen saver automatically displays.

You may see additional tabs in your Display Properties dialog box depending on your hardware and which version of Microsoft Windows you have. The four tabs described here are the most important.

Now that you know what you can do to change the appearance and display of your PC, you're ready to customize the way Microsoft Windows looks.

Note

The procedures here assume you have Windows Me, the latest version of Windows. However, unless otherwise noted, the steps will work with Windows 95 or 98 as well.

Tip

You can also open the Control Panel from My Computer.

Note

AOL is designed to look best when your colors are set at High Color (16 bit) or higher, and the dimensions of the screen area are at least 800 x 600 pixels.

Troubleshooting

If your display becomes severely distorted after you adjust the color settings, wait ten seconds for Microsoft Windows to restore your old settings.

Troubleshooting

Increasing the screen area may cause your screen to flicker and will also cause text and icons to be smaller and harder to see. Check the documentation for your monitor for recommendations on screen area settings.

Adjusting Your PC's Display Settings

The number of colors that your PC can display depends on the capabilities of your monitor and video card. Likewise, the optimal resolution settings depend on the size and quality of your monitor, as well as your own vision. You'll probably want to adjust these settings right away, especially if you plan to spend a lot of time using your computer.

You can adjust the following settings:

▶ **Colors:** When Windows was installed on your PC, a color setting was chosen automatically based on the hardware that your PC detected. Often this default setting is best suited to your PC, but sometimes your hardware may be capable of a higher color setting. Higher settings (such as High Color or True Color) are often preferable because they provide truer-to-life color, but they may also make your screen flicker slightly. Experiment with your settings to find the highest color setting that will display without causing flicker.

▶ **Screen area:** Screen area settings are based on resolutions. Higher settings (1280 x 1024 pixels, for example) show more screen area, while lower settings (640 x 480 pixels, for example) show less screen area. You may want to see as much of the screen as you can, but the higher you set the screen area, the smaller the objects appear on-screen. Lower resolutions tend to be much easier on the eyes. Depending on your needs, you may feel comfortable with a 640 x 480, 800 x 600, or 1024 x 768 setting.

If you use the 640 x 480 screen area setting, you may find that Web pages and other online content runs off the edge of your screen. Try a higher setting — AOL is best viewed at an 800 x 600 or higher resolution.

To begin adjusting the color and screen area settings for your PC:

1. Open the Display Properties dialog box as described in the earlier section, "Using the Display Properties Dialog Box."

2. Click the Settings tab, shown in Figure 5-1.

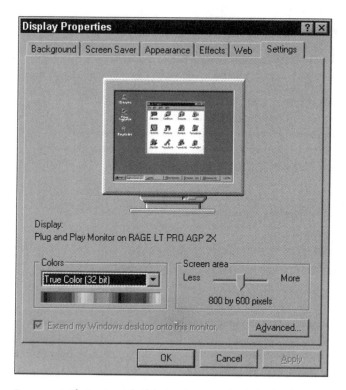

Figure 5-1. The Settings tab of the Display Properties dialog box lets you customize the display to your equipment.

3. Choose a color setting from the Colors drop-down list.

4. Adjust the Screen Area that will be displayed by clicking the slider and moving it to the left and right. Moving the slider to the left makes fewer objects appear on-screen, but those objects look larger. Moving the slider to the right makes more objects appear on-screen, but those objects look smaller.

5. Click Apply to see the effects of your changes.

6. If you adjusted the Screen Area slider, a warning message appears, explaining that the adjustment may take a few seconds. Click OK to test the new setting.

7. The screen changes, and you see a dialog box asking if you want to keep the new settings. Click Yes if you like the settings, and click No if you don't.

8. When you are done adjusting the settings, click OK.

Customizing the Appearance of Microsoft Windows

After you configure Microsoft Windows so that the color setting and screen area are best suited to your hardware and personal tastes, you can begin customizing the way Microsoft Windows looks. You can change the actual colors that are used for the Microsoft Windows desktop and program windows. You can add a picture to the desktop and set up a screen saver to display when your PC is inactive. The following sections describe how to customize the appearance of Microsoft Windows on your PC.

Choosing a New Color Scheme: The Appearance Tab

An easy way to personalize your PC is to change the display's color scheme. The color scheme affects the color of the Microsoft Windows desktop, toolbars, menu and icon names, scroll bars, and more. Using custom color schemes, you can color coordinate Windows to the rest of your home or office! Windows has a variety of built-in color schemes.

If you want to create your own color scheme, choose the item that you want to customize from the Item drop-down list. Then, use the boxes next to the drop-down list to indicate the color or size that you want.

To choose a new color scheme:

1. Open the Display Properties dialog box from the Control Panel, as described in the section, "Using the Display Properties Dialog Box," earlier in this chapter.

2. Click the Appearance tab, shown in Figure 5-2.

3. Choose a color scheme from the Scheme drop-down list. You can preview the color scheme in the upper part of the dialog box.

4. Click the Apply button when you've found a color scheme that you like, and click OK to close the dialog box.

Adding a Background

In addition to Microsoft Windows' built-in color schemes, you can add pictures and custom graphics to the background of the desktop. AOL has many free backgrounds — also called *wallpaper* — that you can download. The following sections show you how to add a new background to your desktop.

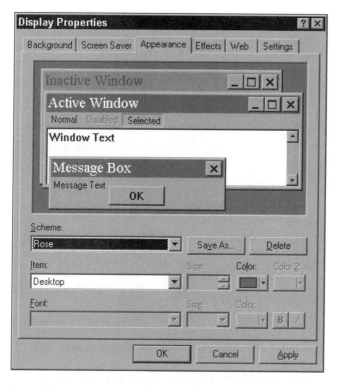

Figure 5-2. The Appearance tab lets you customize the color scheme.

Downloading Wallpaper from AOL

You can download wallpaper from AOL and use the wallpaper as a background for your Windows desktop. To locate and download wallpaper, follow these steps:

1. Launch AOL and sign on.

2. Go to AOL Keyword: **Wallpaper**. The Desktop Makeover window appears.

3. Click the link for free Windows Wallpaper. A Graphic Arts window opens, listing categories of wallpaper.

4. Double-click a wallpaper category to view it. A window listing individual wallpapers appears, as shown in Figure 5-3.

5. Click a wallpaper to select it. In Figure 5-3, a wallpaper called July 4th Fireworks is selected.

6. Click the Download Now button.

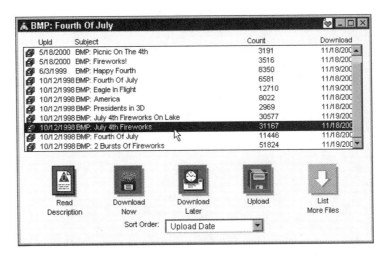

Figure 5-3. AOL offers a variety of wallpaper, which you can download for free.

Note

Saving wallpapers in the `C:\Windows` folder makes them easier to find later.

7. In the resulting Download Manager window, choose the Windows folder of your C: drive from the Save In drop-down list, as shown in Figure 5-4. Make a note of the filename and click Save. The wallpaper downloads.

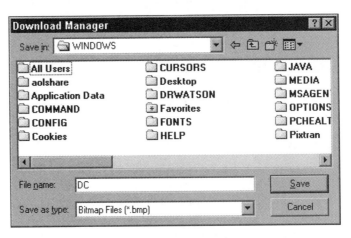

Figure 5-4. Save the wallpaper in the Windows folder.

8. Close the picture preview that appears after the download. Then sign off and close the AOL program window.

Adding a Background to Your Desktop

The process for adding a background to your desktop is the same whether you download wallpaper from AOL or select one of the Microsoft Windows options. To add a background to your desktop:

1. Open the Display Properties dialog box from the Control Panel as described in the section, "Using the Display Properties Dialog Box."

2. Click the Background tab to bring it to the front. Scroll down the list of backgrounds until you find the one you want to use for your wallpaper.

    If you want to use a picture that is not saved in your C:\Windows folder, you have to click Browse to locate the picture file.

3. Select the item to preview it, as shown in Figure 5-5.

4. Click OK to close the Display Properties dialog box. The new wallpaper appears on your desktop.

Tip

If you want to cover the entire desktop with copies of the wallpaper, choose Tile from the Picture Display drop-down list.

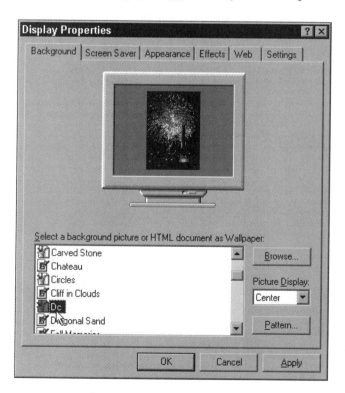

Figure 5-5. Use the Background tab to add custom wallpapers to your desktop.

Disable screen savers whenever you are performing a
long download or installing a
new program. This will help
prevent a system crash.

Using Screen Savers

A problem called *screen burn* used to plague computer monitors. When a display didn't change for hours on end, ghost images of dialog boxes, text, and whatever else was on-screen
became permanently "burned" onto the monitor. To combat
this, programs called *screen savers* were invented. After a few
minutes of inactivity, screen savers immediately start up with a
graphic that moves all over the screen, ensuring that no one
spot remains unchanged for long periods of time.

Modern monitors are less susceptible to screen burn, but
screen savers are still a fun way to improve the appearance of
your PC when you aren't using it.

Setting Up a Screen Saver

Windows has built-in screen savers that are easy to activate:

1. Open the Display Properties dialog box from the
   Control Panel.
2. Click the Screen Saver tab to bring it to the front, as
   shown in Figure 5-6.
3. In the Screen Saver area, choose a screen saver from
   the drop-down list.
4. In the Wait box, click the up or down arrow to adjust
   the amount of time before your PC shows the screen
   saver. A time between five and ten minutes is good.
5. Click OK when you're done.

When you've been away from your PC for the specified time
period, the screen saver automatically turns on. Make the
screen saver go away by wiggling the mouse.

If you assign a password to
your screen saver, make sure
that the password is something you'll remember!

You can protect your PC from prying eyes by assigning a password to your screen saver. Click in the Password Protected
check box on the Screen Saver tab to put a check mark in the
box. Then click the Change button to set up a password.
When the screen saver activates, you have to enter your password to deactivate your screen saver and return to Microsoft
Windows.

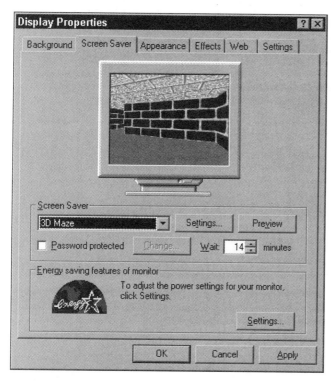

Figure 5-6. Give your PC something to do when you aren't using it by setting up a screen saver.

Downloading Screen Savers from AOL

AOL offers fun and free screen savers that you can download easily. Here's how:

1. Launch AOL and sign on.

2. Go to AOL Keyword: **Screensavers**.

3. The AOL Screensavers window appears. Click a featured screen saver if it looks interesting and move on to step 6 of this list. Otherwise, click the PC Screensaver Libraries link.

4. Double-click a category of screen savers. If you're not sure which one to choose, try Scenery Savers.

5. Select a screen saver and click Download Now.

6. Click Save in the Download Manager window. The download may take a few minutes.

Tip

As with wallpaper, screen savers are easier to find later if you save them in the `C:\Windows` folder.

7. When the download is complete, you'll probably see a message telling you that the file has been decompressed. A message asks if you would like to locate it. Click Yes.

8. A window similar to the one shown in Figure 5-7 appears. Double-click any Read Me and License Agreement icons that you see and read the information they contain. Make sure that you agree with the license agreement.

9. Double-click the Setup icon for the screen saver. The icon is similar to the one in shown in Figure 5-7. Follow the on-screen instructions to complete the setup.

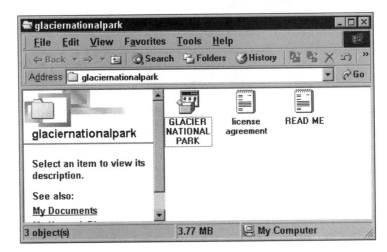

Figure 5-7. Double-click the setup icon (in this case, Glacier National Park) to install your new screen saver.

Most screen saver setup programs automatically set themselves as the active screen saver. If the screen saver you've downloaded does not do this, you can find the screen saver by opening the Display Properties dialog box, clicking the Screen Saver tab, and following the instructions in "Adding a Background to Your Desktop," earlier in this chapter.

Making Windows More Accessible

If you have a disability, Microsoft Windows' accessibility features may help you use your PC. Special features make

Windows more accommodating if you have a vision, hearing, learning, mobility, or other disability. A special Wizard helps you customize Microsoft Windows to your own needs.

Using the Accessibility Wizard

The Accessibility Wizard is the easiest way to set up features in Microsoft Windows to better suit your needs.

1. Choose Start⇨Programs⇨Accessories⇨Accessibility⇨ Accessibility Wizard.
2. The wizard helps tailor Microsoft Windows to your needs and preferences. As you answer questions about the type of disability you have, Microsoft Windows tailors subsequent steps of the wizard to your needs.

Freedom Scientific (`www.hj.com`) makes software that helps vision impaired users make better use of PCs. Check out the screen reader, JAWS, which works with AOL.

Using Windows Accessibility Tools

Even if you don't run the Accessibility Wizard, Windows Me has a couple of neat tools that are readily available from the Accessibility menu. They are

▶ **On-Screen Keyboard:** Choose Start⇨Programs⇨ Accessories⇨Accessibility⇨On-Screen Keyboard to activate this tool. The On-Screen Keyboard, shown in Figure 5-8, is helpful if you are mobility impaired because you can operate a keyboard using only a pointing device (such as a mouse).

▶ **Magnifier:** Choose Start⇨Programs⇨Accessories⇨ Accessibility⇨Magnifier to activate this tool. The screen splits and a magnified view of the screen appears at the top, as shown in Figure 5-9. Notice that the magnification area follows the mouse pointer as you move the mouse around your screen. You can hide the Magnifier Settings box by minimizing it.

Find It Online

Visit AOL Keyword: **Accessibility** to find out more about making AOL accessible, and see how you can become a tester for AOL.

Cross-Reference

If you don't see the Accessibility menu, you need to install the Accessibility component of Windows from your Windows CD. See Chapter 16 for details.

Cross-Reference

If you use the mouse with your left hand, see Chapter 10 for information on customizing your mouse.

Note

The Shift, Ctrl, and Alt keys on the On-Screen Keyboard stick down when you click them, and stay down until you click another key.

Figure 5-8. The On-Screen Keyboard lets you access keyboard keys using only a pointing device.

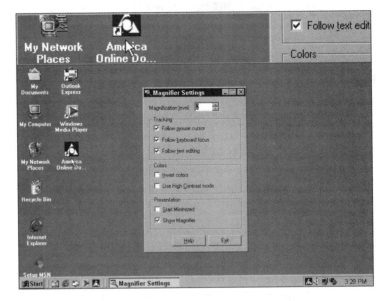

Figure 5-9. The Magnifier provides a magnified view of Microsoft Windows and your other programs.

Summary

Customizing Microsoft Windows is a great way to make your PC feel more like your own. You can tailor Microsoft Windows to your monitor, and add colors, backgrounds, screen savers, and accessibility options to suit your tastes and needs. In the next chapter, you'll gain even more control over your PC by learning how to manage files, folders, and programs.

Quick Look

▶ **Create Folders to Store Files**   **page 90**

Files on your PC are organized into folders. Folders on your hard drive are like
folders in a file cabinet because they help you make sense of your files. Here you
learn how to create new folders of your own.

▶ **Open Files and Folders**   **page 91**

One of the most important things that you can do with files on your computer is
open them in a program so that you can work on them. Opening a file is easy,
and you'll find out how to do it here.

▶ **Search for Files**   **page 92**

The hard drive in your computer has literally thousands of files on it. How do
you sort through all those files to find the one you need? Find out in this section.

▶ **Move and Copy Files**   **page 94**

You'll frequently make copies of files and move them to new locations. Find out
how to copy and move files in just a mouse click or two with Windows Explorer.

▶ **Delete Files**   **page 96**

If you have files that you don't need or want anymore, you'll probably want to
delete them. This section helps you make sure you're deleting the right files, and
shows you how to delete them.

Chapter 6

Organizing Files and Folders on Your PC

Every time you perform a task on your computer, whether you read e-mail online or type a letter, your PC is working with behind-the-scenes information called *data*. Every time you open a program, save some work, or download software from AOL, a *file* full of data is saved on your hard drive. You don't need to understand the data or how it is saved, but you do need to know how to work with these files.

In this chapter, you learn the basics of working with files, including how to organize them in folders, copy them, and move them from one location to another. You also find out how to delete files — and how to get them back again if you didn't really mean to delete them.

Understanding Files and Folders

Everything you do with your PC is saved as a file. A file may be a picture from your most recent family reunion, a text document that lists all the people you want to send holiday cards to, or the Web page of your favorite online retailer. Even the actual programs on your PC are stored as program files. When you launch a program such as AOL or WordPad, a program file springs into action to make the program appear on-screen. Most programs have dozens of program files stored on your hard drive, but you don't need to worry about opening them; most program files work in the background.

A file could be as small as 1K (*kilobyte,* which is 1,024 bytes), or as large as many *megabytes.* (Abbreviated as MB, a *megabyte* is 1,000 kilobytes.) These may seem like huge numbers, but your computer's hard drive probably already contains thousands of files — and it can handle thousands more.

 Definition

A *bit* is the smallest piece of information your computer uses. A *byte* consists of eight bits.

What's a File Extension?

Filenames in Microsoft Windows usually end with a three- or four-digit extension. The *extension* is the portion of the filename that follows the period (.). So if a word processing file is named memo.doc, the extension is .doc. The extension actually helps Windows identify the type of file it is. Depending on how Windows is configured on your PC, the extensions for many common file types are hidden when you view files in My Computer or Windows Explorer, but you'll still see file extensions if you receive a file in an e-mail or download one from AOL.

Why are file extensions important? Usually they aren't, but you should be especially wary of any files you receive in e-mail that have a .doc or .exe extension. Files with .doc extensions are word processing documents designed to be used with Microsoft Word and WordPad, but they can also contain computer viruses. But far more dangerous are files with the .exe extension. These are called *executable* files, which means they are actual programs. They are commonly used to infect your PC with a virus, even though they appear harmless when you double-click them. Be wary of any .exe files that people send you in e-mail, even if the sender is someone you know.

Note

The more programs you have installed on your PC, the more files and folders you will see on your C: drive.

Tip

If you don't see a My Documents icon on your desktop, open My Computer and locate the My Documents folder on your C: drive.

With thousands of files of all different types on your PC, finding just the files you need can seem daunting. Luckily, Windows has already organized many of your existing files into *folders* on your PC's hard drive. The folder system is not unlike the filing cabinet you use at work or home to organize important documents, such as monthly bills and tax returns. You can even create your own folders if you wish, as described later in this chapter.

Windows has even created a folder specifically designed for storing your own document files; it's called My Documents. You can usually access this folder by double-clicking the My Documents icon on your Windows desktop. My Documents is a great place to store word processing documents, pictures, and other files that you are working on.

To begin exploring some of the files and folders already on your PC, double-click the My Computer icon on your desktop and then double-click the icon for your C: drive (which is your main hard drive). The window that appears (yours probably looks similar to Figure 6-1) shows plenty of files and folders.

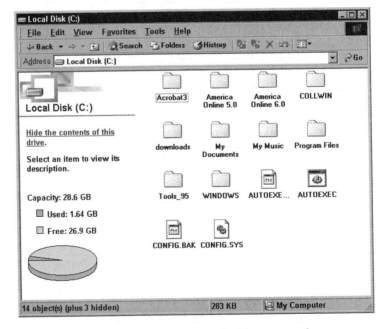

Figure 6-1. Folders help keep the files on your hard drive organized.

Using Windows Explorer

As you use your PC more and more, you'll find that you are constantly working with files. You may discover that you need to make a copy of a file or move a file from one folder to another. Or you may want to delete old files that you don't need anymore. Windows Explorer can help.

The best way to organize your files is to use Windows Explorer, the Windows file-management tool that comes with the Microsoft Windows operating system. To launch Windows Explorer, choose Start⇨Programs⇨Accessories⇨Windows Explorer. Windows Explorer opens, as shown in Figure 6-2.

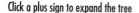
Click a plus sign to expand the tree

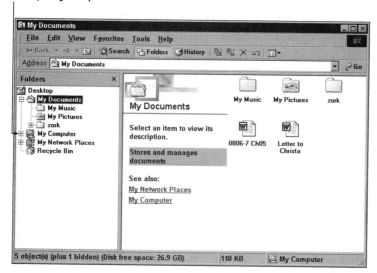

Figure 6-2. Windows Explorer helps you manage the files on your PC.

The Windows Explorer window is divided into two halves:

▶ **Folders list:** A list of folders, disk drives, and other locations on your computer appears on the left side of the window. Click an icon or folder here to view its contents. Click a plus sign (+) next to a folder or item to see subfolders.

▶ **File list:** The contents of folders you select in the Folders list appear on the right side of the window. If the folder contains subfolders, they also appear here.

Before you can do anything to a file — copy it, move it, or delete it — you have to select it. The easiest way to do that is simply to click the file once with the left mouse button. You can tell that a file (or folder) has been selected because the selected folder looks different. For example, in Figure 6-2, the My Documents folder is highlighted on the left side of the screen.

Tip

To deselect a file or group of files, just click once on a blank part of the screen.

But what if you need to select more than one file? That's easy, too, and you can do it several ways. Try each of these techniques with files in the My Documents folder:

▶ Click and hold the left mouse button and drag it so that you draw a box around the desired files. Release the mouse button, and all the files inside the box are selected.

▶ Hold down the Ctrl key on your keyboard as you click once on each file you want to select. The Ctrl key is located in the lower-left corner of most keyboards.

▶ To select several files in a list, click the first file to select it. Then hold down the Shift key on your keyboard and click the last file. All the files in that range are selected.

Creating Folders

Folders provide a great way to keep files organized on your hard drive. Windows provides some folders for you, but you can also create your own folders to organize the files that you create and use. For instance, you may want to create a folder where you store memos to and from your boss, and another folder to store the pictures your kids download or draw. To create a folder, follow these steps:

1. Open Windows Explorer by choosing Start⇨Programs⇨ Accessories⇨Windows Explorer.

2. In the Folders list on the left side of the window, click the location where you want to create a new folder. If you aren't sure where you want to create the new folder, just click the My Documents folder — you can move the new folder later.

3. At the top of the window, choose File⇨New⇨Folder. A folder called *New Folder* appears in the file window on the right side of the screen.

4. Type a name for the folder. Make the name descriptive; it can be up to 256 characters long.

5. Double-click the new folder to open it.

Working with Files

When you do some work in a program — for example, write a letter or a résumé — you need to save your work so you can open it up and work on it again later, or share it with a friend or coworker. To create and save a file, follow these steps:

1. Open a program and do some work. If you're not sure what program to use, open WordPad by choosing Start⇨Programs⇨Accessories⇨WordPad.

2. At the top of the program window, choose File⇨Save. A Save As dialog box appears, which looks similar to Figure 6-3. Most programs automatically try to let you save your work in the My Documents folder, and that's usually the best place to save it.

3. Enter a name for the file in the File Name text box. The filename can be descriptive if you like; filenames can be as long as 256 characters, but a filename that long would look silly. Also, some special characters are not allowed in filenames, including these:
   : \ / ? * " < > |.

4. Click Save. The file is saved.

Opening Saved Files

In Windows, all you have to do is double-click a file to open it — and the same is true if you want to open a folder to see what files are stored in it. Follow these steps to open any file (such as a letter you typed and saved using WordPad):

1. Double-click the My Documents icon on the Windows desktop (if you don't have a My Documents icon, choose Start⇨Programs⇨Accessories⇨Windows Explorer; Windows Explorer will open up to the My Documents folder).

2. If the file was saved in a subfolder, double-click the subfolder to open it.

Tip

If you don't see WordPad in your Accessories menu, click the little arrow at the bottom of the menu to see more program listings.

Note

The procedure for saving a file is almost exactly the same no matter what Windows program you are using.

Caution

If you aren't sure what a file is, don't try to open it. Program files can be damaged if they are opened improperly.

Troubleshooting

If you'd like to save your file to a different disk (such as a floppy), click the down arrow at the top of the Save As dialog box next to the Save In drop-down list and choose the desired disk drive. The floppy drive is the A: drive.

Folder where file will be saved　　Filename

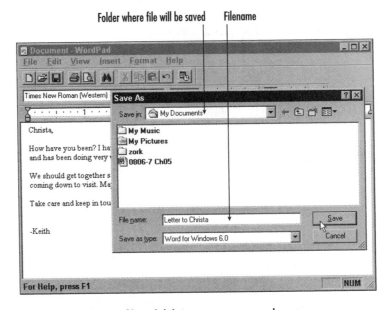

Figure 6-3. Name your file and click Save to save your work.

3. Double-click the icon for the file you want to open (see Figure 6-4). Windows automatically determines which program should be used to open the file. In a few seconds, the appropriate program starts, and the file appears in it.

4. Click the Close button in the upper-right corner of the program window to close it.

If Windows can't decide which program to use to open a file, you may receive a warning message that asks you to select a program to use. Click Cancel if you see this warning.

Searching for Saved Files

Inevitably, you'll save a file and then forget where you saved it. Don't worry; this happens to everyone at some point. Thankfully, Windows makes your files easy to find. Here's how:

1. Choose Start⇨Search⇨For Files or Folders. A search window appears.

2. On the left side of the window, type a search term in the Search for Files or Folders Named text box.

Tip

If you don't find the file you're looking for, try a shorter, less specific word in your search. For instance, try *Judy* rather than *Letter to Judy*.

Click file icon

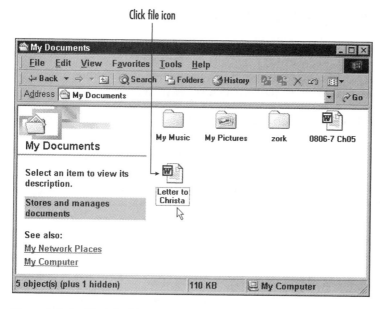

Figure 6-4. Double-click a file icon to open it.

3. Click the Search Now button. After a few seconds, the filename (or a list of filenames if there is more than one match) appears in the lower-right corner of the window, as shown in Figure 6-5.

4. If you have more than one file with a similar name, you may see a list of filenames. Double-click the file you're looking for to open it.

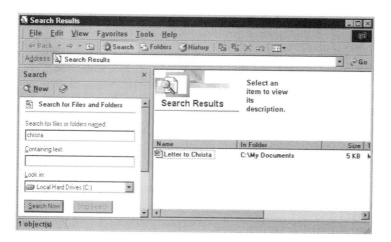

Figure 6-5. Windows lets you search for files on your computer.

Troubleshooting

If you have Windows 95 or 98, choose Start⇨Find⇨ Files or Folders. The search window that appears will be simpler than what is shown here, but works on roughly the same principles.

6

Organizing Files and Folders on Your PC

Cross-Reference

Learn more about download-ing cool software from AOL in Chapter 17.

Tip

If you can't find the file you want in the Downloads folder, see the previous sec-tion, "Searching for Saved Files."

Finding Files You Downloaded from AOL

If you have visited AOL's Download Center (AOL Keyword: **Download Center**), you already know that you can find a lot of cool files and programs online. Where do the things you download from AOL go? They're easy to find:

1. Double-click the My Computer icon on your Windows desktop.

2. Double-click the icon for your C: drive.

3. Locate the Downloads folder and double-click it to open it. The Downloads folder is where AOL automati-cally stores the files you download.

Changing the Appearance of Files in Windows Explorer

When you first open Windows Explorer, files appear as large icons (refer to Figure 6-4). However, you can choose one of four other ways to view your files. To change the way your files appear, click the Views button, shown in Figure 6-6, and choose one of the following view options:

▶ **Small Icons:** Because the icons are smaller, this view lets you see more files at the same time.

▶ **List:** This option is useful if you want to see many files at one time.

▶ **Details:** This view (shown in Figure 6-6) gives you in-formation about each file, such as its size, what kind of file it is, and when it was last modified. You may need to scroll left and right in the window to view all the details.

▶ **Thumbnails:** In Windows 98 and higher, some files, such as pictures and movies, can show a tiny preview on the icon, called a *thumbnail*. In Windows Me, this is the default viewing option in the My Pictures folder.

Copying and Moving Files

Note

The techniques for moving and copying files are the same whether you are working with one file or several files.

You'll probably find yourself constantly moving files or copy-ing them. For instance, you may want to copy a picture file onto a floppy disk, or move an old word processing document into an archive folder. To move a file to a different folder, fol-low these steps:

1. In Windows Explorer, locate the file you want to move.

2. Click the file without releasing the left mouse button. Then drag the selection to its new location.

3. When the folder to which you want to move the file is highlighted, release the mouse button. The file moves to its new folder.

Tip

If you want to move or copy a file to another disk drive (such as a floppy drive), click the plus sign (+) next to My Computer in the Folders list. Then drag the files to the desired disk drive just as if they were folders.

Views button

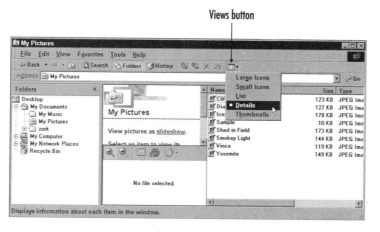

Figure 6-6. Windows Explorer gives you several useful options for viewing your files.

But what if you just want to place a copy of a file in another folder or disk rather than move it? To copy and paste a file, follow these steps:

1. In Windows Explorer, locate the file you want to copy and click it once.

2. Choose Edit⇨Copy.

3. Locate the folder or disk to which you want to add a copy of the file and double-click it.

4. Choose Edit⇨Paste. A copy of the file appears in its new location.

Changing a File's Name

Coming up with creative and descriptive filenames can be difficult, especially if you're not used to doing it. If you find yourself constantly opening files to find out if they're actually what you're looking for, you may want to change the way you name files in the future. For instance, if the file is a memo you typed to your boss about the poor quality of coffee in the office, a

Note

A good rule to remember is to change only the names of files you created. That way, you won't inadvertently change the name of a file that's necessary to keep one of your programs up and running.

Troubleshooting

Remember, a filename can have as many as 256 characters in it, but it cannot include the following special characters: **: \ / ? * " < > |**.

Note

These techniques also work when you use My Computer to view files.

good file name might be Memo to James Smith about coffee. That's a lot more descriptive than a file name like Memo, Smithmemo, or Coffee, and should make the file easier to identify. Best of all, you're never married to any filename you give. You can easily change filenames by following these steps:

1. Locate the file you want to rename with Windows Explorer or My Computer.

2. Right-click (that is, click with the right mouse button) on the file and choose Rename from the menu that appears.

3. Type a new name and press Enter when you're done.

Deleting Files

Eventually, you may want to get rid of files that you don't need anymore. To delete files, open Windows Explorer and select the file you want to delete. Then try one of these options:

▶ Press the Delete (Del) key on your keyboard. The Delete key is located to the right of the Enter key on most standard keyboards.

▶ Click the Delete button, which looks like a large X, on the Windows Explorer toolbar (see Figure 6-7).

▶ At the top of the Windows Explorer window, choose File⇨Delete.

▶ Drag the file to the Recycle Bin in the Folders list.

▶ Drag the file to the Recycle Bin on the Windows desktop (if it's visible).

No matter which option you choose, Windows asks you if you really want to delete the file. Click Yes if you're sure. If the file is being deleted from your hard drive, it will probably be sent to the Recycle Bin, which is described in the next section.

Using the Recycle Bin

What if you accidentally delete a file that you really wanted to keep? Don't worry; Windows gives you a second chance. When a file is deleted from your hard drive, it is actually sent to the Recycle Bin. To see what's inside the Recycle Bin, double-click the Recycle Bin icon on your Windows desktop. The Recycle Bin window appears, as shown in Figure 6-7.

Delete button

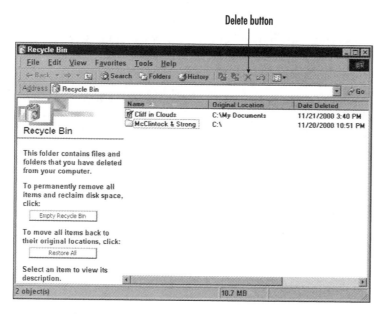

Figure 6-7. The Recycle Bin holds onto your recently deleted files just in case you need them back.

The Recycle Bin basically lets you do two things:

> ▶ **Restore:** If you want to recover all the files in the Recycle Bin, click the Restore All button on the left side of the window. If you want to recover only one file, click the desired file to select it. The Restore All button changes to the Restore button; click the Restore button to restore the file.

> ▶ **Empty Recycle Bin:** If you're certain that you don't need any of the files in the Recycle Bin, click the Empty Recycle Bin button on the left side of the window. Be careful — after you empty the Recycle Bin, the files are gone forever.

You can leave files in the Recycle Bin indefinitely, but if your hard drive starts to get full, Windows automatically starts clearing files from the Bin. In other words, if you send a file to the Recycle Bin, don't count on it being there forever.

Caution

If you delete a file from a removable disk such as a floppy or Zip disk, you won't be able to get the file back — it's gone for good.

6

Organizing Files and Folders on Your PC

Summary

Understanding how to work with files in Windows helps you take charge of your PC. Thankfully, Windows Explorer makes file management easy to do. With Windows Explorer, you can access your files, move them around, copy and paste them to new locations, create new folders in which to store them, or get rid of the files altogether.

The Recycle Bin can give you a second chance if you accidentally delete the wrong file or if you discover you still need it. In the next chapter, you find out how to install, customize, and manage AOL on your PC.

7

INSTALLING AND USING AOL ON YOUR PC

Quick Look

▶ **Upgrade AOL or Install It on a New Computer**   **page 100**
AOL is constantly improving its software by adding new tools and capabilities. Upgrading AOL is easy, and this section shows you how. You also find out how to add your AOL account to another PC if you just bought a new computer.

▶ **Add a Screen Name**   **page 103**
With your AOL account, you can have up to seven unique screen names, meaning each person in your family or household can have a unique online identity. Learn how to add screen names to your account here.

▶ **Block Unwanted E-Mail**   **page 106**
Are you getting e-mail from someone who you'd rather not be bothered by? In this section, you find out how to remove spam and other unwanted e-mail from your online experience.

▶ **Set Parental Controls**   **page 107**
The Internet is a big place, and AOL provides ways to help you protect your family from viewing inappropriate material online. This section shows you how to set up Parental Controls.

Chapter 7

Installing and Using AOL on Your PC

Most computer programs can be tailored to suit individual needs, and AOL is no exception. AOL provides flexibility by letting each member of your family have his or her own online identity, and AOL helps you control which services you and your children can access. In this chapter, you find out how to set up Parental Controls to customize AOL to meet your family's needs, but first, you learn about upgrading the AOL software on your PC and keeping AOL connected even if you move or sign on away from home.

Upgrading or Adding AOL to Your PC

Upgrading America Online on your PC or adding the software to a new PC that you just bought couldn't be easier. The simplest way is to use an AOL CD-ROM that was mailed to you or that you pick up for free from participating retailers (use AOL Keyword: **Upgrade** to find out where you can find a free CD).

Insert the CD in your CD-ROM drive and wait for the setup
program to begin. If the AOL Setup program doesn't launch
automatically, follow these steps:

1. Double-click the My Computer icon to open My
   Computer.
2. Double-click the icon for your CD-ROM drive. The icon
   probably has an AOL logo on it.
3. The setup program launches. If the setup program
   doesn't launch, look for the icon called SETUP and
   double-click it. The setup window, shown in Figure 7-1,
   appears on-screen.

Find It Online

You can download upgrades
directly from AOL. Visit AOL
Keyword: **Upgrade** to see if
a new version is available.

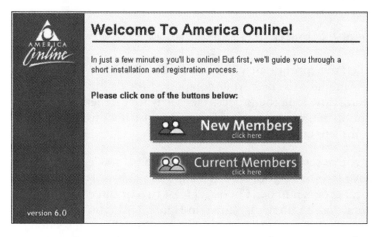

Welcome To America Online!

In just a few minutes you'll be online! But first, we'll guide you through a
short installation and registration process.

Please click one of the buttons below:

New Members
click here

Current Members
click here

version 6.0

Figure 7-1. When you place a new AOL CD in your CD-ROM drive, you see a window
that looks like this.

After the welcome screen for the AOL setup program appears,
click the Current Members button. The next screen (shown in
Figure 7-2) gives you three options:

▶ **Upgrading to a New Version of AOL on This
   Computer:** Choose this option if you just want to upgrade AOL on a computer that already has your AOL account installed on it.

▶ **Adding Your Existing AOL Account to This
   Computer:** Choose this option if you just bought a
   new computer and want to install AOL on it.

▶ **Creating an Additional AOL Account on This
   Computer:** Use this option only if two or more people
   in your household with separate AOL accounts use the
   same computer.

Troubleshooting

Before you install a new version of AOL, make sure that
all other programs are
closed. You should also disable your antivirus software,
as described in Chapter 20.

7

Installing and Using AOL on Your PC

Note

Don't confuse creating a new
account (which involves paying for AOL service) with creating a new screen name,
which you can find out about
later in this chapter.

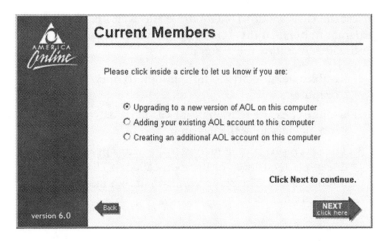

Figure 7-2. Choose the option that best fits what you want to do.

Click the appropriate choice and then click Next. AOL takes a few minutes to check your computer for existing AOL software. How long the process takes may vary depending on the option you've chosen. Just follow the instructions on-screen to complete installation.

If you're setting up your AOL account on a new computer, you have to provide your screen name and password and choose a local access number. Choose at least two or three access numbers close to home, as shown in Figure 7-3. If you're having trouble finding an access number, see the following section.

Note

Be sure to choose a local access number that will not cause you to incur long-distance or toll charges when you use AOL.

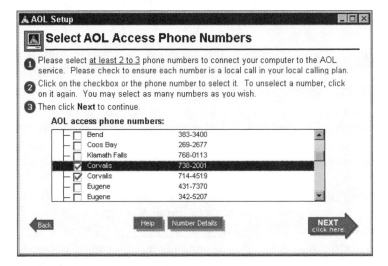

Figure 7-3. Choose two or three access numbers that are local calls for you.

When the setup process is complete, you're asked whether you want the new version of AOL to be the default browser for the Web, e-mail, and newsgroups. Click Yes.

When the setup process is complete, AOL launches. Congratulations! You're ready to go online!

Changing Your Local Access Number

If your computer uses a dial-up modem connected to your phone line, that modem must dial an *access number* to access AOL. The access number is answered by another modem connected to one of AOL's computers. Be sure that the number you choose is a local number. Even though the access number may be in your area code, you could still incur a large phone bill if the number is a toll or long-distance call for you.

If you move, you may need to choose a new local access number. Here's how:

1. Sign on to AOL and choose Help⇨AOL Access Phone Numbers.
2. In the AOL Setup window, type your area code and select your country of residence. Click Next to continue.
3. A list of access numbers appears on-screen (refer to Figure 7-3). Choose two or three numbers that are local calls for you.
4. Confirm your selections and then click Next.
5. In the Confirm Current Location window, select the numbers for your old location and click Delete. Make sure that you delete all of your old access numbers and leave the new ones. Click Finish when you're done.

Adding a Screen Name to Your Account

Your AOL account allows you to have up to seven unique screen names, enabling you to set up screen names for everyone in your family. Each screen name has its own Online Mailbox, Buddy List, and chat identity. If you set up screen names for your children, be sure to also set up Parental Controls as well. I explain how Parental Controls work later in this chapter.

Tip

If you're not sure whether an access number is local or long distance, call your local operator (dial 0) to find out.

7

Installing and Using AOL on Your PC

Setting Up Access Numbers on Your Laptop

If you have a laptop that you routinely take with you when you travel, you may want to configure separate access numbers for each location that you visit. This will help you avoid long-distance charges when you travel.

To set up access numbers for a new location, click the Setup button on the Sign On screen, and then click Add Location. Give the location a name that you'll remember, select the option that lets you choose access numbers for the new location, and click Next. Then simply follow the procedure for selecting access numbers. When you arrive in the new city and want to go online, select the desired location from the Select Location drop-down list on the Sign On screen.

The AOL Keyword: **Screen Names** works for master screen names only.

If you're having a hard time choosing a screen name that isn't already taken, try adding some numbers to the screen name.

To set up a new screen name, follow these steps:

1. Sign on to AOL using your master screen name (the one that you created when you first signed up for AOL) and visit AOL Keyword: **Screen Names**. A list of your current screen names is displayed.

2. Click Create a Screen Name.

3. You're asked if you're creating the new screen name for a child. If you're creating the screen name for an adult, click No and skip ahead to Step 5. Otherwise, click Yes.

4. If you clicked Yes in the previous step, a window appears on-screen providing information about how you can safeguard your children's privacy. Read it and then click Continue.

5. In the next window that appears, click Create Screen Name to begin a series of online steps.

6. In the first step (Step 1 of 4), type a screen name that you would like to use and click Continue. The screen name can be 3 to 16 characters long and may contain both letters and numbers. When you're done, click Continue.

7. If the name is already being used by someone else, a message appears, telling you to pick another name.

8. In the next step, choose and type a password that is between six and eight characters long. Then click Continue.

9. Next, choose a Parental Controls category for the screen name and click Continue. Here are your choices:

- **General Access (18 +):** Allows full, unrestricted access to AOL and the Web.
- **Mature Teen (16–17):** Web sites and newsgroups with mature content are blocked.
- **Young Teen (13–15):** Restricts access to age-appropriate content. Instant messages and some chat rooms are blocked.
- **Kids Only (12 & Under):** Restricts access to age-appropriate content. Instant messages and most chat rooms are blocked.

10. If you chose the General Access option, you are given the option to make the screen name a master screen name. Choose Yes or No. A person signed on using a master screen name has the power to adjust Parental Controls and add new screen names, so consider this choice carefully. When you're done, click Continue.

11. Review the settings that you created and click Accept Settings if everything is correct. Otherwise, click Customize Settings to set up Parental Controls.

Repeat these steps for each new screen name. When you're finished, all the screen names for your account appear listed in the screen names window, as shown in Figure 7-4.

Troubleshooting

Don't choose a password that others can easily guess, such as a birth date or the name of your pet. Use combinations of unusual words and numbers to ensure others won't guess the password.

Note

The AOL staff will never ask for your password or personal information in an e-mail, chat, or phone conversation.

7

Installing and Using AOL on Your PC

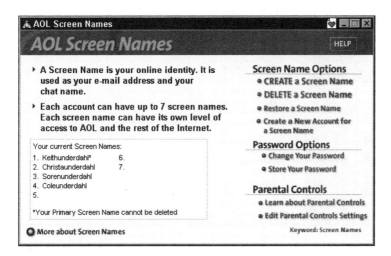

Figure 7-4. This account has four screen names set up.

Customizing AOL

AOL isn't just easy to use; it's also easy to customize. You can keep unwanted e-mail out of your Online Mailbox, and you can safeguard your children's privacy. The following sections show you how.

Setting Mail Controls

Definition

Just as everyone has a postal address, every entity on the Internet has an *Internet domain*. Your e-mail address (user@aol.com) takes on AOL's domain name. AOL is the Internet's largest domain.

Find It Online

To find out more about avoiding unwanted e-mail, use AOL Keyword: **Spam**.

Mail Controls enable you to control the mail that you receive. You can block junk e-mail (also called *spam* in online jargon), mail from specific people or Internet domains, or even file attachments and pictures in e-mail. Mail Controls can only be configured when you are logged on using a master screen name. Here's how to set up Mail Controls:

1. Sign on to AOL using a master screen name (see the section on creating screen names earlier in this chapter).

2. Visit AOL Keyword: **Mail Controls**.

3. Click the Set Up Mail Controls button.

4. In the screen that appears, click Next.

5. In the next screen that appears (shown in Figure 7-5), select a screen name from the drop-down list and choose a control option. You can choose to allow all mail or to block all mail. If you want to allow some (but not all) mail, choose the third option and click Next.

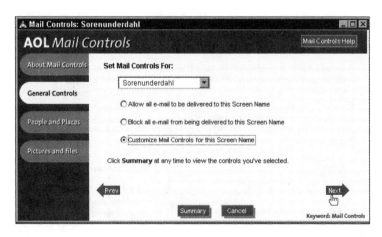

Figure 7-5. Choose a screen name that you want to customize Mail Controls for here.

6. On the next screen, click one of the blocking options. If you decide that you want to block mail from particular AOL screen names, domains, or Internet e-mail addresses, you must type them into the text box shown in Figure 7-6 and click Add. Click Next when you're done.

Blocked addresses appear here

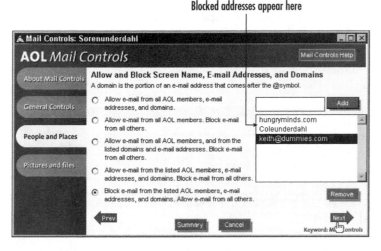

Figure 7-6. You can block or allow mail from specific screen names, e-mail addresses, or domains here.

7. Choose whether the screen name can send and receive attachments (such as pictures) in e-mail. Then click Next.

8. Review the Mail Controls that you set up and click Save to confirm them. You can make changes by clicking Prev.

9. In the final screen, click Return to Mail Controls to return and set up Mail Controls for another screen name, or click Close to leave Mail Controls.

You can set up Mail Controls for any of your screen names. If you are receiving a lot of junk mail from the same domain or person, add that domain or person to your list of blocked e-mail sources.

Safeguarding Your Family with Parental Controls

The Internet is an important tool for your entire family, and AOL's Parental Controls help you take the worry out of accessing the online world. By setting up Parental Controls for the

Note

Remember, viruses are often exchanged in e-mail attachments.

Cross-Reference

Before you set up Parental Controls, make sure that you have set up a unique screen name for each person who will use the computer. See the earlier section on creating screen names.

7

Installing and Using AOL on Your PC

screen names on your AOL account, you can ensure your children's online safety. You can also customize when your family members can sign on and for how long they stay online. To set up Parental Controls, follow these steps:

1. Sign on to AOL using a master screen name and visit AOL Keyword: **Parental Controls**.

2. In the window that appears, click the Set Parental Controls link. The Parental Controls window appears, as shown in Figure 7-7.

Click to scroll up or down

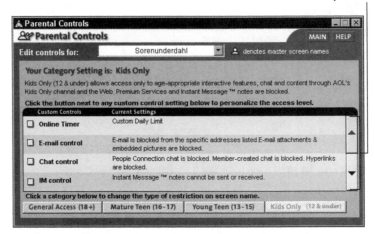

Figure 7-7. Use Parental Controls to control content and features on your computer.

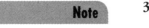

Note

Note that master screen names have a unique icon next to them in the screen name selection menu.

Tip

Each set of controls has a unique wizard to guide you through configuration; just follow the on-screen instructions.

3. Choose a screen name from the drop-down list at the top of the window to set controls for that screen name.

4. To set controls for a specific type of activity on AOL (such as e-mail, chats, and Web browsing), click a button next to a control listing. You may need to scroll down in the window to see all the controls. These controls include

   • **Online Timer:** Controls the total amount of time per day that a screen name can spend online

   • **E-Mail Control:** Configures mail controls

   • **Chat Control:** Blocks certain types of chat rooms

   • **IM Control:** Blocks instant messages

   • **Web Control:** Controls access to certain types of Web sites

- **Additional Master:** Sets a screen name as a master screen name
- **Download Control:** Controls whether files can be downloaded
- **Newsgroup:** Blocks adult-oriented newsgroups
- **Premium Services:** Controls whether the screen name has access to AOL Premium Services

5. Click the Close button in the upper-right corner of the window when you're done customizing the Parental Controls.

Summary

Although you may be happy with the way that you currently have AOL set up on your PC, you can customize your online experience whenever you want. This chapter showed you how to upgrade the AOL software and add AOL to a new computer. You also learned how to choose a new access number and how to add screen names for members of your family. One of the most important things that you can do is customize AOL to safeguard your family from spam and other unwanted material. In the next chapter, you'll learn more about using many of AOL's features and services.

Quick Look

▶ **AOL Keywords**   **page 113**
You don't have to memorize complicated Web addresses to navigate AOL; you
can just use keywords. This section introduces you to keywords on AOL.

▶ **Instant Messages**   **page 122**
If you're tired of racking up high long-distance phone charges, try chatting with
your friends and family online using instant messages. Instant messages let you
converse by typing and reading messages in real time, without having to pay the
phone company.

▶ **AOL Anytime, Anyplace**   **page 123**
With AOL Anywhere, you can check e-mail, stocks, news, weather, and more by
using another computer, a telephone, Mobile Communicator, pager, or a cell
phone. Find out just how easy it is here.

▶ **Shopping Online**   **page 126**
If you're tired of the crowds and hassles of shopping at the local superstore, try
shopping online with Shop@AOL. The prices are great, the selection is tremen-
dous, and the sales staff is always knowledgeable — plus, your transactions are
guaranteed to be safe!

Chapter 8

Using AOL

America Online is much more than an Internet service. With AOL, you can get to know the AOL community and use services that aren't available on the Internet. You can use AOL to communicate directly with friends and family and to go shopping online. And now, thanks to AOL Anywhere, you can take advantage of AOL even when you aren't using your PC.

This chapter introduces you to many of AOL's most popular features. If you need help setting up your AOL account and preferences, see Chapter 3.

Using Keywords to Surf AOL

Popular culture today is filled with references to the Internet. Many of those references can get confusing, filled with lots of dots and *w*s. AOL offers an easier way to browse the online world: keywords. Just type a keyword into the Address box on the navigation bar, and AOL takes you where you want to go.

Just about every AOL feature has its own AOL keyword. If a feature has a keyword, the keyword appears in the bottom-right corner of the feature's main window. Literally thousands of AOL keywords exist. For a complete list, visit AOL Keyword: **Keywords** and click Keyword List.

To begin browsing AOL using keywords, follow these steps:

1. Start AOL and sign on.
2. Click the Address box on the AOL navigation bar, as shown in Figure 8-1.
3. Enter a keyword. If you don't have a keyword in mind, just enter a word or phrase that you're interested in, such as Sports, Shopping, or Slingo.
4. Press Enter on your keyboard or click Go on the navigation bar. After a few seconds, a window for the keyword appears.

Cross-Reference

Another great way to surf AOL is to browse AOL's channels. See Chapter 3 for more on using AOL channels.

Tip

One quick way to get to the Keyword window is to press the Ctrl key and the letter K on your keyboard at the same time.

Finding Friends and Family on AOL

AOL is a great way for you to keep in touch with your friends and family. The People Directory makes finding people easy, even if you don't know their screen names. To use the People Directory, follow these steps:

1. Choose People⇨People Directory from the AOL toolbar. The Member Directory window appears.
2. Enter search information in the appropriate text box in the Member Directory window:
   • If you're looking for someone with similar interests, use the Search Entire Profile text box.
   • If you're looking for a specific person, use the Member Name text box
   • If you're looking for someone who lives near, use the Location text box.

Note

The People Directory searches only AOL members who have completed profiles. If you haven't filled out a profile for yourself yet, do so by clicking the My Profile button in the Member Directory window.

8

Using AOL

3. Click Search. A list of results appears. Double-click a listing to view a person's entire profile. When you find the person you're looking for, make a note of his or her screen name.

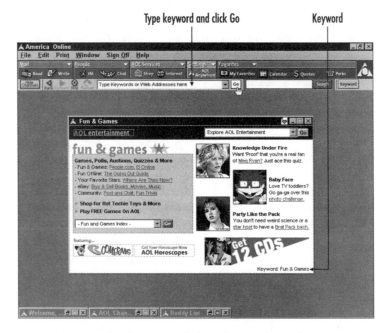

Figure 8-1. Keywords make it easy to find your favorite places on AOL.

Searching AOL and the Internet

AOL gives you access to millions of keywords, Web pages, and other locations all over the Internet. But finding the exact needle that you're looking for in what amounts to the world's largest haystack can sometimes seem challenging. Don't worry; follow these steps to get started:

1. Type a word or phrase (for example, *Tae kwon do*) in the Search box on the right side of the navigation bar.

2. Click Search. After a few seconds, a window listing the search results appears, as shown in Figure 8-2.

Figure 8-2. Search results appear based on the word or phrase that you type in the AOL Search box. Click a blue link to open it.

3. Click a blue link to view a result. If the page that appears isn't quite what you're looking for, click the Back button on the navigation bar to return to the search results.

If your search results are too broad, use more words to narrow the search. For instance, to find sites about the Queen of England, type **Queen England** in the search box and click Search. AOL will search for Web pages that contain both of those words.

You can also enclose words in quotes to make AOL search for that exact phrase. For instance, **"Minnesota Vikings"** will only produce results pertaining to the football team, whereas **Minnesota Vikings** will also yield a lot of Web pages about the state and ancient Norsemen.

If you want to visit a specific Web page on the Internet, type its address — such as **www.hungryminds.com** — in the Address box and then click Go.

Using AOL to Keep in Touch with Friends and Family

AOL offers a variety of communication tools to help you stay in touch with your friends and family, as well as to make new friends online. This section shows you how to use e-mail, chat,

8

Using AOL

and instant messaging. You also find out how to stay in touch with buddies all the time by using your Buddy List.

Using AOL E-Mail

E-mail is short for *electronic mail.*

Of all the things people do online, e-mail is perhaps the most popular activity. E-mail is a great way to communicate with other people because it combines the best aspects of traditional mail:

▶ The delivery system is reliable.

▶ You can read messages at your leisure.

▶ You can hang on to messages for as long as you want.

But the best part is that you don't have to pay postage. And unlike postal mail (called *snail-mail* by many e-mail users), e-mail arrives in the recipient's mailbox almost immediately.

Understanding E-Mail Addresses

When it comes to e-mail addresses, spelling counts (but capitalization doesn't). If you get just one letter wrong, the e-mail will not go to the intended recipient.

AOL e-mail lets you communicate with AOL members and Internet users. As long as you know a member's screen name or an Internet user's complete e-mail address, you can send and receive messages. Keep in mind that when you send messages to other AOL members, you only need to use their screen names — you can omit the aol.com.

As with postal mail, e-mail must be properly addressed. A pair of typical e-mail addresses looks like this:

▶ keithunderdahl@aol.com is the e-mail address my Internet friends need when they send me mail.

▶ keithunderdahl is all my AOL friends need to send me mail.

▶ keithunderdahl@hungryminds.com is an example of what an Internet e-mail address looks like. You need to type the entire address, including everything after @.

You can also set up an Address Book with the e-mail addresses of all the people that you keep in touch with. Use AOL Keyword: **Address Book** and click New Contact to get started.

Reading and Writing E-Mail

AOL provides you with an Online Mailbox where the mail you receive and read is stored and where you can compose and send mail of your own. The Mail menu on the AOL toolbar is

Cross-Reference

You can configure AOL to download new mail automatically while you're away by using Automatic AOL. See Chapter 17 for details.

devoted to your Online Mailbox. Just click the Read button, and your mailbox appears, as shown in Figure 8-3.

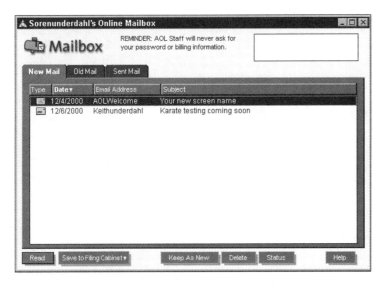

Figure 8-3. AOL provides this electronic mailbox for your e-mail.

To write and send e-mail, follow these steps:

1. Click the Write button on the AOL toolbar.
2. The Write Mail window appears, as shown in Figure 8-4. Type the e-mail address or screen name of the recipient in the Send To box and then press the Tab key twice.

   If you'd like to send a *carbon copy* of the message to someone else, type the e-mail address or screen name in the Copy To box.
3. Type a subject in the Subject box, press Tab, and type your message.
4. When you're finished with the message, click the Send Now button.

Handling File Attachments in Mail

One of the neatest things you can do with e-mail is send and receive files as e-mail *attachments*. This is a great way to exchange pictures with friends and family or send a word processing document to your boss when you can't get to the office.

Caution

Never download an e-mail attachment if you don't know the person who sent it or what the file is. E-mail attachments are often used to infect PCs with computer viruses.

8

Using AOL

Type e-mail address or screen name here

Message body   Subject   Send

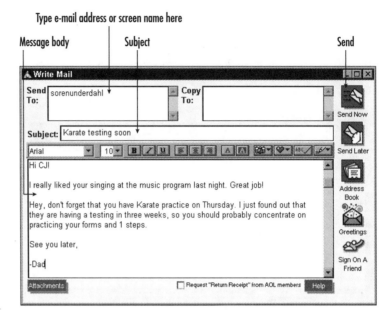

Figure 8-4. Compose your message in the Write Mail window.

If you receive an e-mail message with an attached file, you'll see the name and size of the file listed in the header portion of the e-mail, as shown in Figure 8-5. To download it, follow these steps:

The Download button only appears at the bottom of e-mail messages that have files attached.

1. Click the Download button at the bottom of the mail window and choose Download Now from the pop-up menu that appears.

2. A warning screen from AOL appears, describing some of the potential pitfalls of e-mail attachments. Read this warning and click Yes if you want to download the file. The Download Manager dialog box appears.

3. In the Download Manager dialog box, make a note of the filename and the folder it's being saved in and then click Save. By default, attachments are saved in the `C:\America Online 6.0\download` folder.

   The file is downloaded to your PC, and you see a File Transfer progress meter. If the file is a picture, it automatically appears in its own window when it's done downloading.

To find downloaded files quickly, choose Start⇨ Documents.

File name and size

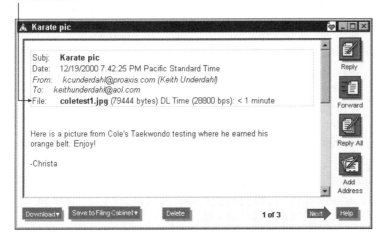

Figure 8-5. You can send and receive files such as pictures with AOL e-mail.

You can also attach files to e-mail that you send out. But before you send an e-mail attachment to an online buddy, make sure that the recipient is willing and capable of receiving your attachment. Some Internet services don't allow file attachments, and most people need some advanced warning before you send a large attachment via e-mail.

Just follow these steps to attach a file to an e-mail message:

1. Begin writing a new e-mail message. Don't forget to address the message as described in the previous section.

2. Click the Attachments button in the lower-left corner of the mail window.

3. In the Attachments window, click the Attach button.

4. In the Attach dialog box, locate the file that you want to attach, click it once to select it, and click Open.

5. Repeat Steps 3 and 4 for any additional files that you want to attach. Click OK in the Attachments window when you're done.

6. When you're done composing your message, click the Send Now button.

Replying to and Forwarding Mail

When friends send you e-mail messages, you'll often want to respond to what they wrote or sent. Or you may want to forward a message to someone else who may find it interesting.

Troubleshooting

In AOL 6.0, if you try to send an open file as an attachment, you are alerted that the file is open and the e-mail isn't sent.

8

Using AOL

When you're reading a message that you've received, you'll see three reply options along the right side of the window:

- ▶ **Reply:** Click this button to reply to the person who sent you the e-mail.
- ▶ **Forward:** Click this button to forward a message that you received to someone else.
- ▶ **Reply All:** If you receive a message that was sent to other people as well, click Reply All to send your reply to *all* of the original recipients.

When you click one of these buttons, a new mail message window appears with the subject already filled in. If you click Reply or Reply All, the Send To box will already be filled in, but if you click Forward, you'll have to provide an e-mail address or screen name for the person that you want to send the message to.

If you forward a received message to another online buddy, make sure you get permission from the original sender first.

Using the Filing Cabinet to Save Mail

Mail in your Online Mailbox is actually stored on AOL's computers, or *mail servers*. This procedure enables you to read your mail from almost any computer with access to AOL.

Before you delete messages from the server, you may want to save some of them on your hard drive. You can save mail for future reference by using the Filing Cabinet. To save a message in the Filing Cabinet, follow these steps:

1. In the Online Mailbox window, select the message that you want to save.
2. Near the bottom of the Mailbox window, click the Save to Filing Cabinet button and then choose Mail from the pop-up menu that appears.
3. The message is saved to your Filing Cabinet. You can access the Filing Cabinet by choosing Mail⊏⟩Filing Cabinet from the AOL toolbar.

Chatting in AOL

Another popular online activity is chatting. Unlike e-mail, *chat* takes place in real time, like a telephone conversation. AOL chat rooms let you chat with many people at once. You never know who you'll find in a chat room, so to be on the safe side, don't give out any personal information in chat rooms, and remember that AOL personnel will never ask you for your password or billing information.

The People menu is dedicated to Chat and other community activities. To begin chatting online, follow these steps:

1. Click the Chat button on the AOL toolbar. The People Connection window appears.

2. Click Find a Chat.

3. On the left side of the Find a Chat window, choose a category and then click the View Chats button.

4. Select a chat room from the list on the right and click the Go Chat button. After a few seconds, a chat room window opens, as shown in Figure 8-6.

5. Read the activity, and make some posts of your own. When you're done chatting, click the Close button in the upper-right corner of the chat window.

Caution

People sometimes post offensive material in chat rooms. If you see something that you feel is inappropriate, click the Notify AOL button or leave the chat room.

Chat activity   Chat participants

Type post here

Figure 8-6. Chat rooms can get a bit unruly, but they can also be a great way to talk with people that share your interests.

During a chat, someone in the room may try to have a private chat with you. You can even initiate a private chat with

8

Using AOL

someone by selecting a screen name in the screen name list and clicking Private Chat. Keep in mind that all the same rules that apply to "public" chat rooms apply to private chats as well. If you're new to chatting, click the New to Chat link in the People Connection window to get an overall sense of what to expect and to learn the lingo.

Keeping a Distance When You Don't Want to Chat

You don't always have to chat with everyone you meet online. If you encounter someone in a chat room who's annoying you in some way, or if you simply don't want to chat, you can use AOL's Ignore feature, which allows you to block any further conversation with the person you specify. If you're in a chat room and you want to use the Ignore feature, follow these steps:

From the list of members in the chat room that appears on the right side of the chat window (refer to Figure 8-6), double-click the screen name of the person you want to ignore. A small window appears, offering you several options.

Click the **Ignore Member** check box and close the window. Although others in the chat room will still see comments from that person, you will not.

Using Instant Messaging

Note

If you want to exchange instant messages with a buddy, both of you must be online.

If you have visited any online chat rooms, you've probably noticed that keeping up with all the conversations can be challenging. If you'd rather just chat with an online buddy that you know, use AOL Instant Messenger. Instant messaging is similar to chat in that it works in real time, but it's much more private.

To send someone an instant message, choose People⇨IM from the AOL toolbar. Enter your buddy's screen name in the To box, type a message, and click Send. If the person is offline, a message appears, telling you so. If he or she is online, you see an instant message window appear.

You can chat with Internet friends using the AOL Instant Messenger℠ service. They can download AOL Instant Messenger at www.aol.com.

Using the Buddy List

If you don't feel like memorizing your buddies' screen names, add them to your Buddy List. The Buddy List automatically appears every time you launch AOL and sign on. Follow these steps to add a person to your Buddy List:

1. Click the Setup button at the bottom of the Buddy List window.
2. In the Buddy List Setup window, choose a category (Buddies, Family, or Co-Workers) that you want to add the person to and click Add Buddy.
3. Enter the Buddy's screen name and click Save.
4. Close the Buddy List Setup window when you're done.

When your buddies are online, their screen names appear in the Buddy List. To send a quick message to a buddy, select that person's screen name in the Buddy List and click the Send IM button.

Getting the Information You Want with AOL Anywhere

One of the problems with many forms of electronic communication is that you have to be at your computer to communicate. But AOL is turning that assumption upside down with AOL Anywhere, an innovative service that enables you to access e-mail, send instant messages, and check news and weather by using a telephone, cell phone, pager, television, Mobile Communicator, handheld computer, or Gateway Connected Touchpad with Instant AOL.

To begin using AOL Anywhere, follow these steps:

1. Visit AOL Keyword: **AOL Anywhere** or click the AOL Anywhere button on the AOL toolbar.
2. In the window that appears, click the Go button to start AOL Anywhere. Your My AOL page — part of AOL Anywhere — appears. It contains news headlines, weather, horoscopes, stock portfolios, and your calendar.
3. If this is the first time that you have started My AOL, you'll see a window asking for your zip code and birth date. Enter this information and click Submit so that My AOL can display local news and weather, as well as your personalized horoscope.

Find It Online

If you don't see your Buddy List, visit AOL Keyword: **BuddyView**.

Find It Online

If you're just interested in accessing AOL e-mail and some other features by telephone, visit AOL Keyword: **MyAOLbyPhone**.

8

Using AOL

Troubleshooting

If you don't see a box asking for your zip code and birthday, click My Preferences to personalize My AOL.

To change the My AOL sections that are displayed, click the Personalize My AOL button in the upper-right corner of the page. In the Personalize My AOL window that appears, place a check mark next to items that you want, and remove check marks next to items that you don't want. For example, if you're interested in sports, check the Sports option for up-to-the-minute scores. Click Save at the bottom of the Personalize My AOL window to close it.

To personalize an individual section of My AOL, click the Personalize button that appears in the upper-right corner of that section. For instance, if you want to keep tabs on specific stocks that you own, click the Personalize button and then choose Customize to open the My Portfolio window. From there, click the Create button and then follow the on-screen instructions.

You can access My AOL from any computer that has Internet access. Simply launch the Web browser on that computer and visit www.aol.com. You'll see a screen similar to Figure 8-7. Enter your screen name and password and click Go to sign on and check your e-mail, My Calendar, My AOL, and more.

Tip

When you're done using AOL Anywhere on someone else's computer, make sure that you click the Sign Out link on any of the AOL Anywhere pages.

Find It Online

Now you can have an AOL-trained technician come to your house to setup, register, and demonstrate how to use AOL products or devices. Visit AOL Keyword: **IHS** to get more information about *AOL In Home Support* and to find out about the availability of the service in your area.

Figure 8-7. Visit www.aol.com from any computer to access your AOL account using AOL Anywhere.

AOL Anywhere enables you to access AOL from more than just another PC. You can also access various features of AOL Anywhere using a cell phone, a regular telephone, a handheld PC, AOLTV, and more. To find out more about the other AOL

Anywhere services, click the AOL Anywhere button on the AOL toolbar and click a button for the service that you're interested in.

Planning Your Day with My Calendar

You probably have a special place where you record all of your important appointments and dates. Maybe it's a calendar on your wall or on your desk. Wouldn't it be great if you could keep track of your schedule and be able to access it anywhere? You can with AOL's My Calendar feature, shown in Figure 8-8. To begin using My Calendar, click My Calendar on the AOL Welcome Screen or click the Calendar button on the AOL toolbar.

Tip

Remember, you can access My Calendar using AOL Anywhere, meaning that you can check your calendar using any computer with Internet access.

Figure 8-8. My Calendar helps you plan your busy day.

The first time that you use My Calendar, a series of setup screens appears and helps you set up My Calendar. The setup screens ask you a series of simple questions that help My Computer better match the time zone and city that you live in.

To add an event to the calendar, click the number for a day and click Add Appt in the little window that appears. Fill in information about the appointment or event and click OK to add it to the calendar.

Shopping Online

Shopping can be both fun and necessary. But it can also be frustrating if the product you want isn't in stock. If you're tired of shopping hassles, try shopping online with Shop@AOL. You can visit Shop@AOL by clicking the Shopping Channel button on the Channels toolbar or by using the AOL Keyword: **Shopping**.

Troubleshooting

Click the Customer Service link on any shopping category page to find out more about shopping online, AOL Certified Merchants, and the AOL Guarantee.

All your transactions are secure when you shop online with AOL. You can browse Shop@AOL several ways:

▶ Click a category on the left side of the window. Most categories have subcategories that appear in a menu when you click the category title.

▶ Click one of today's specials in the main portion of the window.

▶ Type a product or brand name in the search box near the top of the window and then click Search.

You can sign up for the AOL Quick Checkout service from any Shop@AOL page. AOL Quick Checkout allows you to safely store your personal information so that when you make a purchase from a participating AOL Merchant, you don't have to manually enter this information. Click the About Quick Checkout link to learn more.

Shop@AOL provides a great way to find your favorite items, even things that are really hard to find in your local stores. And even if you intend to buy locally, Shop@AOL is a great way to research products before you spend your hard-earned cash.

Summary

AOL is literally packed with features to make your PC fun and useful throughout your daily life. You have access to a world of information using AOL keywords and Internet search tools, you can shop online, and you can stay in touch with friends and family with communication tools like e-mail and instant messages. AOL Anywhere gives you access to AOL's services even when you aren't at your PC, and My Calendar helps you plan your day. Now that you're familiar with AOL and Windows, the next part of this book will help you get familiar with the hardware of your PC.

Quick Look

Chapter 9

Understanding Your PC's Components

I f you own a car, you know that it has many components that help you get around. The gas tank holds fuel, the engine provides power, the brakes help you stop, and the seats (hopefully) keep you comfortable. Just like a car, your computer consists of many separate parts that all work together. It has disk drives for storing information, processor chips to handle that data, a monitor and speakers to help you see and hear what's going on, and a keyboard and mouse to let you take control.

As a computer owner, it's important to recognize each part of your PC and know what the parts do. With this knowledge you'll better understand the capabilities of your PC and use it more effectively.

This chapter introduces you to the basic components of your PC by showing you how to recognize the parts of your computer, explaining what they do, and deciphering the alphabet soup of words that is often used to identify various PC components.

The Motherboard

You spend nearly all your computer time wiggling the mouse, typing on the keyboard, and viewing the monitor, but all of the real activity takes place inside the box that everything plugs into. You may not understand how your car engine works, but you do know that if you don't put gas in it, it won't run. Likewise, you don't need to know *how* your PC's memory or sound system work, but you need to know enough about the whole system to be able to tell if there's a problem.

If you were to open up that box that houses your PC's inner workings, you would see a mess of chips, spikes, and connectors. Figure 9-1 shows a less complicated version of this mess. The following sections explain what all these parts do.

Just as your heart is the part of your body that all blood flows to and from, the *motherboard* of a PC is the main circuit board in your computer that everything else plugs into. The motherboard houses the *central processing unit* (CPU), which controls your computer's actions, as well as your PC's *random access memory* (RAM), which gives the PC enough working space to act on your commands.

The motherboard is filled with sockets and slots, including

- ▶ A socket or slot for the CPU to be plugged in to.
- ▶ Slots (called *DIMM* or *SIMM* slots) for system RAM to be plugged in to.
- ▶ Slots for adapters, also called *expansion cards,* that allow you to add new capabilities to your computer. For example, you can add sound cards, network cards, and so on.
- ▶ Connectors, commonly called *ports,* for a keyboard, mouse, printer, and other devices. These ports are usually oriented to align with holes on the PC case so that the mouse, keyboard, and printer can be connected without actually opening the case.
- ▶ Ports for disk drive cables. These ports — and the cables that connect to them — stay inside the case.

Caution

PC components are delicate, so don't open the case without the help of a professional or someone with PC hardware experience. Also, check your warranty information to ensure you aren't voiding the warranty by opening the PC.

▶ A small battery (just like the battery that you use in a watch) to power the PC's internal clock.

▶ Power connectors. These take power from the PC's power supply, also located inside the case.

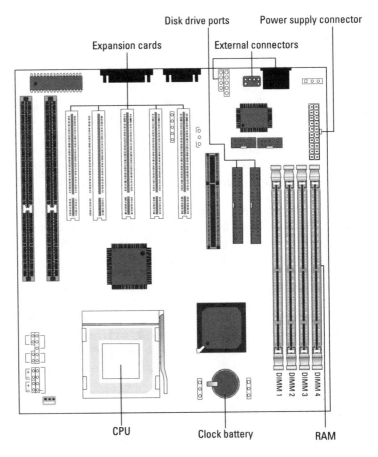

Figure 9-1. The motherboard of your computer might look something like this.

Note

In addition to the basics, some motherboards also include a built-in display adapter (or video card), a built-in sound controller, and a special AGP *(Accelerated Graphics Port)* for advanced display adapters.

The motherboard is housed inside the PC case, sometimes called the *console*. The case must protect your computer's components from exposure and dust, guard against electrical hazards, and be sufficiently ventilated so that your PC doesn't overheat. The case also incorporates the power supply, which controls the flow of electricity through your computer. Some cases are small and fit easily on top of a desk, while others are larger and designed to sit on the floor under or next to a desk.

The CPU

If the motherboard is your PC's heart, then the CPU is most definitely your PC's brain. When people ask how fast your computer is, they really want to know how fast the CPU, or *central processing unit,* is at processing commands. The CPU oversees just about everything that the computer does. The speed of the CPU is usually expressed in *megahertz* (MHz) or *gigahertz* (GHz).

The two most successful CPU manufacturers today are Intel and AMD, and the processor in your computer probably comes from one of these companies.

Definition

A *megahertz* (MHz) is a unit of measurement equal to a million electric pulses, or cycles, per second. One *gigahertz* (GHz) is equal to 1,000 MHz.

RAM

When you work on a complicated math problem, you probably use scratch paper to work out the equations and come up with an answer. Whenever your PC's CPU handles data, it also requires a workspace similar to your scratch paper. That working space is called *random access memory,* or RAM, and without enough RAM, your PC will be sluggish and prone to crashing. RAM is different from storage (described later in this chapter) because it serves as only a temporary working space for the CPU, and anything there disappears when the PC's power is turned off.

RAM in modern PCs usually comes on a narrow circuit board called a DIMM (dual in-line memory module). A DIMM snaps into a special slot on your motherboard and looks similar to Figure 9-2. The physical dimensions (length, height, and so on) of DIMMs are standardized, so the size of a DIMM is measured in how many megabytes (MB) of RAM it holds.

Definition

A *megabyte* equals 1,000 kilobytes. A *kilobyte* equals 1,024 bytes. A *byte* is a single piece of data (such as a numeral, letter, or dot of color in a graphic) on your PC.

Figure 9-2. This memory module plugs into a special DIMM slot on the motherboard.

Troubleshooting

Many older PCs use smaller memory modules called SIMMs (single in-line memory modules). If you're not sure what kind of memory modules your PC uses, consult a professional.

The reason DIMMs are so handy is that if you ever need to add more RAM, you can do so by simply replacing a DIMM with one of higher capacity. Or better yet, you can add to the existing RAM by snapping a new DIMM into an empty slot if one is available on your motherboard.

The more RAM you have, the better off your computer will be. Here's why:

▶ More RAM gives your computer a bigger working space, meaning that you can run more and bigger programs simultaneously.

▶ Greater amounts of RAM also help your PC run faster, so you can still have several programs running and have each of them run quickly.

Here's some RAM information to keep in mind:

▶ Your PC needs at least 32MB of RAM (64MB is better) if you plan to run several programs at the same time.

▶ You should be aware of the amount of RAM required by major programs. Check the program's documentation for details.

To run AOL 6.0, your PC should have at least 32MB of RAM installed on your PC.

▶ Always make sure your PC exceeds a program's minimum RAM requirements by at least 16MB. Following this rule may not protect you entirely from having your system involuntarily shut down (or *crash*), but it can make a huge difference.

Devices That Connect You to the Internet

Find It Online

Discover more about high-speed online access at AOL Keyword: **AOL PLUS**.

Most computers connects to America Online using a *modem*. The most common type of modem is a dial-up modem that connects at 56.6 Kbps (kilobits per second) using a telephone line. A modem has two phone jacks; one connects to the phone company, the other to a regular telephone. You don't have to connect a telephone to the second jack if you don't want to, but it will let you use the line for regular phone calls when your PC is offline.

Most dial-up modems are located inside your computer, so look for the phone jacks on the back of your PC's case.

Dial-up modems are easy to use but not terribly fast. In reality, most dial-up modems connect at speeds much slower than 56.6 Kbps. Actual connection speeds vary depending on the quality of your telephone line and your distance from the phone company's main office. Other, faster types of modems include

- ▶ ISDN
- ▶ DSL
- ▶ Cable modems

Your phone or cable company provides these high-speed modems, which usually connect to a network adapter on your PC. Companies that offer high-speed access offer installation of the modem and the software that runs it, a nice feature because ISDN, DSL, and cable modems can be complicated to install. They'll even install a network card in your PC if it doesn't already have one. Check with the provider to find out if the service is available in your area.

Getting High-Speed Access with AOL PLUS

AOL offers its own high-speed access (also called *broadband* access) called AOL PLUS (AOL Keyword: **AOL PLUS**). AOL PLUS costs an additional $19.95 per month but lets you download Web pages and other online content up to 50 times faster than a regular dial-up modem.

The service includes your choice of a DSL modem, DirecPC, or satellite modem. Soon, you'll be able to use a cable modem. Make sure that your PC has a network card installed (see Appendix C to take an inventory of your PC) before signing up for this service.

 Find It Online

For your added convenience, AOL now offers *AOL In Home Support*. Upon request, an AOL trained technician will come to your house to setup, register, and demonstrate how to use AOL products or devices. *AOL In Home Support* prices vary for different services. You can visit AOL Keyword: **IHS** to get more information, find out about the availability of service in your area, and to request the service.

Your PC's Storage Drives

Unlike RAM, which disappears the second you shut down your PC, storage is what saves your documents so that you can review, edit, and share them with others later. As long as your

Note

Unlike random access memory, which holds on to bits of files for short periods of time, storage drives hold on to your files forever — or until you delete them.

storage drives are working, you can locate and open documents that you save, even if you shut down and restart your PC.

Your PC has two different kinds of storage components. These components are interchangeably called *disks* or *drives* — they both mean the same thing. Drives that are permanently mounted inside your PC are called *hard drives*. Drives that use removable disks (such as CD-ROMs or floppy disks) are called *removable disk drives*. The following sections explore these storage options. To access the drives on your PC, double-click the My Computer icon on your Windows desktop. My Computer opens as shown in Figure 9-3.

Your My Computer window may look slightly different depending on which version of Windows you have and how many different disk drives are installed on your PC.

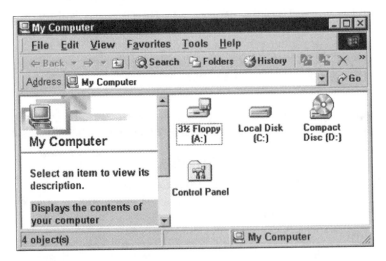

Figure 9-3. My Computer shows you the disk drives that are on your computer.

Hard Drives

The hard drive is an essential component of your PC because it stores all your documents (such as that letter you're writing) and programs (like AOL, Microsoft Windows, and Microsoft Office). Information remains on the hard drive even when the power is turned off — provided that you save it before you shut down, of course.

How big should your hard drive be? Program files for Windows 95 may require as little as 80MB, while Windows Millennium Edition can use over 600MB. AOL 6.0 requires another 113MB of disk space (130MB if you have Windows 95). All other programs you install on your PC take up disk space, and of course you'll want plenty of storage space for files you work on and software you download from AOL. Add up the disk space requirements for all the programs on your PC, estimate how much free space you think you'll want for your own files, and then triple the total. This should give you a good *minimum* amount of hard disk space that you'll need.

Removable Disks

Computer data can be stored on many kinds of disks. And although hard drives (which also store information and are sometimes called *hard disks*) generally stay inside the PC, other kinds of disks can be removed. These removable disks can include the following:

- ▶ **Floppy:** The 3½-inch disks aren't actually floppy, but the name has stuck from the early days of personal computers. Every PC has a floppy drive (always the A: drive). Most floppy disks hold just 1.4MB, which isn't very much. Floppies can be used to store small files like word processing documents, which can then be easily transported to another PC.

- ▶ **CD-ROM:** *Compact disc-read only memory* discs look exactly like music CDs. In fact, your CD-ROM drive can be used to play music CDs. Most new computers have CD-ROM drives, which Windows usually calls the D: drive. CD-ROMs are *read only* because you can't save your own files on them. CD-ROMs are often used for in-stalling program files.

- ▶ **DVD-ROM:** *Digital versatile disc-read only memory* drives are beginning to take the place of CD-ROM drives on more expensive PCs. DVD-ROM drives can read CD-ROM discs, as well as movie DVDs and DVD-ROM software discs.

- ▶ **CD-R or CD-RW:** A *CD-R* (compact disc-recordable) or *CD-RW* (compact disc-rewritable) drive lets you record data onto blank CDs. A blank CD can hold up to 650MB of information, so CDs are great for archiving and shar-ing large files. You can also use a CD-R or CD-RW drive

Definition

One *gigabyte* (GB) equals 1,000 megabytes (MB). The size of most hard drives is measured in gigabytes, meaning a 15.8GB hard drive can hold 15,800MB of data.

Cross-Reference

Many other types of remov-able disk drives exist. See Chapter 11 for more on work-ing with removable disks.

to record your own music CDs, which can then be played in any music CD player. CD-R and CD-RW drives usually only come with the most expensive PCs, but you can have one installed for less than $200 if you wish.

Adapters of All Kinds

Cross-Reference

For details on identifying all of the external connectors on the back of your PC, see Appendix C.

Many of the capabilities of your PC are handled by adapter cards. *Adapter cards* (also known as *expansion cards*) slide into special *expansion slots* on the motherboard (refer to Figure 9-1), and since they're inside the PC case all you usually see of them are external connectors on the back of the console. Common adapter cards include

▶ **Sound Card:** Your sound card processes the audio that you hear through speakers when you listen to music, watch a movie, or play a game on your computer. The back of the sound card has connectors for speakers, a microphone, a *line input,* and usually a joystick. A typical sound card looks similar to Figure 9-4. The line input usually isn't used for anything, unless you have another device (like an external music player) that is designed to connect to it.

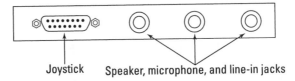

Joystick   Speaker, microphone, and line-in jacks

Figure 9-4. Your sound card usually has connections for speakers, a microphone, a line input, and a joystick.

Definition

Video cards are sometimes also referred to as *display adapters.*

▶ **Video Cards:** All PCs have a video card. The video card usually has just one connector that looks like Figure 9-5. This is the connector that your monitor plugs in to.

Figure 9-5. Your monitor plugs into this connector on your video card.

▶ **Network Adapters:** If you have more than one computer and you want to connect these computers together to form a network, then each computer has to have a network adapter. The network adapter is an *expansion card,* and it probably has a port (or connector) on the back that looks like a wide telephone jack. Network adapters are also used to connect high-speed modems like DSL, ISDN, and cable modems to your PC. A network adapter is not critical to your PC's operation, so you might not have one.

▶ **Other Adapter Cards:** Hardware manufacturers produce a dizzying array of cards to fill vacant expansion slots on your motherboard. You can find everything — even FM radio tuners. The important thing is that you have an available expansion slot of the correct type on your motherboard before you try to install any new cards. And of course, if you've never installed PC hardware before you should consult a professional because the components are very delicate.

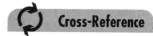

Cross-Reference

See Appendix C to determine which kinds of slots are available on your computer.

External Components

The components inside your computer might do all the hard work, but the monitor, keyboard, speakers, and mouse allow you to interact with your PC. Many other external components help you make better use of your computer as well. Common external components include

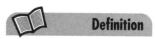

Definition

External PC components are often called *peripherals,* because they exist out on the periphery of your system.

▶ **Monitors:** If the monitor on your computer resembles your television, that is no mistake. Many early personal computers were designed to plug into regular TVs. Computer technology has come a long way in the last two decades, and PC-specific monitors have improved tremendously. Their quality and resolution cause far less eyestrain than TV tubes of yore, and new flat-panel designs conserve space and electricity.

When buying a monitor, try to get one with the highest refresh rate possible; 75 kilohertz (KHz) or higher is best. Higher refresh rates mean less screen-flicker, which is a major cause of eyestrain.

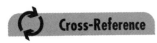

Cross-Reference

Your mouse and keyboard need special care to stay in tip-top working condition. See Chapter 18 for more information.

▶ **Keyboards and mice:** Virtually all your interaction with the computer happens by typing on the keyboard and moving the mouse. The mouse is technically called a *pointing device* because you use it to move a cursor or arrow and point at things on the screen. A mouse that fits in your hand is the most common type of pointing device, but in place of a mouse, you can use a trackball, touch pad, or toggling device.

▶ **Printer:** A printer lets you print out letters, reports, pictures, e-mail, Web pages, and many other kinds of documents you use and read on your PC. Next to a monitor, keyboard, and mouse, a printer is probably the most important peripheral you will own.

▶ **Digital camera:** Many people are now replacing their old film cameras with filmless digital cameras. You can take pictures with your digital camera, and then connect it to your PC and transfer the pictures from the camera right to your hard drive.

▶ **Scanner:** If you already have some printed pictures that you want to get in your computer, you can scan them using a scanner.

▶ **MP3 player:** MP3 is a popular electronic storage format for music, and MP3 players are small portable devices that can play music that is in MP3 format. You can buy and download MP3 music online, and store the music on your hard drive. Then connect the MP3 player to your PC and transfer the music from your hard drive to the player so you can take the music with you.

▶ **Handheld computer:** Tiny computers that rest in the palm of your hand can be used to maintain your address book and daily calendar, check e-mail and send Instant Messages with AOL, and more. Popular types of handhelds include Palmtops and Pocket PCs.

▶ **Network hubs:** To set up a home network with two or more PCs, connect a network cable from the network adapter on each PC to a central hub. The hub acts as an intersection where files and data transfer between the computers on the network. Figure 9-6 illustrates a typical home network arrangement.

Tip

If you're thinking about setting up your own network, the easiest way is to buy a networking kit that includes all the network cards, cables, and a hub.

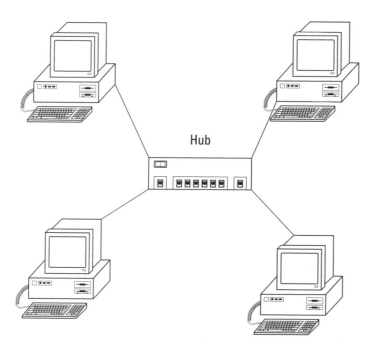

Figure 9-6. Computers can network with each other by connecting to a common hub.

Summary

Many components come together to make your computer
work for you. In this chapter, you learned about internal components of your PC, such as the CPU, RAM, hard drives, and
video card. You also learned about your monitor, keyboard,
mouse, and the other devices (called *peripherals*) that attach
to the outside of your computer. In Chapter 10, you can find
out even more about some of these items, in particular the
ones that help you take control of your PC.

Quick Look

▶ **Monitors** **page 146**

The monitor is one of your computer's most important components, because it enables you to see what the PC is doing. In this part of the chapter, you find out about the different types of monitors that are available and how to use them.

▶ **Keyboards** **page 149**

Your computer's keyboard resembles that of a typewriter, and enables you to type letters and access important functions of the PC. Several different kinds of keyboards are available, and this chapter helps you select the best one for you.

▶ **Mice** **page 150**

Virtually all PCs come with a mouse, and many different kinds of mice are available. When choosing a new mouse, how do you know if you need a mouse with two buttons or three? What about trackballs and touchpads? What kind of mouse can you use with your PC? Find out in this section.

▶ **Speakers and Microphones** **page 153**

Modern PCs are true multimedia tools. Computer speakers are available for every budget and listening taste. Find out all about speakers and microphones and how to connect them to your PC.

Chapter 10

Interfacing with Your PC

Remember the computers used in old science fiction movies? They were huge, gray cases consisting of hundreds of unlabeled buttons and blinking lights. How did anyone make sense of those things?

Thankfully, the designers of modern PCs didn't refer to those old films when they created your computer. Your PC has a display screen and speakers that present information in a way that is easy to understand. Moreover, the mouse and keyboard are simple to use, allowing you to easily take control of your PC. This chapter helps you understand the devices that make interfacing with your PC easy and enjoyable.

Viewing Your PC's Display

Your PC's monitor is easily one of its most important components. The monitor lets you see what is happening on your

PC. Most monitors are designed to fit on a desk, use energy efficiently, and reduce eyestrain. The following sections show you how to select and set up your monitor, as well as how to customize your monitor to your liking.

Comparing Monitor Types and Sizes

A majority of PC monitor screens use a *cathode ray tube* (CRT) similar to the picture tube in a television set. CRT monitors are affordable and available in a variety of sizes, but they take up quite a bit of space on your desk and produce a lot of heat.

Many laptops, on the other hand, use flat-panel displays, which are designed with LCD (liquid crystal display) technology for a flatter, more compact design. Flat-panel monitors are now available for desktop PCs as well, but they're expensive. They usually provide superior display quality, take up less space on your desk, produce less heat, and use less electricity.

Keep in mind that most flat-panel monitors require a special type of video card that outputs a digital signal. Most conventional PC video cards output an analog signal.

When choosing a monitor, keep several key factors in mind:

▶ **Size:** The size of the monitor is measured in inches diagonally across the screen. Bigger monitors let you see more windows, icons, pictures, and other on-screen elements at once, meaning you don't have to scroll up and down or left and right in your programs as often. Seventeen-inch monitors provide the best balance of screen area and cost.

▶ **Dot pitch:** The display on a CRT is actually made up of millions of tiny dots, and the display clarity of a monitor is measured in *dot pitch*, the distance between each tiny dot. The smaller the dot pitch, the better; try to get a monitor with .28 dot pitch (meaning the distance between each dot is .28 mm) or lower.

▶ **Refresh rate:** If the monitor's refresh rate is too slow, the display will flicker and strain your eyes. Try to get a monitor with a refresh rate of at least 75 Hz (you can usually find a refresh rate frequency listed on a monitor's specifications chart). *Hertz* (abbreviated Hz) is a measure of frequency for electromagnetic cycles in a device such as your monitor.

Find It Online

Visit AOL Keyword: **Computing** to research your next monitor. Just type **monitor** in the product search box.

10

Interfacing with Your PC

Note

Dot pitch and size are less important considerations with flat panel displays because they usually offer much higher clarity and resolution.

Look at the connector carefully to make sure you're plugging it into the right port. Other ports on the back of your computer may look similar, but if you look closely, you'll see that other similar connectors have fewer small holes.

Connecting a Monitor to Your PC

Virtually all PC monitors are connected to computers using a cable. The end of the cable has a connector that corresponds to a *port* on the back of the PC. The port on the back of your computer that the monitor cable plugs into looks like the one in Figure 10-1, and as you can see, it's made up of rows of small holes. Now look at the connector at the end of the monitor cable. It's made up of the same number of rows of pins, which fit into the holes in the port.

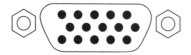

Figure 10-1. Notice that the monitor connector and port each have three rows of five small holes.

Nothing about plugging your monitor into your PC is complicated. Just be sure the PC's power is turned off before you connect or disconnect the monitor, and you're ready to go.

Adjusting the Display Controls on Your Monitor

Start up your computer and wait for Microsoft Windows to load. Then take a good, hard look at your monitor. Does Windows fill the entire screen area, or can you see a lot of black space around the edges? Does the screen seem tilted slightly, or is the shape of the display distorted? You may be able to fix some of these problems with the controls on your monitor.

Tip

Check your documentation for a complete description of all the controls on your specific monitor.

Sometimes these controls are simply a row of knobs across the bottom of the monitor, or you may have to use arrow buttons on the front of the monitor to bring up an on-screen menu full of controls. Each knob or control probably has a picture next to it, similar to the ones shown in Table 10-1 (which describes each control's function).

Table 10-1. Monitor Display Controls

Control	Function
← →	Controls the width of the display area
▢	Centers the display horizontally
↕	Controls the height of the display area
▭	Centers the display vertically
)(	Distorts the middle of the display in or out to fit your monitor
⬳	Distorts the trapezoidal shape of the display area
▱↓	Tilts the display clockwise or counterclockwise

Your monitor may have some or all of these controls, or even some that aren't shown here. Adjust the controls as you see fit to make your display better fit the screen.

Selecting a Keyboard

Keyboards are cheap and easy to replace. Generally speaking, you have a choice of either a standard rectangular-shaped keyboard or a curved ergonomic keyboard. Many people — especially experienced typists — prefer ergonomic keyboards because they enable you to place your hands in a more comfortable position; but other people are more comfortable with the more traditional types of keyboards. You may want to try using both types to see which one suits you best.

Some keyboards have special buttons tailored to your PC. If you have one of these special keyboards and want to replace it with an identical one, you'll probably have to get it directly from your PC's manufacturer.

When you connect your keyboard to your PC, you must make sure that you plug it into the right place. Figure 10-2 shows the two most common types of connectors used for keyboards. The round connector is older and more common. It's called a *PS/2* connector. Some newer keyboards use a small, rectangular connector, called a *USB*. Check the back of your PC to see if you have a port for one or both of these connector types, and

Cross-Reference

If the keyboard you want to buy has a USB connector, make sure that you have an open USB port on your PC. See Appendix C for more on USB ports.

review the documentation that came with your PC to see which connector you should use for the keyboard.

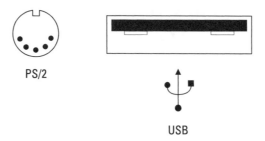

PS/2

USB

Figure 10-2. Most keyboards use either a PS/2 or USB connector.

Using a Mouse

Cross-Reference

To prolong the life of your mouse, see the section on cleaning your mouse in Chapter 18.

A mouse is important because it makes AOL and your PC easy to use. To say that you can't do anything without a mouse may seem like an exaggeration, and of course, you can use your keyboard rather than a mouse to move around programs and applications. However, the best way to open a program on your computer or to visit a *hyperlink* (in the online world, a clickable picture or piece of text that takes you to another Web site or page) is to point and click.

Because PC mice are such an important part of PC use, manufacturers have come up with several twists on the original concept. All these variations on the mouse do the same thing — they allow you to point and click to do things with your computer.

Because the mouse (or other point-and-click device) is used so frequently, it can wear out quickly, and you may eventually need to replace it. The following sections give you all the information you need to be able to select the right mouse (or other point-and-click device) for you and connect it to your PC.

Tip

Don't forget to use a mouse pad under your mouse. A rubber mouse pad gives the rolling ball under your mouse more traction and helps keep it clean.

All PC mice and other point-and-click devices have at least two buttons, aptly called the left and right mouse buttons. (One-button mice are for Macintoshes.) And some mice have three buttons. Here's what the buttons on a mouse do:

▶ Use the button on the left to double-click icons, select items, click tool buttons and menus, and click hyperlinks.

▶ Use the button on the right to open menus full of shortcuts to various commands.

▶ The button in the middle usually doesn't do anything. Most three-button mice are actually designed to be used with the UNIX and Linux operating systems instead of Microsoft Windows. If you buy a three-button mouse, you should be able to use it with your PC and Windows.

A few mice also have a rolling knob that helps you scroll through pages in your documents and online without having to move the mouse over great distances on your desk.

Understanding Other Pointing Devices

A mouse isn't the only kind of pointing device that is available. In fact, if you have a laptop, it probably has a different kind of pointing device built in. The two most common types of pointing devices installed on laptops are

▶ **A pointing stick:** This is a small rubber knob in the middle of the keyboard that you toggle with your finger. It looks kind of like the eraser head from a pencil. When you want to left- or right-click, press the button near the pointing stick.

▶ **A touchpad:** Many laptops have a flat, square-shaped tool for pointing. Place your finger on the touchpad and move it around to move the mouse pointer. Often you can simulate clicks by tapping on the touchpad, but you can also use the left- and right-click buttons located next to (or beneath) the touchpad.

Another kind of pointing device that you may want to try on your PC is a trackball. A trackball looks like an upside-down mouse, because it has a ball on the top that you roll to move the pointer. Some people find trackballs more comfortable because you can use just your fingers to move the ball rather than your whole hand.

Whatever type of pointing device you use, it'll probably take some practice to get used to it. Touchpads, pointing sticks, trackballs, and mice all feel a little different, but after you've used one type for a while, it will feel natural in your hand.

Connecting Your Mouse to Your PC

The type of connection you use to connect your mouse to your PC depends on the type of mouse you have. Figure 10-3

Tip

Most laptops also have provisions for connecting a mouse to the back of the computer through either a serial or USB port. Check your documentation to see if this is an option for your laptop.

Find It Online

Shop online for a new pointing device at AOL Keyword: **Computer Shop** and choose Printers, Software, & Accessories in the Computers menu.

10

Interfacing with Your PC

shows the three connector types most often used for mice: serial, PS/2, and USB. Look on the back of your PC's console to see which types are available. Your PC may have one, two, or all three types of connectors. Also check the documentation that came with your PC to see which kind of connector is recommended for a mouse.

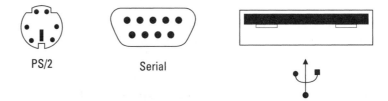

PS/2   Serial

Figure 10-3. A mouse may use a PS/2, serial, or USB connector.

Of these three connectors, PS/2 and serial are the most common. In fact, many mice come with a little adapter that allows the same mouse to connect to either one of these ports. If you buy a new mouse or another kind of pointing device, make sure that you get one that has the same kind of connector as your current mouse, and always follow the recommendations in your PC's documentation.

Customizing the Mouse

Microsoft Windows lets you customize the way your mouse works. You can change the speed for double-clicks, and even swap button operations between the left and right buttons, which is especially handy if you use your mouse with your left hand. To customize the mouse, follow these steps:

1. Choose Start⇨Settings⇨Control Panel.

2. In the Control Panel, double-click the Mouse icon. The Mouse Properties dialog box appears, as shown in Figure 10-4.

3. In the Button Configuration area, indicate whether you use your mouse with the right hand or left hand.

4. In the Double-Click Speed area, move the slider left or right to speed up or slow down the speed required for double-clicks. Double-click the jack-in-the-box on the right to test the new speed setting.

5. When you're done making changes, click OK to save your changes and close the dialog box.

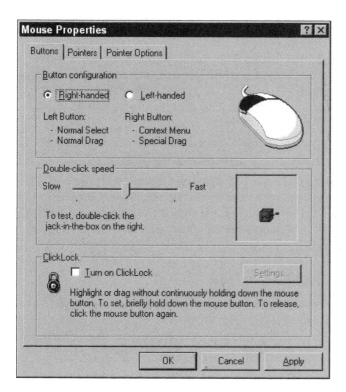

Figure 10-4. Use the Mouse Properties dialog box to customize the way your mouse works.

The Mouse Properties dialog box also has a Pointers tab that lets you customize the pointer's appearance, and a Pointer Options tab where you can adjust the pointer speed and other options. Experiment with these settings to change the way your mouse pointer appears on-screen.

Choosing Audio Devices

To produce audio, your computer needs an adapter (commonly called a *sound card*), that allows you to hear music. Of course, you also need speakers so that you can hear audio. The speakers may be built into your PC hardware or you may need to purchase and plug them in yourself.

Your PC — and all of its applications, including AOL — will work even if no sound card or speakers are installed. However, multimedia technology has made audio as important to many

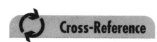

Cross-Reference

If your PC doesn't have a sound card, see Chapter 21 to find out how to install one. If you're not sure if your PC has a sound card, check out Chapter 9.

10

Interfacing with Your PC

programs as a mouse is to your daily computing. AOL, for instance, produces an audible "You've Got Mail" notification when new mail arrives. This message can be handy if you're using another program at the same time that AOL's running in the background. Because AOL periodically checks for new mail automatically, this audible notification helps you know when new mail has arrived.

Evaluating and Selecting Speakers

Tip

In general, if you're looking for PC speakers, you should shop in the computer section of your local electronics store rather than the home audio section.

Computer speakers are available for any budget. You can find a pair of simple, battery-powered speakers for less than $10. If you want better sound quality, you can easily spend hundreds of dollars for high-end speakers that sound so good you may stop listening to music on your home stereo altogether. A good place to start looking for PC speakers is at AOL Keyword: **Computer Shop**.

For the best balance of sound quality and value, look for speakers that have a separate subwoofer, as shown in Figure 10-5. The subwoofer produces low-frequency sound, leaving the left and right speakers free to produce clear mid- and high-frequency sound.

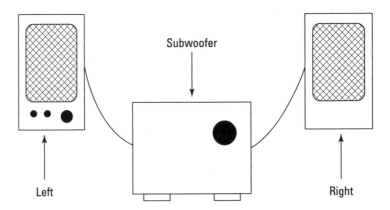

Subwoofer

Left   Right

Figure 10-5. Speaker sets with a separate subwoofer provide the best sound.

Choosing a Microphone

Your sound card should contain a connection for a microphone. A microphone is less important than speakers, but it can be useful nonetheless. For example, a microphone enables you to do the following:

▶ Record narration for a video project in Windows Movie Maker (a video editing program that comes with Windows Me; see Chapter 15 for details).

▶ Use your PC as a telephone. You can download programs from AOL Keyword: **Download Center** that enable you to use your PC as a phone.

▶ Talk to buddies online using AOL. If you have a teleconferencing program such as Intel Video Phone or Microsoft NetMeeting, a microphone lets other people hear your voice.

You probably don't need to spend a lot of money on a fancy microphone for your PC unless you want to record high-quality audio.

Connecting Audio Components to Your Sound Card

Most PC speakers use standard audio jacks, but you should double-check the connectors on the back of your sound card to make sure that any speakers you buy are compatible. The connectors on most sound cards look like the connectors shown in Figure 10-6. Each jack on the sound card should be labeled, so check closely before connecting your speakers or microphone.

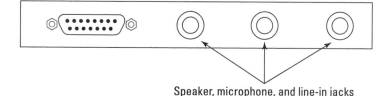

Speaker, microphone, and line-in jacks

Figure 10-6. Your sound card usually has connections for speakers, a microphone, and a line input.

Summary

Your PC is more than just an expensive box with blinking lights; it's an advanced tool that you can use throughout your daily life. Interface devices such as monitors, keyboards, mice, and speakers make PCs easy and enjoyable to use. In the next chapter, you'll learn about another component of your PC: storage. Storage devices include hard drives and other disk drives.

Quick Look

▶ **Disk Drives**
Your PC stores information on many different kinds of disk drives. Learn how to use Windows to identify your disk drives and how to determine how much free space is available on each one.

▶ **Hard Drives**
Your PC's main disk drive is called the *hard drive,* on which you store software programs and files. Find out what you need to know about your hard drive, as well as how to explore it.

▶ **Removable Disk Drives**
Unlike the hard drive, some other types of disk drives use removable discs. The two most common types are floppy drives and CD-ROM drives, but there are many others. Learn how to use removable drives with your PC.

Chapter 11

Mastering Storage Devices

Consider for a moment all of the information that your computer needs to perform its work. It must access program files to load Windows and launch AOL. If you do some work in a word processor, you probably want to save the work so that you can use it again later. Your PC has to store all of this information on *disk drives*, which you can think of as your PC's long-term storage. Some types of drives are mounted permanently inside the computer, and others are removable. In this chapter, you learn about the different kinds of storage used by your PC.

Working with Drive Letters in Windows

Personal computers can store files in many different places. Windows keeps track of all those places by assigning each place a unique letter. Usually, each letter represents a different disk drive attached to your computer. Your PC can have many separate drives, but you probably have at least three.

The following sections tell you more about your disk drives, how to locate them, and what they do.

Using My Computer to Identify Your Disk Drives

Double-click the My Computer icon on your Windows desktop. You should see a window similar to Figure 11-1, but probably with fewer disk drives listed.

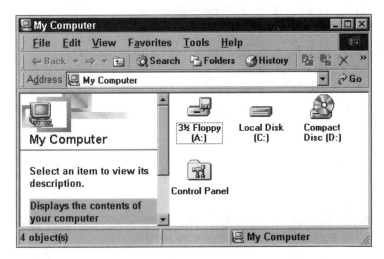

Figure 11-1. My Computer shows you all of the different disk drives attached to your computer.

Several different types of drives are shown in Figure 11-1. They are

► **(A:):** On a PC running Windows, drive A: is always a 3½-inch floppy disk drive. You can store files on floppy disks to take with you and use on another PC.

► **(C:):** The *hard drive,* where you store files on your PC is always C:. Program files for Windows and your other programs are also stored here. Chances are that your C: drive is your only hard drive.

▶ **(D:):** Virtually all PCs have a CD-ROM or DVD-ROM drive, and it's usually labeled D:. If your computer has additional disk drives, such as a second hard drive or a Zip drive, your CD-ROM drive might have a different letter, such as E: or F:.

Take a moment and study the disk drives that My Computer lists on your own PC. Make a mental note of how many hard drives you have, what the letter is for your CD-ROM drive, and whether or not you have any other special kinds of drives installed.

Finding Out How Much Free Space Your Disk Drives Have

One of the most common questions you will have to answer about your computer is how much free storage space is available on your disk drives. My Computer makes it easy to check:

1. Launch My Computer.
2. Right-click the icon for the drive you want to check (such as your C: drive) and choose Properties from the menu that appears. You should see a dialog box similar to Figure 11-2.

Understanding Bits and Bytes

Computers are not very smart. Whereas you have no problem understanding such basic concepts as alphabets and numeric systems, all a computer understands is on or off, or one or zero. Your computer performs its tasks by working with *bits*. Because bits use a *binary* (or *base-two)* system — your computer has no other choice but to express information as a combination of its only two options — one and zero (or on and off). Eight of these bits combined together make a *byte,* a single piece of data in your computer.

Storage space on a computer disk drive is measured in bytes. A *kilobyte* (KB) consists of 1,024 bytes; a *megabyte* (MB) equals 1,000 kilobytes; and 1,000 megabytes makes a *gigabyte* (GB). Most hard drives sold today hold many gigabytes of data.

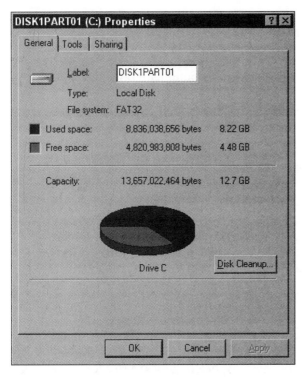

Figure 11-2. This hard drive has 4.48GB of free space.

3. Note the amount of free space that is listed.

4. Click OK to close the dialog box when you're done.

You can check the amount of free space on any disk shown in My Computer by following the instructions above. But the C: drive — your hard drive — is the most important one because that is where most of your important program files are stored. Make sure you have a few hundred megabytes of free space on your C: drive at all times so that you can ensure better performance and prevent crashes.

Understanding Your Hard Drive

Every PC has a hard drive that resides inside the main PC case and provides storage space for program files — including Windows and AOL. In Windows, the main hard drive is identified by the letter C:. Most of the storage locations provided by

Note

Some computers have more than one hard drive, in which case each additional hard drive has its own drive letter.

Windows, including My Documents and the Recycle Bin, are located on the hard drive. To begin exploring your hard drive

1. Double-click the My Computer icon on your desktop.

2. In My Computer, double-click the icon for your C: drive.

3. You see a variety of folders on the C: drive, including

   • **My Documents:** This is the folder you use to store files.

   • **America Online 6.0:** Program files for AOL are stored in this folder. The America Online folder has a sub-folder called *download,* which stores all the files you download from AOL's Download Center. File attachments you download from AOL Mail are also stored here.

   • **Program Files:** When you install new software on your PC, the software's program files usually go into a sub-folder in the Program Files folder. Avoid changing or deleting files in this folder unless you are specifically told to do so by a program's instructions.

   • **Windows:** Program files for Microsoft Windows are stored in this folder. As with Program Files, don't modify files or subfolders in the Windows folder unless you are specifically told to do so.

4. Click the Close button in the upper-right corner of the window to close it.

Definition

RAM stands for random access memory, your PC's short-term memory.

You should always keep at least a few hundred megabytes of free space available on your hard drive. Windows frequently uses free space on the hard drive to augment the capabilities of system RAM, and if your hard drive is full, you will encounter slow performance and frequent system crashes.

Using Removable Storage Devices

Hard drives are called *hard* because they are generally considered a permanent part of the PC, which presents some limitations:

- ▶ You are limited to the storage capacity of the hard drive.
- ▶ If you want to take the data with you when you travel, you must bring the whole computer.
- ▶ A hard drive is difficult to lock in a cabinet or safe if you have security concerns.

Removable storage can solve these problems. *Removable storage* drives are drives from which the disk or other storage media is easily removable and transportable. These include floppy disks, CD-ROMs, DVD-ROMs, CD-RWs, and other removable formats. In most cases, your storage capacity is limited only by the number of blank disks you can afford.

Floppy Disks

All PCs have a 3½-inch floppy disk drive, which Windows identifies as A:. The disks themselves are not very floppy; the name dates to older 5¼-inch and 8-inch disks that were indeed flexible, or *floppy*. Most floppy disks hold 1.4MB of data. That's not a lot of space, but floppies are big enough to hold a few JPEG pictures or as many as a dozen typical word processing files.

CD-ROMs

Virtually all modern PCs have CD-ROM (Compact Disc-Read Only Memory) drives. CD-ROMs look exactly like music CDs, and you can use your CD-ROM drive to play music CDs in your computer.

CD-ROMs are called *read only*, because you cannot modify or erase files on a CD. Nor can you save your own files on a CD-ROM disc. They are usually used for distributing software, and today virtually all programs you buy for your PC will come on a CD-ROM.

Cross-Reference

In Chapter 19, you find out how to use a special floppy disk called an *emergency startup disk* to troubleshoot problems with Windows.

Cross-Reference

To learn more about installing programs on your PC from a CD-ROM, see Chapter 16.

11

Mastering Storage Devices

Note

Both CD-R and CD-RW drives can read regular CD-ROM discs.

Cross-Reference

See Chapter 21 to learn how to add a CD-R or CD-RW drive to your own PC.

Recordable CDs

As you read in the previous section, you cannot save files on a CD-ROM. However, if you have a special CD-R (Compact Disc-Recordable) drive, you can record, or *burn,* your own CDs. Blank CD-R discs are available at most computer and consumer electronics stores. Most discs hold 650MB of data, but 700MB discs are also available. That's a lot of space, making recordable CDs a great way to back up or share large files.

You can also use CD-R drives to record your own music CDs. CD-R drives come with programs called *disc-mastering software* to help you set up and record CDs. Some disc-mastering software, such as Adaptec's Easy CD Creator 4 Deluxe (available at most office and computer supply stores), lets you record music CDs that can be played in any CD player. Easy CD Creator 4 Deluxe even converts MP3 music into the correct format so that it can be played on regular CD players.

A CD-R can be recorded only once. This means that you cannot modify the data stored on it, but it also means that you can use it in any CD-ROM drive. Most newer CD-R drives are also CD-RW (Compact Disc-ReWritable) drives. CD-RW discs can be recorded on and erased multiple times. CD-RW discs are a bit more expensive, and they don't work in some CD-ROM drives.

Backing Up Your Important Files

Although modern PCs are pretty reliable, it's still a good idea to take precautions against losing all of your important files to a system crash or hard-drive failure. Taking the time to back up your important files on a regular basis can save you hours, days, or even weeks of work later if your PC crashes.

It's probably not reasonable to back up your entire hard drive, but you should back up your most important files — word processing documents, pictures, and other files that aren't easily replaceable — on a regular basis. One of the best ways to do this is to copy them onto a large disc such as a CD-R.

Other Storage Devices

Many other types of removable storage devices are available for your PC. They include LS-120 SuperDisks from Imation, Zip disks from Iomega and other companies, Orb drives from Castlewood Systems, and others. If you're looking for removable storage, you should consider several important things:

> ▶ **Price:** Check not only the price of the disk drive, but also the disks that go in it. Can you afford to buy enough blank disks to suit your needs?

> ▶ **Storage capacity:** Are the disks big enough to hold the amount of information you need?

> ▶ **Sharing:** If you need to share files with other people, do they also have a disk drive that will accept the media you give them?

> ▶ **Connection:** Does your PC have an open connection of the correct type for the drive you want to buy?

Cross-Reference

If you're not sure that your PC has an open connection that the removable drive can plug into, see Appendix C.

Find It Online

Use AOL Keyword: **Shop Direct** and click Computer Upgrades to find and purchase storage devices.

Summary

In this chapter, you reviewed the different types of disk drives that your computer can use to store files. These include hard drives inside your computer, as well as drives that use removable media, such as floppy drives, CD-ROM drives, and others. You learned how to identify those drives using My Computer. In the next chapter, you find out about using digital cameras and scanners with your PC.

11

Mastering Storage Devices

Quick Look

Chapter 12

Working with Cameras and Scanners

Think about how fun it would be to store all of your pictures on your computer. You could print extra copies and mail them to your friends and family, attach pictures to e-mail messages, or even add pictures to your Web page to share them with the world. After you have the pictures in your PC, you can do all of these things and more.

To get the pictures into your PC, you need some type of digital camera, scanner, desktop cam, or digital camcorder (because your PC can only work with digital images). In this chapter, you find out about these different options that enable you to get images into your PC.

What Is a Digital Camera?

Digital cameras operate similarly to everyday point-and-shoot cameras except that digital cameras don't use film. Instead of storing pictures on film, digital cameras store pictures electronically so that the pictures can easily be copied to your PC. Once inside your PC, you can put those pictures to almost endless use — from sharing them with friends and family via AOL to creating your own personalized wall calendar.

Balancing Price, Features, and Quality: Choosing a Digital Camera

Choosing the right digital camera means balancing several factors: You need to find a reliable camera that fits your budget and includes the features that will be most useful to you. A great place to start your search for a digital camera is AOL Keyword: **Digital Camera Store**, shown in Figure 12-1.

 **Find It Online**

Digital cameras come in a variety of models. To get help finding the right camera for your needs, check out AOL Keyword: **Digital Camera Decision Guide**, where you are asked a series of questions to help determine what camera may be best for you.

Figure 12-1. You can find lots of great digital camera deals on AOL.

Here are some points to consider when shopping for a digital camera:

▶ **Resolution:** You don't need to know a lot about resolution, but you should know that it measures the number of dots that make up the picture. More dots mean higher-quality pictures, but also a higher camera price.

12

The lowest-resolution digital cameras generally have only 640 x 480 resolution. You will probably want a resolution of at least 1024 x 768 for acceptable quality images.

▶ **Zoom capabilities:** A zoom lens allows you to zero in on a subject so that it fills the frame. Digital cameras often have both optical and digital zoom. Optical zoom brings the subject closer without getting fuzzy; digital zoom tends to make pictures fuzzy. Look for a camera that has at least a 3X optical zoom. You'll pay a little more for a camera with zoom capability, but you'll find that the camera is far more useful.

▶ **Memory:** Don't you hate it when you run out of film? Even though a digital camera stores pictures on small memory cards instead of on film, eventually the memory will become full. And the higher the resolution of the picture, the more memory the picture takes up, meaning that a few pictures can take up a lot of memory. Make sure your digital camera has *removable memory cards,* which are kind of like floppy disks for your digital camera. You can carry extra memory cards with you when you shoot pictures. That way, you don't have to stop taking pictures when the memory card is full — instead, just pop in a new card and start shooting.

▶ **Battery power:** Batteries can be a considerable expense with digital cameras because digital cameras use a lot of energy. You can save money by using rechargeable batteries as opposed to using disposable ones. So consider buying a digital camera that can use rechargeable batteries.

▶ **Price:** Digital cameras are generally quite a bit more expensive than film cameras, so you need to consider your budget when buying a digital camera. You can find some digital cameras with very limited features for under $100, but expect to pay $300 to well over $1,000 for digital cameras with high resolution and optical zoom features.

▶ **Software compatibility:** Your digital camera must be able to work with your PC so you can copy pictures from the camera to your PC. In most cases, compatibility isn't a problem, but you should make certain that the camera's specifications say that it works with the version of Windows that is on your PC.

▶ **Type of connection to your PC:** In addition to making sure the software works with Windows, the camera

Tip

Buy the highest capacity memory card you can afford for your digital camera. Doing so allows you to store more pictures at higher quality settings.

you choose must be able to connect to your PC. Most digital cameras connect to your PC with a USB connection, called a *port*, although a few cameras use a serial port. All modern PCs have USB ports, but a few lack serial ports, so the safest thing to do is to make sure the camera uses a USB port.

Definition

USB stands for *Universal Serial Bus* and allows for a Plug and Play connection between your computer and devices such as digital cameras, scanners, and printers.

Connecting the Camera to Your PC

Your PC may have only one or two USB ports, but you can add an inexpensive USB hub to increase the number of USB devices (such as printers, desktop cams, or external modems) you can connect to your PC. Check out AOL Keyword: **USB** (shown in Figure 12-2) to find out more about USB ports.

Cross-Reference

To find out more about the types of connectors your PC has, check out the diagrams in Appendix C.

Cross-Reference

Appendix C also offers additional information on USB ports.

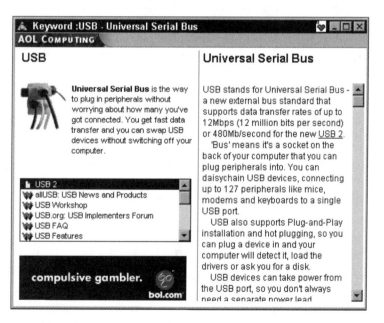

Figure 12-2. AOL Keyword: **USB** tells you more about what you can do with your USB connector.

To connect your digital camera to your PC, follow these steps:

1. Plug the USB cable into your PC (or into the USB hub if you are using one).
2. Plug the other end of the USB cable into your camera.

Downloading Images from Your Camera

Note

After you purchase your digital camera and read the instructions that come with it, install the camera's software on your PC. For more on installing software, see Chapter 16.

After you take some pictures with your digital camera, you need to *download* them to your PC. After connecting the cable to your camera and PC (as explained in the preceding section), start the software that came with your camera. You may have to click a button that says something such as "Click Here to Download Pictures" to start the download process. Because each brand of camera is slightly different, you need to consult the camera's documentation to learn the exact procedure for your camera. Generally, you just need to follow the on-screen prompts.

After you download your pictures, you may want to edit them. Your digital camera probably comes with some photo-editing software that will allow you to do basic editing, such as cropping and changing the brightness or contrast. If your camera doesn't include photo-editing software, you may want to try IXLA Digital Camera Suite, Adobe PhotoDeluxe, Kai Photo Soap, MGI PhotoSuite, Ulead Photo Express, or Microsoft Picture It! — all of which are inexpensive programs you can buy online on AOL. Check out AOL Keyword: **Digital Photo** to find links to tips, chats, and software for digital photo editing.

After you download the pictures from your digital camera and they are safely stored on your PC, erase those pictures from your camera's memory to make room for more pictures.

Purchasing, Hooking Up, and Using a Scanner

Another way to get images into your PC is to use a scanner. A scanner is an electronic device that converts a photograph into a digital image that you can use in your PC. Scanners are especially useful when you have existing photographs (taken with a traditional film camera) that you want to convert into digital images. For example, you could use a scanner to scan photos from an old family album. Then you can upload those images to the "You've Got Pictures" service to share them with other family members.

Getting the Features You Want

The most common type of scanner is the flatbed scanner. This type of scanner looks and works like a small copy machine. You lift the scanner's lid and then place photos face down on the glass for scanning.

Here are some points to consider when purchasing a scanner:

▶ **Type of connection to your PC:** One important item to consider when you're buying a scanner is the type of connection between the scanner and your PC. The three common types of ports are USB, parallel, or SCSI. (See Appendix C for information on identifying which type of ports are on your PC.) Scanners that connect by using the USB port are the easiest to install on your PC.

▶ **Resolution:** Virtually all scanners can scan in color and with a high enough resolution for home use. Scanner resolution is rated in *dots per inch* (dpi), and inexpensive scanners typically scan at 600 dpi or higher. You can usually choose the resolution setting when you are scanning, and you may want to choose a lower resolution when scanning images for online use to keep the file size (and download time) at a reasonable level.

▶ **Price:** Scanners are one of the less expensive peripherals you can add to your PC. Prices start at under $100, and there's little reason to spend more than $250.

For help picking the right scanner, check out AOL Keyword: **Scanner Decision Guide**, shown in Figure 12-3.

Installing a Scanner

After selecting a scanner, you need to install the software that's provided and connect the scanner's cable to your PC. The scanner software enables your PC to control the scanning process, so you must install it before you can use the scanner. In most cases, the scanner comes with a CD-ROM that you use to install the software.

12

Working with Cameras and Scanners

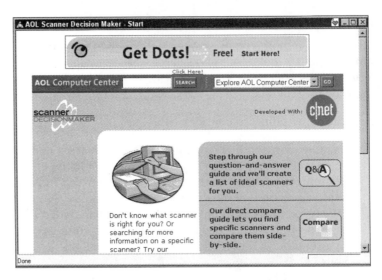

Figure 12-3. Use the Scanner Decision Guide to find the right scanner for your needs.

Scanning an Image

After the software is installed and the scanner is connected to your PC, you can scan any flat object, such as a photograph. Just lift the lid of the scanner, place the photo face down on the glass, close the lid, and then click the Scan button in the scanner software on your PC.

To learn more about using scanners, check out AOL Keyword: **Scanning** to visit the Image Scanning Resource Center.

Working with Desktop Cams

Desktop cameras (called *desktop cams* for short) are small cameras that are always connected directly to your PC. You can use desktop cams to take still images as well as send moving images. You can even use a desktop cam to make video phone calls as I'm about to do in Figure 12-4.

You need a fast connection such as ISDN, DSL, or a cable modem to send lifelike full-motion videos from your desktop cam. If you use a dial-up connection with a modem, your videos will be poorer in quality.

To ensure that you don't get a crooked image of the photo, make sure that you place the photo squarely against the top and side scanning guides.

To find out more about high-speed connections, check out AOL Keyword: **AOL PLUS**.

Figure 12-4. With a desktop cam, you can let others see who they are talking to.

Most desktop cams connect to your PC via the USB port. After the cam is connected, your PC shows the cam in Windows Explorer. You can view the image from the cam by clicking the icon for the cam in Windows Explorer. You may need to click the My Computer icon to see the desktop cam icon in Windows Explorer.

Your desktop cam probably includes software that enables you to make video phone calls over the Internet. To do so, you first connect to AOL and then start the video phone software. Your buddy on the other end of the call must also be using video phone software in order to see you, and he or she must have a desktop cam to be able to send images to you.

If you don't have video phone software, you can use Microsoft NetMeeting (which comes with all versions of Windows) to place a video phone call over the Internet. To find NetMeeting, choose Start➪Programs➪Accessories➪Communications. You can use NetMeeting to receive video from a buddy who has a desktop cam, even if you don't have one.

12

Working with Cameras and Scanners

Using a Digital Camcorder with Your PC

If you have a digital camcorder, you can create movies that you can use on your PC. You can, for example, create a movie that you can include on your AOL home page so that others can view your movie.

Digital camcorders require a special type of connection to your PC. This connection is known as FireWire or IEEE-1394. If you own a newer PC that was built with digital moviemaking in mind, it may have a FireWire connector already. (To see if your PC has a FireWire connector, check out the diagrams in Appendix C.) Otherwise, you may need to have a FireWire adapter card installed in your PC. A FireWire card costs about $100 (plus installation if you don't want to add it yourself).

To create your own movies, copy your recording from your digital camcorder to your PC and then edit the movie in a program such as Windows Movie Maker, which comes with Windows Me. When you edit your movie, you connect various scenes together to tell a story, and you can even add a soundtrack to make the movie more fun. After you finish your editing, Windows Movie Maker assembles all the clips into a complete movie that you can view or share. (See Chapter 15 for more on using moviemaking software.)

Sharing Pictures Online

Find It Online

You can quickly navigate to your online pictures by using AOL Keyword: **Pictures**.

You can share your pictures online so that your friends and family can enjoy them, too. These may be pictures you took with your digital camera, ones you scanned with your scanner, or images from your film camera if you had the film developed by a participating "You've Got Pictures" film processor.

If you have your film developed by a "You've Got Pictures" developer, you'll hear the message "You've Got Pictures" when your pictures are available online.

If you want to upload pictures from your digital camera or scanner to the "You've Got Pictures" service, follow these simple steps:

1. Click the "You've Got Pictures" icon on the AOL Welcome Screen.

2. On the "You've Got Pictures" main page, click the Learn How link (see Figure 12-5) for information on uploading and exchanging pictures online.

Tip

You can also have your online photos printed on items, such as coffee mugs and T-shirts.

Figure 12-5. From the main "You've Got Pictures" window, you can get photo tips and start sharing pictures online.

Summary

In this chapter, you found out about different ways to create digital images with your PC. You also discovered how to share those images with family and friends online by using the "You've Got Pictures" service on AOL.

12

Working with Cameras and Scanners

USING PRINTERS AND OTHER PERIPHERALS

Quick Look

▶ **Working with Printers** **page 181**

A printer enables you to print out copies of your documents and pictures. Here, I tell you how to choose and install your printer.

▶ **Handheld Computers and Your PC** **page 185**

If you're thinking of buying a handheld computer, you probably want to know how to pick the right one. Here, I show you how to compare handheld PCs and how you can use one as a useful companion to your desktop PC.

▶ **Downloading Music to an MP3 Player** **page 190**

A portable MP3 player makes it possible for you to carry along your favorite music wherever you go. I show you how to find music on AOL and how to copy music from your desktop PC to your MP3 player.

▶ **Using a Battery Backup** **page 190**

If your PC is going to be useful, it needs a reliable source of power. Here, I show you how to choose the right battery backup system to ensure that your PC always has the power it needs.

Chapter 13

Using Printers and Other Peripherals

Y ou can make your PC even more useful by adding peripherals — extras like printers and portable music players that give your PC additional capabilities. To get the most from your PC, you need to choose the add-ons that best suit your needs.

To help you decide what extras you want and need, you may want to create a list of things that you like to do — not just with your computer, but also when you're just hanging around the house. You'll soon discover (if you haven't already) that a wide range of available extras can turn your PC into a stereo system, a companion to your handheld PC or portable MP3 player, or your own personal printing press. In this chapter, you see how to determine what you need and how to make the options that you choose work together with your PC. Check out Chapter 12 if you're interested in finding out how to use PC extras to save, edit, and transfer digital images.

Choosing and Setting Up a Printer

A printer is probably the most common extra that you can add to your PC. With a printer, you can print documents, digital photos, labels for shipping or organizing, your family tree, and signs and banners that you've created. You may need additional software for some of these tasks, and one great place to find what you need is the AOL Computer Center Channel.

Evaluating Different Types of Printers

To choose the right printer for your needs, you need to know how the different types of printers compare to each other and which printers are best at the type of printing you do most. Here are some important things you should know about printers:

▶ **Inkjet** printers are the most common home printers. Inkjet printers are usually quite inexpensive. However, they can be expensive to use if you do a lot of printing because the ink cartridges typically don't last very long and are expensive. Most inkjet printers also print in color. Inkjet printers range from about $69 to $1000.

▶ **Laser** printers are more expensive than most inkjet printers, but laser printers are the more economical choice if you do a lot of printing. Because laser printer toner cartridges last for many more pages than do inkjet cartridges, the actual cost to print each page is far lower. For example, it may cost as little as 2 cents per page to print on a laser printer, and anywhere from 10 cents to a dollar per page on an inkjet printer. Laser printers usually print somewhat faster than inkjet printers. Most laser printers cannot print in color, although some of the more expensive models do print in color. Laser printers range from about $400 to $4000.

▶ **Photo inkjet** printers are inkjet printers that are specifically designed to print digital images, although photo inkjet printers can print text, too. Photo inkjet printers generally print a bit slower than other inkjet printers, but they print photos that look extremely lifelike. Photo inkjet printers typically range from $250 to $1500.

Find It Online

If you want additional help choosing the right printer, visit AOL's Printer Decision Guide at AOL Keyword: **Printer Decision Guide**.

Find It Online

To find printers, cables, and supplies online, check out AOL Keyword: **Printers & Accessories** to visit Shop@AOL's Printers, Software, & Accessories Department.

Caution

When you choose a printer, make certain you choose one that is fast enough for your needs. Selecting a slow printer because it is inexpensive may not be your best choice.

Cross-Reference

If you need help identifying the connectors on your PC, see Appendix C.

Note

A few printers include an *infrared* port that enables them to receive data from a laptop PC without using a cable. You're most likely to find an infrared port on portable printers that are intended for mobile use, but even some desktop printers include this option.

So how do you decide which printer is best for you? Start by deciding what type of printing you're most likely to do. If you're going to write a novel and plan to print a lot of drafts as you go along, the speed and economy of printing on a laser printer makes the most sense. If you're going to print digital photos to enter in a photo contest, you'll want the photo quality printing of a photo inkjet printer. If you want some color so you can print your own calendars, buy a standard inkjet.

In the next section, "Connecting a Printer to Your PC," I show you another important thing you need to know about a printer — how it connects to your PC.

Connecting a Printer to Your PC

Before you can print documents on your printer, you must connect your printer to your PC. In most cases, you connect your printer to your PC with a cable. You need to make certain that your PC and your printer both have the same type of connection so that you can connect them.

Printers typically use either a *parallel* connection or a *USB* connection to your PC. Parallel connectors are shaped like the letter D and are about 2 inches wide. USB connectors are rectangular and about a half-inch wide. In most cases, both of these connectors are located on the back of your PC, and some newer PCs also have USB connectors on the front of the system. A few printers include both types of connections. Check to see which type of connection is available on your PC before you buy a printer.

To plug your printer in to your PC, first make sure your PC is turned off. Then, securely attach the cable to the printer port and screw the connector in to the back of your PC (if you are using a parallel connection) or simply plug the USB cable into the USB port (if you are using a USB connection).

Printers typically do not include the cable that is needed to connect to your PC. Check to see if the printer you buy includes a cable and buy the correct cable when you buy your printer so that you don't have to make an extra shopping trip if it does not include the cable. If the printer's description does not specifically say that a cable is included, then you probably need to buy the cable separately.

Enabling Your PC to Recognize Your New Printer

After you've connected the cable between your PC and your printer, you need to tell your PC that you have a new printer. To do so, follow these steps:

1. Start your PC and choose Start⇨Settings⇨Printers.

2. When the Printers window opens, click the Add Printer icon to start the Add Printer Wizard, shown in Figure 13-1.

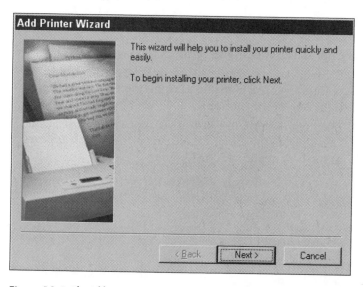

Figure 13-1. The Add Printer Wizard sets up your new printer in a few minutes.

3. Follow the instructions and click Next to continue.

4. You need to tell the wizard the type of printer you have. To do so, you need to know the brand and model of your printer. Just choose that specific brand and model from the drop-down list on-screen when the wizard asks you to do so.

5. After you've identified the brand and model of the printer and clicked Next, the Printer Wizard prompts you to print a test page. Print the test page. That way, you can be sure your new printer is working properly.

Setting a Default Printer in Windows

Households that have more than one computer often have more than one printer. Because Microsoft Windows is set up to let you connect as many printers to your PC as you want, you should designate a printer as the *default* (or automatic choice) — even if you only have one printer.

Setting a default printer can help you print items quickly and hassle-free. If you don't take this extra step, your PC may ask you which printer you want to use whenever you print something — even if you only have one printer.

To set a printer as the default, follow these steps:

1. Choose Start⇨Settings⇨Printer.
2. Right-click your printer's icon by moving the mouse pointer over the icon and clicking the button on the right side of the mouse.
3. The menu shown in Figure 13-2 appears. Choose Set as Default from the menu. (Make sure a checkmark appears in the box next to Set As Default.)

Figure 13-2. Make an automatic choice about which printer to use.

Reviewing Your Printer Settings

Your printer has a number of options that control things such as print quality, paper size, and print layout. Although different types of printers offer different sets of options, you access those options the same way for every printer. To access your printer's settings

1. Choose Start⇨Settings⇨Printers.

Find It Online

For more help on using your printer and to find printing supplies, use AOL Keyword: **Print** to visit AOL's Print Central.

2. Right-click the printer icon.

3. Choose Properties on the menu (refer to Figure 13-2).

4. After the Properties dialog box opens, select the print quality, paper size, layout, and other options you want to use. Different brands of printers offer many different sets of options, so you'll need to examine the available options carefully to see which settings fulfill your needs.

Using a Handheld Computer with Your PC

A handheld computer (also called a *personal digital assistant* or a *PDA)* is a great companion for your PC. With a handheld computer, you can carry your Address Book, My Calendar, and messages from your Online Mailbox in your pocket. And you can easily share all that information with your desktop PC automatically. Check out AOL Keyword: **PDA** to find information and resources about handheld computers.

Definition

Handheld PCs are also called *PDAs* — Personal Digital Assistants.

Selecting the Right Handheld for You

Many different handheld computers are on the market, but you need to decide whether you want a handheld that runs the Palm operating system or one that uses a version of Windows. The handheld PCs that run a version of Windows are also called Pocket PCs. Table 13-1 demonstrates some of the important differences between Palm PCs and Pocket PCs.

For more help deciding which handheld PC is right for you, check out AOL Keyword: **Handheld Decision Guide** to visit the PDA Decision Guide. To buy a handheld PC online, visit AOL Keyword: **Pocket PC Center** at the AOL ShopDirect Handheld Center, shown in Figure 13-3.

Table 13-1. *Evaluating Palm PCs and Pocket PCs*

Feature	Palm PCs	Pocket PCs	Bottom Line
Resolution	Have monochrome screens with a screen resolution of 160 x 160 pixels.	Have color screens with a screen resolution of 240 x 320 pixels.	Overall, Pocket PCs have three times as many pixels, which results in a clearer display.
Organization	Include built-in software to handle basic tasks, such as keeping your schedule and address book.	Include built-in software to handle basic tasks, such as keeping your schedule and address book.	Both can handle the basics, but Pocket PCs have more memory, enabling them to hold more data than a Palm PC. Also, because Pocket PCs are set up similarly to the Windows desktop, they may be easier to use.
Other software	Are limited to basic PDA functions. You can buy some additional programs, however.	Have additional programs that are built-in, including things like pocket versions of Microsoft Word and Excel.	If all you want is a PDA, the Palm may fill your needs, but if you want a PDA that is more like a computer, the Pocket PC is a much better choice.
Power	Typically have processors that are about 30 MHz and include 2MB to 8MB of memory.	Run between 150 MHz and 206 MHz and include 16MB to 32MB of memory.	The Pocket PC has the memory and power to do many different types of computing tasks, while the Palm PC has only enough power for simple organizational tasks.
Accessories	Generally lack easy expansion options.	Allow easy expansion with add-on memory cards, modems, network adapter cards, digital camera cards, and so on.	If you want to expand your handheld easily, a Pocket PC is a far better choice.
Price	Range from about $250 to $500.	Range from about $350 to $600.	You may pay between $50 and $100 more for a Pocket PC than for a Palm PC.

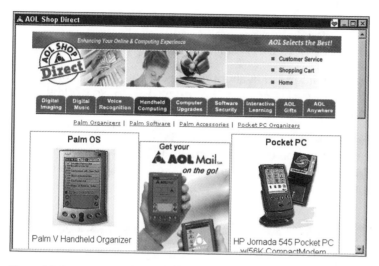

Figure 13-3. Buy your own handheld PC at AOL ShopDirect.

Synchronizing Your Handheld with Your PC

You want to keep your desktop PC and your handheld PC *synchronized* to make certain that they both hold the same information. When you update an address in your Address Book, for example, you want that same address update to appear on your handheld PC, too.

Keeping your handheld PC and your desktop PC synchronized is very easy, and all handheld PCs come with software and a cradle that enable you to keep important information current. The cradle also enables you to hook your handheld PC to your desktop computer when the batteries in your handheld need to be recharged. Here's how you synchronize your handheld and your desktop PC:

1. Install the desktop portion of the synchronization software that came with your handheld onto your desktop PC.

2. Take your handheld PC with you on the road. Feel free to use it as much as you need to.

3. When you're back home again, place your handheld device into the desktop cradle. The information that

Definition

Synchronization means copying the most recent information changes between your desktop PC and your handheld PC.

you've changed in the handheld PC is automatically updated to your computer, and any changes you've made to your PC data is updated in your handheld PC.

For more information about the specifics of using a Pocket PC, check out *Pocket PCs For Dummies* (IDG Books Worldwide) by Brian Underdahl, one of the co-authors of this book.

Figure 13-4 shows an HP Jornada 545 Pocket PC sitting in the synchronization cradle. This cradle attaches to your PC using the USB connector (usually located on the back of your desktop PC).

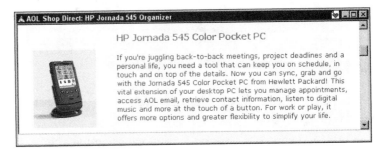

Figure 13-4. When you place your handheld in the cradle, as shown here, your files synchronize automatically.

Using AOL Anywhere on Your Handheld

The AOL Anywhere service (www.aolanywhere.com) offers members access to many of AOL's features and services, even when you're using a computer that doesn't have the AOL software installed. With AOL Anywhere, you don't have to worry about missing an important e-mail when you're away from home. You can also receive these benefits of AOL Anywhere with your handheld PC.

Because your handheld PC is fast, easy, and convenient, your handheld PC e-mail can be available wherever you go. To find out about the variety of ways you can gain access to AOL when you're not using your home PC, use AOL Keyword: **AOL Anywhere**.

Note

Most handheld PCs need a modem that you purchase separately in order to send and receive e-mail. Use AOL Keyword: **Handheld Center** to reach the AOL Shop Directs Handheld Center.

To download the software that enables you to send and
receive AOL Mail using your handheld PC, follow these steps:

1. Log on to the Internet and type **www.aolanywhere.
   com** in the address box.

   Or if you're logged on to the Internet using AOL, type
   AOL Keyword: **AOL Anywhere** and click the
   Download Now button associated with the type of
   handheld PC you have. Then skip ahead to Step 3.

2. You're taken to the AOL Anywhere site. Click the
   Handheld button.

3. A page like the one shown in Figure 13-5 appears
   showing three handheld PC devices: Palm, Windows
   CE, and Pocket PC. Choose the link that matches the
   type of handheld PC you have and click the Download
   Now button.

Cross-Reference

See Chapter 8 for more on
using AOL Mail.

Find It Online

To go directly to the AOL
Mail download center, use
AOL Keyword: **Palm Mail**.

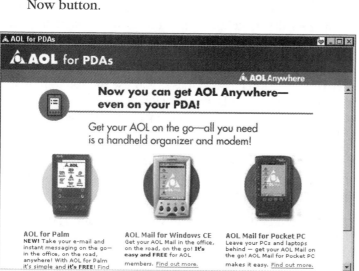

Figure 13-5. You can use AOL Mail to send and receive e-mail from your PDA.

4. It takes just a few minutes to download the AOL Mail
   software. After you download and install the AOL Mail
   software, you can sign on and read your mail in your
   Online Mailbox.

Downloading and Listening to Music Online

Note

MP3 stands for Motion Pictures Expert Group Type 3 — a method of compressing music files to make them smaller. To find MP3 music files that you can download, check out AOL Keyword: **Music Download.**

If you're like most people, you probably want to listen to the music you like rather than whatever happens to be playing on the radio. With a portable MP3 player — a small portable device that plays music that you download from your PC — or a Pocket PC, you choose the music you want to hear offline, or you can use AOL's Media Player to listen to your favorite music online.

You can download many different music tracks on AOL. To introduce new albums, music groups often provide songs that fans can download so that they can check out the music before they buy. But remember that downloadable music files are subject (like anything else) to copyright laws. Check out AOL Keyword: **Copyright** to find out more information about which materials are protected by copyright and which can be freely distributed.

Tip

Because the AOL Media Player is periodically and automatically updated along with the rest of your AOL software, you don't need to worry about being able to play different types of online music. You simply click the link to begin playback.

After you have downloaded music, you use the software that came with your MP3 player or Pocket PC to copy the music from your desktop PC to your MP3 player or Pocket PC.

Even if you don't have a portable MP3 player or a Pocket PC, you can still enjoy online music using the AOL Media Player (see Figure 13-6). The AOL Media Player automatically plays music when you click a link to a music track.

If you want to know more about your PC's sound system, see Chapter 10 for details.

Tip

Even if your PC is connected to a UPS battery, be sure to shut down your PC as soon as possible when the lights go out because the UPS battery is only designed to power your PC for a few minutes.

Using a Battery Backup

Computers need a constant supply of power to keep running. If the lights go out — even for a second — your PC stops working and you have to restart your PC to continue using it. In addition, you may lose anything you were working on when the power went out if you haven't saved your work recently.

To prevent your PC from losing power, you can add a battery backup unit — also known as a *UPS* or *Uninterruptible Power Supply* — that provides power to your PC even when the lights go out.

Figure 13-6. You can play music online using the AOL Media Player.

Don't plug printers — especially laser printers — into your
UPS because printers often draw more power than the UPS is
designed to provide.

Battery backup units come in different power capacity sizes,
and the capacity is listed using measurement units called *VA*
or Volt-Amps. You want a unit that can provide enough power
to keep your PC running for several minutes. For an individual
PC, 280VA is the minimum recommended size. A large capacity, such as 500VA, will keep your PC running for a longer time.

Summary

In this chapter, you reviewed some of the peripherals that you
can use to get even more from your PC. You first saw how to
choose and install the printer that suits your needs. Then, I
described how handheld PCs allow you to do some of the activities that you do on a desktop PC while you're on the road.
This chapter helped you distinguish between Palm devices
and Pocket PCs and explained how you can share information
between handhelds and your desktop PC. Finally, you learned
about using an MP3 player to listen to and download music
from AOL. In the following chapters, you can find out about
the different kinds of PC software you can use.

P A R T

IV

FINDING AND USING THE RIGHT PC SOFTWARE

Quick Look

Chapter 14

Understanding Software Types

You need *software* — programs — to do almost anything with your PC. Software is the set of instructions that tells your computer how to perform various tasks. You can use many different types of software on your PC, and each different type makes it possible for your computer to do different things. For example, one program makes it possible for you to write letters to your friends, and another enables you to view the interesting things you see on AOL.

To make your PC do what you want, you need to use the right software. In this chapter, you find out how to open the programs on your PC, and how to determine which software you need to perform various tasks.

Choosing Programs That Help You Get Work Done

You can choose many different programs to run on your PC, depending on the kinds of things you want to accomplish. If you're not yet sure what you want your PC to do, you may want to consider your personal interests — your PC can enrich just about any hobby. In the following sections, I show you some of the more common types of programs that you may already have on your PC, as well as some additional programs you may want to purchase.

Locating the Programs That Are Already Installed on Your PC

Some programs may already be installed on your new PC. Before you spend money on new software, check to see if the manufacturer of your PC has already installed the programs you need. For example, if you want to write a letter, you need to use a word processing program. You use a spreadsheet program to perform calculations and a database program to organize your list of baseball cards or old records. You'll find icons for many of the programs on the desktop, but the surest way to locate the programs that are installed is to look at the Programs menu, which you can open by choosing Start⇨ Programs.

Word Processing Programs

You use *word processing* programs to write letters, novels, term papers, and other types of *documents* that primarily are made up of words. You can choose from several popular word processing programs:

- ▶ **Microsoft Word** is the most common word processing program you are likely to encounter. Microsoft Word is one of the programs in Microsoft Office.
- ▶ **Corel WordPerfect** is another popular word processing program that is a member of the Corel PerfectOffice package.
- ▶ **Lotus WordPro** is a part of the Lotus SmartSuite package.

Be sure that any new software programs you purchase are compatible with your PC's operating system. For example, if you're using Windows Me, make certain that new software is intended for use with Windows Me.

To see the latest Windows programs, check out AOL Keyword: **Windows**.

14

Understanding Software Types

For help getting the most from your word processing program, check out AOL Keyword: **Word Document**.

To see how to add a printer so you can print out copies of your word processing documents, see Chapter 13.

No matter which of these word processing programs you choose, you will find that each program contains similar tools to help you create documents. For example, you can

▶ Check your spelling and grammar.

▶ Apply special formatting and fonts to give documents a unique style.

▶ Insert digital pictures, graphs, charts, and even live hyperlinks to Web sites.

▶ Create newsletters that you can send to your friends and family — you can either print them out and send them through the postal service or send them as e-mail attachments by using AOL Mail.

▶ Add tables of contents, indexes, and other professional elements to help readers navigate long documents.

Figure 14-1 shows a document I am creating in Word.

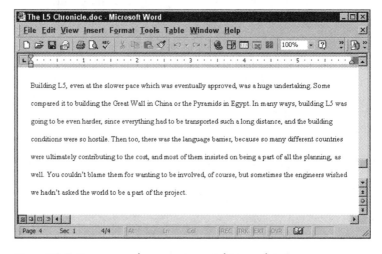

Figure 14-1. You use a word processor to create letters and stories.

Spreadsheets and Database Managers

In addition to word processing, you can use your PC to do numerical calculations and to manage information.

To see what you can do with a spreadsheet, visit the PC Spreadsheet Computing Forum at AOL Keyword: **Spreadsheet**.

For numerical calculations, you use a *spreadsheet* program such as Microsoft Excel, Corel Quattro Pro, or Lotus 1-2-3. Spreadsheet programs display the data and the results of your calculations in *rows* and *columns*. The intersections of these rows and columns are called *cells*. Figure 14-2 shows how I use a spreadsheet to calculate payments on an auto loan.

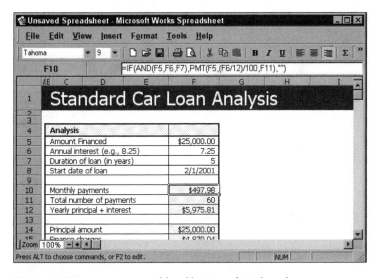

Figure 14-2. You can use a spreadsheet like Microsoft Works to do numerical analysis.

To manage groups of related information, you use a *database* program. A database program is more complex than a spreadsheet because it is intended to track information rather than to simply perform calculations. That is, a database program must maintain lists of related information about groups of items. For example, you could use a database program to keep track of your music collection or to maintain a membership list for an organization you belong to. In Figure 14-3, I am using a database program to keep track of my favorite family recipes.

In addition to the Microsoft Works database, shown in Figure 14-3, other common database programs include Microsoft Access, Corel Paradox, and Lotus Approach.

Desktop Publishing Programs

Even though you can create unique documents in a word processing program, you may need a program that focuses specifically on larger-scale projects. For example, if you want to create fancy documents, such as a club newsletter or personalized greeting cards, a *desktop publishing program* may

Find It Online

You can find out more about databases at the PC and Mac Database Computing Forum (AOL Keyword: **Database**).

Find It Online

To get help with desktop publishing, check out AOL Keyword: **Desktop Publishing**.

be a better bet because this type of program makes creating and laying out your document much easier. One of the reasons desktop publishing programs are easier to use for these projects is because they often have ready-made *templates,* or models, which you can customize to meet your specific needs.

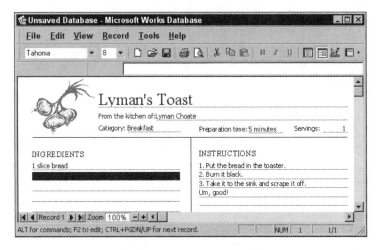

Figure 14-3. You use a database program to organize information.

Some typical desktop publishing programs that you may want to consider for home use include Corel Print House, Microsoft Picture It! Publishing, and Serif Page Plus. Each of these programs has plenty of features but is easy enough to use that you won't spend hours trying to figure out how to do simple tasks.

You can often find *demo* versions of desktop publishing programs. Demos don't usually have all the functionality of full versions, but they are usually free. That way, you can try out the program before you buy it. Visit the manufacturer's Web site to see if a demo is available.

Find It Online

You can download one of the most popular shareware graphics editing programs at AOL Keyword: **Paint Shop Pro**. Just double-click the application icon in the menu.

Graphics Editing Programs

If you have a digital camera or a scanner, or if you want to use graphic images from some other source (such as digital photos someone e-mailed you or that you downloaded from AOL), you probably need a *graphics editing program,* which enables you to modify those images.

Here are some of the things you can do with a graphics editing program:

- ▶ **Reduce red-eye:** You can remove the red spots that often appear in the eyes of people in a flash picture.
- ▶ **Crop out the unnecessary parts of a picture:** You can reduce the size of an image by removing extra (and often distracting) parts of the image around the main subject.
- ▶ **Adjust brightness and contrast:** You can adjust the brightness of an image to make it appear lighter or darker. In addition, you also can change the contrast level.
- ▶ **Adjust hue:** You can change the balance of the different colors in an image to adjust for things such as skin tones that don't look quite right.

To find more information about graphics editing programs, visit the Computing Graphic Arts Forum (AOL Keyword: **Graphics**).

Opening a Program in Windows

Now that you have an understanding of what programs you can use, as well as what programs you already have, you can get started using them. In Windows, you can open programs several different ways:

- ▶ Double-click the program *icon* (the little picture that represents the program) on the Windows desktop. To double-click, move the mouse pointer onto the icon and then rapidly click the left mouse button twice.
- ▶ Some programs, including AOL, have a small icon that appears on the Quick Launch toolbar, which is just to the right of the Start button. You can open AOL by clicking that icon once.
- ▶ To open a program from the Start menu (which you open by clicking the Start button), move the mouse pointer until the program you want to open is highlighted on the menu and then click once.

If your PC has software that the manufacturer installed, you may already have a simple graphics editing program.

14

Understanding Software Types

See Chapter 4 for more information on the Windows desktop.

For more Windows basics, see AOL Keyword: **Windows**.

To make sure you have the latest version of AOL installed, visit AOL Keyword: **Upgrade**.

Programs That Help You Cruise the Internet

The most important Internet program you need is AOL's *integrated browser.* When you install AOL on your PC, you install a program that has most of the features you need integrated right into the program. That is, AOL includes the *browser* (for viewing Web pages), AOL Mail (for sending and receiving e-mail messages), *instant messenger* (for sharing messages in real time with AOL buddies), and many more useful services. Figure 14-4 shows the AOL 6.0 Welcome Screen. The Web browser controls appear on the Navigation bar, which is located just below the AOL toolbar.

Web browser controls

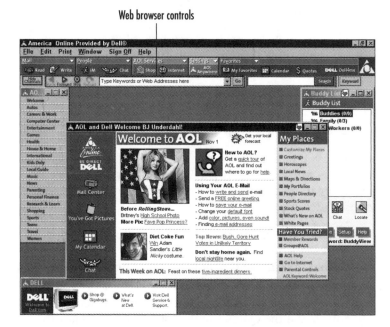

Figure 14-4. AOL's built-in browser has everything you need to browse the Internet.

Adobe Acrobat

Although the AOL integrated browser includes most of the features you need to view Web pages, you may encounter some documents online that were created in a *format* that none of the programs on your PC can open or view. The most common of these document formats is *PDF* — Portable

Document Format. PDF documents are often created for official documents (such as tax forms) and catalogs because they cannot be modified by anyone who views them, and they look just like their hard copy counterparts.

To view these documents, you need a program called *Adobe Acrobat Reader.* The Adobe Acrobat Reader may already be installed on your PC, especially if you installed the *AOL Extras* — special add-ons that you can choose to install when you first install AOL or later by opening the AOL Extras folder on the Start menu. If it isn't already installed, you can download the latest version of Adobe Acrobat Reader for free by visiting the Adobe Web site at www.adobe.com and clicking the Get Acrobat Reader link.

WinZip and Other File Compression Programs

Large files can take longer to send and receive than smaller ones. To reduce the size of files you send and receive, you can *compress* those files by using a program such as WinZip. WinZip is a *shareware* program — meaning that you can try it out for free and then register it for a small fee if you want to keep using it. You can download the latest shareware version of WinZip at www.winzip.com.

AOL can *decompress* the zip file attachments you receive with AOL Mail.

Find It Online

See AOL Keyword: **Zip File** for more information on file compression programs.

Working with System Utilities

To keep your PC safe from problems and running the way it should, you use special *utility* programs. A utility program is a program designed to make your PC easy to use — by keeping it in tip-top shape.

Windows includes several tools that you can use to keep your PC running smoothly. You access these tools by choosing Start⇨Programs⇨Accessories⇨System Tools and then selecting the tool you want to use. The tools you need to know about and use include

▶ **Disk Cleanup:** Safely removes unneeded files that are simply wasting space on your PC.

Caution

Many utility programs can damage your PC if you aren't careful to follow the directions when using them. If you aren't sure about what a utility program does, get help from an experienced user.

Find It Online

For more information on using utility programs, go to AOL Keyword: **Download** and then scroll down to the Utilities category.

▶ **Disk Defragmenter:** Reorganizes your files in a more efficient manner so your PC can open them more quickly.

▶ **Maintenance Wizard:** Enables you to schedule routine maintenance operations so they run automatically in the future. By using the Maintenance Wizard, you don't have to worry about remembering to use these other utilities because they'll run automatically on a regular schedule.

▶ **ScanDisk:** Finds and corrects any errors on your disks.

Antivirus Programs

While some computer viruses are intended to damage or destroy the files on your PC, others can be mildly annoying. Because you never know if a virus-infected file is a real threat to your PC, you need to protect your computer by installing *antivirus* software.

Tip

You may need to temporarily suspend your antivirus software to successfully install new programs. Check your antivirus software for a disable option, and remember to re-enable the antivirus protection later.

Your PC can become infected with a virus in a number of different ways. Opening files attached to e-mail is one of the most common ways. However, recently, viruses have been spread through HTML-based e-mail messages, which don't require readers to open any attachments. In addition, viruses may be attached to other types of files, such as word processing documents. To protect your PC, visit AOL Keyword: **Virus** where you can download trial versions of several popular antivirus programs.

All antivirus programs need regular updates to protect your PC effectively. If you don't update your antivirus software often, you won't be protected against the latest threats. Most people feel that updates about every two weeks will offer reasonable protection.

Programs for Fun

Many programs can make your PC more entertaining. For example, you can

Cross-Reference

See Chapter 17 for more information on downloading software from AOL.

▶ **Play games on your PC:** Game designers have created games to fit almost any interest, from action and adventure games to word games and card games.

To play some games on your PC, you must install a program — usually from a CD-ROM or by downloading a shareware game from AOL. On AOL, you can play online games with other AOL members as your opponents. To see how to play online games on AOL, check out AOL Keyword: **Games Find**.

▶ **Play music or movies:** AOL's Media Player automatically plays music and videos when you're online, but you can also enjoy these types of entertainment when you are not online. To play music and videos when you are not connected to AOL, use a program such as Windows Media Player, shown in Figure 14-5.

 **Cross-Reference**

See Chapter 13 for information on using Windows Media Player to share music with your Pocket PC.

14

Understanding Software Types

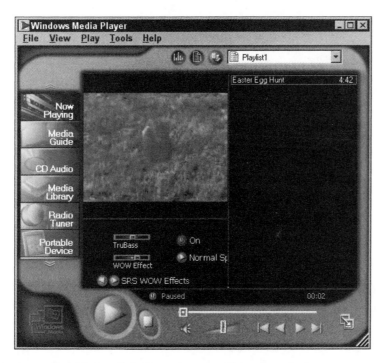

Figure 14-5. Windows Media Player plays your offline music and videos.

Summary

In this chapter, you reviewed some of the types of software that you can use to get the most from your PC. You found how to identify some of the programs you may already have, and learned how to open Windows programs. In addition, you learned about some of the types of programs you may want to purchase for various hobbies and projects. You learned about the programs you use to get the most from the Internet, and then some ideas about programs that help make your PC more fun. Finally, you discovered utility programs that keep your PC running safely and efficiently.

USING SOFTWARE THAT COMES WITH YOUR PC

Quick Look

Chapter 15

Using Software That Comes with Your PC

Your PC came with several useful software programs that enable you to get work done without having to buy additional software. There's also plenty of software built right into your system that's strictly for fun. In this chapter, I show you how to find and use the programs already on your system so you can get the most from your computer without spending a lot of time or money.

Writing a Letter with WordPad

WordPad is a word processor that you can use to create letters or other simple documents. WordPad includes basic text formatting options so you can control how the text looks in your document.

Opening WordPad

To use WordPad to create a document, you first need to open the program. To do so, choose Start⊐Programs⊐Accessories⊐ WordPad. Figure 15-1 shows what WordPad looks like when you first open it.

Note

WordPad is very basic and does not include features like spelling or grammar checking.

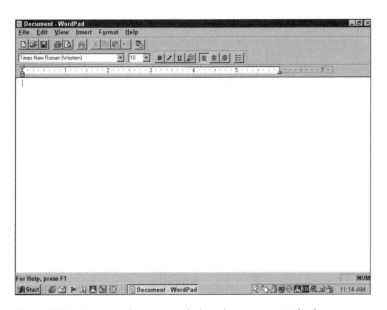

Figure 15-1. You can easily create nice-looking documents in WordPad.

Using WordPad's Menus

WordPad has several menus you can use to create documents:

- ▶ **File:** This menu has all the commands you need to open, save, print, or e-mail a document. It also contains a list of the documents you have most recently opened; just choose one of these documents from the menu to open it.

- ▶ **Edit:** This menu includes commands you use to cut, copy, or paste text in a document. The Edit menu also has commands you can use to find and replace text, as well as commands for controlling objects such as digital images that you've added to your documents.

- ▶ **View:** This menu enables you to select tools such as a ruler and toolbars that appear on the WordPad screen. You can also choose specific options for different types of documents.

15

Using Software That
Comes with Your PC

▶ **Insert:** This menu enables you to add the date and time to a document and to insert an object, such as a picture, into the document.

▶ **Format:** This menu contains options for changing the appearance of the text in your document by applying different fonts, margins, and tabs.

▶ **Help:** This menu opens the WordPad Help system so you can find out more about using the program.

Editing and Formatting

Find It Online

If you're having trouble finding just the right word, you can use AOL Keyword: **Word** to access the Merriam-Webster Collegiate Dictionary.

Tip

To undo an edit, choose Edit⇨Undo. The text in your document goes back to the way it was before you made your last change.

Almost no one creates the perfect document on his or her first try. You'll probably need to edit your documents to correct errors or improve the quality of your text. In addition, you may want to format your documents to improve their appearance.

After you've added text to your document, you can edit it by using the Edit menu commands. For example, if you want to move text from one place to another, follow these steps:

1. Select the text you want to move. To select the text, click at the beginning of the text you want to select and hold down the left mouse button; then drag the pointer to the end of the selection.

2. Choose Edit⇨Cut to move the text to the Windows Clipboard. If you'd rather copy the text than move it, choose Edit⇨Copy.

3. Click in the document where you want the new text to appear.

4. Choose Edit⇨Paste to add the new text.

Formatting your text is just as simple. Follow these steps:

1. Select the text you want to format. To select the text, click at the beginning of the text you want to select and hold down the left mouse button; then drag the pointer to the end of the selection.

2. Click one of the toolbar buttons to apply the formatting you want to use. For example, to make the text bold, click the Bold button. Other formatting options include choosing a different font or text size, applying italic, underlining text, and changing the text color. For more complete control over the formatting, open the Format menu and choose the option you want to use.

Viewing and Printing Documents

After you have finished creating, editing, and formatting your WordPad document, you'll probably want to print it. Before printing, however, you may want to take a look at the layout of the document to make sure the document will look like what you expected; that way, you don't waste a lot of ink and paper.

To preview a document before printing, choose File⇨Print Preview. This command opens a special window that shows how the text will lay out on the page; the dotted lines indicate the margins. Click the Close button to close the Print Preview screen.

To print a document, choose File⇨Print, and then click OK to print the document.

Saving WordPad Documents

After you've gone through all the work to create a document in WordPad, you'll probably want to save that document so you can find it on your hard drive and open it again in the future.

To save your work, follow these steps:

1. Choose File⇨Save to open the Save dialog box.
2. Enter a name for the file in the File Name text box.
3. Click the Save button to save the file.

WordPad saves your documents in the My Documents folder by default. Refer to Chapter 6 for more information on saving files.

Tip

You can open Microsoft Word documents in WordPad even if you don't have Word installed on your PC.

Troubleshooting

If you're using an older version of Windows, you can find the games by choosing Start⇨Programs⇨ Accessories⇨Games.

15

Using Software That Comes with Your PC

Playing Games in Windows

Your PC includes several games that you can play. Windows Me comes with 11 games that you find by choosing Start⇨Programs⇨Games. Here's a list of a few of them:

- ▶ Classic Hearts is a computerized version of the Hearts card game.
- ▶ Classic Solitaire enables you to play Solitaire on your PC without shuffling cards.

▶ FreeCell is a variation of Solitaire.

▶ Internet Backgammon is a version of Backgammon that you play over the Internet against other live players.

▶ Internet Hearts is another version of Hearts that you play on the Internet.

▶ Minesweeper is a board game where you try to avoid clicking on the squares where mines exist.

Find It Online

To find games you can play online, check out the Games Channel (AOL Keyword: **Games**).

To play the Windows games, select the game you want from the menu and use your mouse to click or drag. If you want to know more about the individual games, click Help and then click the menu option that tells you about the game.

Figure 15-2 shows one of the games, Minesweeper, which you play by clicking boxes until you either clear the board or hit a mine. The numbers on the board tell you how many mines are in adjacent boxes.

Figure 15-2. Avoid hitting mines to win this game.

Drawing a Picture with Paint

You can use a Windows program called Paint to draw graphical images on your computer screen. You can also use Paint to modify existing digital images that you download from your digital camera or receive from friends and family.

To use Paint to create a picture, follow these steps:

1. Choose Start➪Programs➪Accessories➪Paint to start the Paint program.

2. Use the tools to the left of the drawing area to create an image. (See the bulleted list that follows for more information on these tools.)

3. Use the color boxes below the drawing area to select colors. Figure 15-3 shows a picture in which I used the *airbrush* tool to apply a spray paint effect to part of the image.

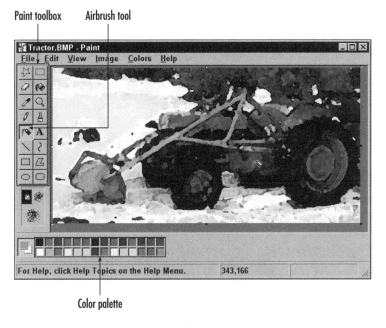

Paint toolbox   Airbrush tool

Color palette

Figure 15-3. You can easily create graphic images in Paint.

4. Choose File⇨Save to save your work.

The Paint toolbox includes the following tools that you can use to edit or create graphic images:

- ▶ **Free-Form Select:** Enables you to select part of the image by dragging
- ▶ **Select:** Enables you to select a rectangular area with the mouse
- ▶ **Eraser/Color Eraser:** Removes areas as you drag the mouse pointer
- ▶ **Fill With Color:** Fills an entire area with the selected color
- ▶ **Pick Color:** Selects the color under the mouse pointer

Troubleshooting

Experiment with the tools. If you don't like an effect, choose Edit⇨Undo to go back to the way the image looked before your last change.

▶ **Magnifier:** Zooms in or out on selected areas of the image

▶ **Pencil:** Draws using a pencil-like tool as you drag the mouse pointer

▶ **Brush:** Draws using a broader, paintbrush-type tool

▶ **Airbrush:** Spray paints on the image

▶ **Text:** Adds text to an image

▶ **Line:** Adds a straight line as you drag the mouse pointer

▶ **Curve:** Adds a curved line as you drag the mouse pointer

▶ **Rectangle:** Adds a box as you drag the mouse pointer

▶ **Polygon:** Adds a multisided form as you drag the mouse pointer

▶ **Ellipse:** Adds a rounded object as you drag the mouse pointer

▶ **Rounded Rectangle:** Adds a box with rounded corners as you drag the mouse pointer

Cross-Reference

See Chapter 13 for information on using Windows Media Player to share music with a portable MP3 player or Pocket PC.

Tip

When you're online, the AOL Media Player enables you to listen to music and to watch videos.

Entertaining Yourself with Windows Media Player

You can use Windows Media Player to play music, watch videos, copy music to your Pocket PC, and to listen to radio stations that broadcast on the Internet. For example, if you insert an audio CD in your CD-ROM drive, Windows Media Player automatically opens and starts playing the music.

To open Windows Media Player, choose Start⇨Programs⇨ Accessories⇨Entertainment⇨Windows Media Player. Figure 15-4 shows Windows Media Player playing music from an audio CD.

Some of the more popular Media Player features appear as buttons on the left side of the Media Player window. (If you don't see all of these buttons, look for a double arrow under the buttons and then click it to expand the list.) The buttons include

Click to see additional features

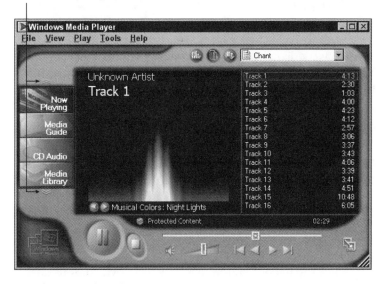

Figure 15-4. You can play your favorite music and videos with Windows Media Player.

▶ **Now Playing:** Displays colors and shapes that change with the beat of the music you're playing or shows the video when you are playing a movie. You can choose View⇨Visualizations to change the display that appears when music is playing.

▶ **Media Guide:** Connects you to the Windows Media Player Web site, where you can choose online content to view or listen to.

▶ **CD Audio:** Plays audio CDs that you insert into your PC's CD-ROM drive or copies audio CDs to your hard drive.

▶ **Media Library:** Organizes your collection of music and videos.

▶ **Radio Tuner:** Allows you to listen to Internet radio stations.

▶ **Portable Device:** Copies music to your portable MP3 player or Pocket PC.

▶ **Skin Chooser:** Allows you to select alternate appearances for Windows Media Player.

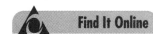
Find It Online

To find audio and video files that you can download, visit AOL Keyword: **New Files** and click the Animation & Video link.

Making Movies Using Windows Movie Maker

Note

Windows Movie Maker movies can be viewed only with Windows Media Player 7, which comes with Windows Me. If you want to share Windows Movie Maker movies with family or friends, make sure that they have Windows Media Player 7.

Tip

If you want to record a soundtrack for your movie, click the Timeline button — the top button to the left of the filmstrip — to change to Timeline view.

If you have a digital camcorder or desktop cam, you can use Windows Movie Maker to create and edit movies. (See Chapter 12 for more information on desktop cams and digital camcorders.

With Windows Movie Maker, you can make your home movies more interesting, and you can share finished movies with family and friends across the Internet — just attach the video files to an e-mail message.

To use Windows Movie Maker, follow these steps:

1. Choose Start⇨Programs⇨Accessories⇨Windows Movie Maker.

2. Click the Record button to record a new video. You can also record a video from a tape in your digital camcorder.

3. When the recording is finished, wait for Movie Maker to split the recording into *clips* — individual scenes from your movie.

4. Drag the clips onto the filmstrip near the bottom of the window in the order you want them to appear.

5. When you're finished creating your movie, choose File⇨Save Movie to save your movie for viewing.

In Figure 15-5, I'm using Movie Maker to assemble a series of clips into a family movie.

Using Other Windows Programs

Your Windows PC has several other handy programs you can use to perform tasks. You find most of these programs in the Programs⇨Accessories section of the Windows Start menu:

▶ **Calculator** is an on-screen calculator that you use to perform calculations. After you have completed a calculation, you can choose Edit⇨Copy to copy the answer to the Windows Clipboard so you can paste the result into a document.

Filmstrip   Record

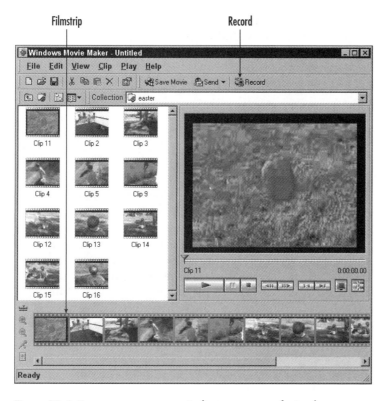

Figure 15-5. You can arrange your movie clips to create a professional looking movie.

▶ **Character Map** makes it easy to add symbols or foreign characters, such as accents, into your documents. Character Map is on the Programs➪Accessories➪ System Tools menu.

▶ **Notepad** is a simple *text editor* — a program you use to edit files whose format must not be altered from *plain text.*

▶ **Phone Dialer** makes your modem dial a phone number so that you can connect to another computer or make a voice call to another person. Phone Dialer stores up to eight entries in a *speed dial* list so you don't always have to enter the same phone numbers when you want to repeat a call. Phone Dialer is on the Programs➪Accessories➪Communications menu.

▶ **Sound Recorder** enables you to record your own messages through your computer's microphone. Sound Recorder is on the Programs➪Accessories➪ Entertainment menu.

Tip

Double-click the speaker icon in the tray near the time display to quickly display and adjust the Volume Control.

15

Using Software That Comes with Your PC

▶ **Volume Control** allows you to adjust the volume level for the different sound sources on your computer. Volume Control is on the Programs⇨Accessories⇨ Entertainment menu.

Summary

Your PC came with many options, tools, and software programs. In this chapter, you got a rundown of the most useful and fun programs you can use. First, you learned about some of WordPad's features so you can get used to the process of writing letters and other documents before purchasing another kind of word processing software. You also found out that your PC already has several different kinds of games to play, some of which you can play with others on the Internet. The Paint program enables you to draw and edit pictures as well. Among some of the other great programs on your PC are Windows Media Player, which allows you to play music and videos, and Movie Maker, which allows you to create your own movies from your digital video camera's footage.

Quick Look

Chapter 16

Installing and Uninstalling Software

The easiest and best way to upgrade your PC is to install new programs, also known as *software.* New programs that you may decide to buy include word processing software, games, tax programs, picture editors, and graphics programs. Or you may download new software from AOL. Most software is easy to install, but there are a few basic things you should know before you begin. This chapter shows you the ins and outs of installing new software on your PC.

This chapter also shows you how to uninstall programs. Getting rid of old programs on your PC that you don't use any more will improve your PC's performance and make it easier to use.

Installing Programs

Software engineers work hard to make the programs they create easy to install. They have to, because the software business is very competitive, and a difficult installation leaves a bad first impression for users. This section shows you what you need to know to make the installation process go even more smoothly.

Of course, the first step in installing any new software is to read the instructions that came with it. Where the instructions are depends on how you obtained the software:

▶ **CD-ROM:** If the software came on a disk or CD-ROM, you may be able to find installation instructions in an instruction booklet, on the inside cover of the CD's plastic jewel case, or even printed on the CD itself.

▶ **Download:** Before you download software from AOL, make sure you click the Read Description button in the Download Center window to find the installation instructions. You may also want to print the instructions by choosing Print⇨Print from the menu bar.

▶ **README:** Most software comes with a file called *README,* similar to the one shown in Figure 16-1. The file contains important information about the software and installation. Use My Computer to navigate to the disk or download folder where the software is located to find the README file. Double-click the README file to open it.

The installation instructions should be straightforward, but before you install the software, you need to do a few things to get your PC ready; see the following section for details.

Getting Windows Ready for an Installation

Windows needs little in the way of preparation before you install new software, but in general, you should do the following:

▶ **Close any programs you have open.** Some programs can be installed while other programs are running; in fact, if you download a program from AOL's Download Center (see Chapter 17), it will probably install automatically as soon as the download is complete. Still, close everything to ensure that the process goes quickly.

Find It Online

Remember, you can find software to download at AOL Keyword: **Download Center**.

Note

Remember, software you download from AOL is automatically placed in a folder called Download in the America Online 6 folder on your C: drive.

Double-click to read

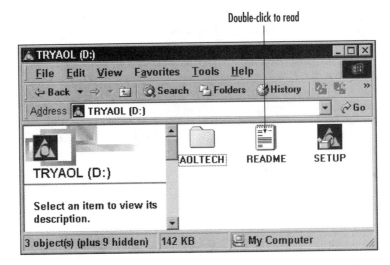

Figure 16-1. Software that comes on a CD (including AOL 6.0) has a README file that contains instructions on how to install the software.

> ▶ **Temporarily disable any screen savers on your PC.** If your screen saver automatically turns on during a download or installation, it could interrupt the process.

> ▶ **If you haven't restarted your PC in the last 24 hours or so, shut it down and restart it before you begin installation.** Doing so will remove any temporary files in your system's *random access memory* (RAM), making the installation process less likely to stall.

Finally, you should disable your antivirus software as described in the following section.

Disabling Your Antivirus Program

Cross-Reference

Chapter 20 shows you how to scan your PC and its disk drives for viruses.

Antivirus programs are important because they protect your PC from being infected by computer viruses. But they can also get in the way of many software installations because some setup programs resemble virus activity. For this reason, most software instructions insist that you disable your antivirus program before installation. Just to be safe, you should scan the CD (or your computer if you downloaded the software) using your antivirus program *before* you install new programs.

The procedure for disabling your antivirus software depends on which program you have, but these general steps work for most programs:

1. Click the icon for your antivirus program in the Windows system tray (it's in the lower-right corner of your screen, next to the clock). If you're not sure which icon is for your antivirus software, slowly move your mouse over the icons until a *ToolTip,* or small box that indicates the name of the program, appears.

2. In the menu that appears, choose Disable, Deactivate, Exit, or a similar option. Figure 16-2 shows the system tray icons and menus for two popular antivirus programs.

3. After you have installed your new software, restart your PC to reactivate your antivirus software.

Some antivirus programs require you to right-click on the system tray icon to see a menu.

Visit AOL Keyword: **McAfee** to learn about McAfee VirusScan. Or learn about Panda Antivirus at www. pandasoftware.com.

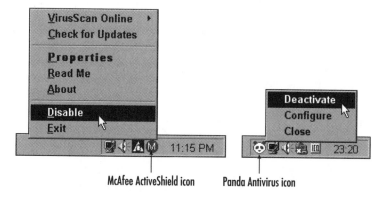

McAfee ActiveShield icon   Panda Antivirus icon

Figure 16-2. Click Disable to temporarily shut down McAfee ActiveShield and click Deactivate to shut down Panda Antivirus.

Installing the Software

After preparing your PC for installation, you're ready to actually install the new software. If the software came on a CD, your PC will probably automatically launch the installation program after you place the disc in your CD-ROM drive. Figure 16-3 shows the setup screen that automatically appears when you place an AOL 6.0 CD in your CD-ROM drive.

If you buy software online, you can always be assured of the best selection of programs. To find great software online, visit AOL Keyword: **Download Center** and click the Buy Software tab to visit SoftwareBuys.com.

16

Installing and Uninstalling Software

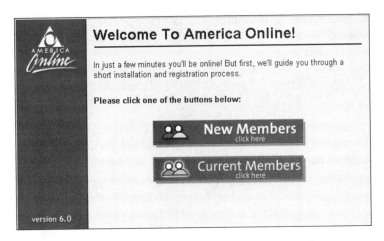

Cross-Reference

For more on downloading software from AOL, see Chapter 17.

Note

If you're installing software you downloaded from AOL, double-click your C: drive and then open the America Online 6.0 download folder.

Tip

If you see several icons labeled Setup or Install, look for the one that looks like a computer.

Note

If you're upgrading to a newer version of a program that is already installed on your PC, check the software's documentation to see if you should uninstall the older version first.

Figure 16-3. When you place an AOL upgrade disk in your CD-ROM drive, a screen like this appears automatically.

If a screen doesn't appear automatically, follow these steps:

1. Double-click the My Computer icon on your desktop.
2. Double-click the icon for your CD-ROM drive (it's usually drive D:). The icon may have a picture of a CD on it, or it may have an icon for the program that's on the disc.
3. If the setup program doesn't launch automatically, look for an icon called Setup or Install, as shown in Figure 16-4.
4. Follow the instructions on-screen to complete the installation. At some point, you may be asked where you want to save the software. For best results, just accept the default location that is shown.

Installing and Removing Windows Components

Windows comes with many useful tools and programs built right in. Most of them are already installed on your PC, but some of them may not be. For instance, the Windows Accessibility features are often not installed on new PCs, or you may find that a previous owner of your used PC removed fun components like games and screen savers. Likewise, you may find that there are some installed components that you don't use, and you'll want to get rid of them to reduce the clutter on the Programs menu and your desktop. One component you'll probably want to remove if you have Windows 98 or Windows Me is Outlook Express, an e-mail program that doesn't work with AOL.

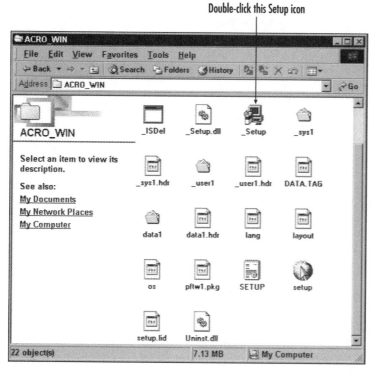

Figure 16-4. To install new software, look for the Setup or Install icon that looks like a computer.

To install (or remove) Windows components, as well as to see a list of components that are available, follow these steps:

1. Place your Windows CD in your CD-ROM drive.
2. Choose Start⇨Settings⇨Control Panel.
3. In the Control Panel, double-click the Add/Remove Programs icon.
4. In the Add/Remove Programs dialog box, click the Windows Setup tab, shown in Figure 16-5.

Note

Most Windows components take up very little hard drive space, but keep an eye on the Space Required and Space Available listings to ensure you don't overfill your hard drive.

16

Installing and Uninstalling Software

Finding and Installing Hardware Drivers

Windows uses *drivers* — special software that enables each piece of hardware on your PC to work. Most of these drivers are built into Windows, but when you purchase some new devices, such as a printer or scanner, you may need to install the driver software.

When you buy a new piece of hardware, you may receive a CD-ROM along with that hardware that includes the drivers. Insert the CD-ROM and then click the Have Disk button when the Add Hardware Wizard detects your new hardware.

Unlike other software, you probably won't have any reason to uninstall and reinstall drivers. About the only time you might need to reinstall a driver is if you reinstall Windows itself.

See Chapter 18 for information on using Windows Update (where you may also find new drivers for some of your hardware). You may also want to check out AOL Keyword: **Computer Tune-up**.

---

5. By clicking the mouse, you can place a check mark next to components you want to add, and remove check marks next to components you want to get rid of. To view subcomponents in a component category (such as Accessories), select the category and click the Details button.

6. When you're done, click OK.

Uninstalling Programs

Software engineers work hard to make programs easy to install, but they usually put less effort into making them easy to remove. However, sometimes software comes with a handy utility that helps you remove, or *uninstall*, the unwanted software, and sometimes it doesn't. The following sections show you what to do in each case.

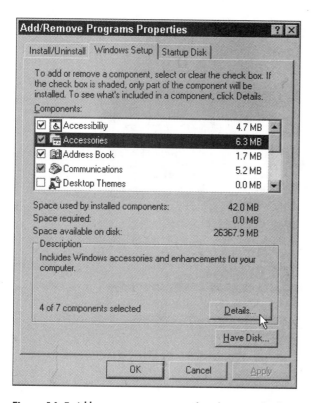

Figure 16-5. Add or remove a component by selecting or deselecting the check box next to it.

Using the Add/Remove Programs Tool

When you want to uninstall software that you don't use anymore, the first thing you should do is try to remove it using the Windows Add/Remove Programs utility:

1. Choose Start⇨Settings⇨Control Panel.
2. Double-click the Add/Remove Programs icon in the Control Panel.
3. The Install/Uninstall tab of the Add/Remove Programs dialog box is selected by default, displaying a list of programs (see Figure 16-6). Locate the program you want to remove in the list. Click it once to select it.
4. Click the Add/Remove button and follow the on-screen instructions to uninstall the software.

Note

When you uninstall a program, a message usually appears on-screen, asking you if you want to remove shared components (components the program shared with other programs). These components are usually safe to remove.

16

Installing and Uninstalling Software

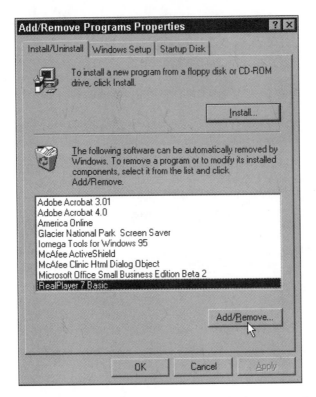

Figure 16-6. Use the Add/Remove Programs dialog box to uninstall software you don't use anymore.

Of course, it's possible that the program you want to remove isn't listed in the Add/Remove Programs dialog box. If it isn't, continue to the following section.

Using a Program's Uninstall Utility

If the Windows Add/Remove Programs dialog box doesn't list the program you want to uninstall, look for an uninstaller utility that came with the program:

1. Choose Start⇨Programs.

2. Click the menu listing for the program you want to uninstall.

3. In the submenu that appears, look for a listing that says Uninstall the *program name* (the name of the program). If you see such an icon, click it and follow

the instructions on-screen to uninstall the program. For example, to uninstall RealPlayer, a popular media player, choose Programs⇨Real⇨RealPlayer⇨RealPlayer Uninstaller.

Alas, some programs don't even have an uninstaller utility. But you can still remove these programs manually, as described in the following section.

Removing a Program Manually

Manually removing a program from your PC can be a little tricky, but it is possible. You should only use this option to uninstall a program if you've been unsuccessful with the options presented in the two previous sections, "Using the Program's Add/Remove Programs Tool" and "Using a Program's Uninstall Utility." To manually uninstall a program, follow these steps:

1. Delete desktop icons for the program by clicking and holding down the left mouse button and dragging the icons to the Recycle Bin.

2. Choose Start⇨Programs and locate the menu listing for the program. Right-click the menu listing and choose Delete. Confirm the deletion; the listing disappears from the Programs menu.

3. Use My Computer to locate the program folder for the program on your C: drive. The name of the folder should closely match the name of the program that you want to get rid of. If the match is questionable and you aren't sure, don't delete the folder.

4. Delete the program folder (see Figure 16-7).

Uninstalling programs by deleting files and folders from your hard drive can be dangerous. If you aren't absolutely sure that the files and folders you are deleting are not used by any other programs, get help from a computer-savvy friend or contact technical support for the company that produced the software.

Caution

Deleting files from your hard drive can be dangerous. Be absolutely certain that any folders or files you delete are only for the program you want to uninstall.

16

Installing and Uninstalling Software

Select a folder to delete   Click Delete

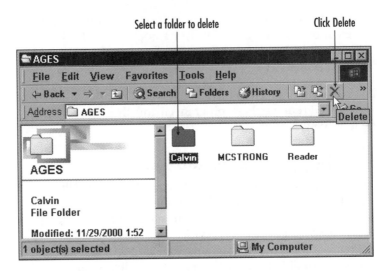

Figure 16-7. I am about to delete a program folder called Calvin.

Summary

By following a few basic steps, you can easily install and unin-stall software on your PC. Removing programs is often more challenging than installing, but by following a few careful steps, you can do it safely. In the next chapter, you see how to download software from AOL.

17

DOWNLOADING SOFTWARE FROM AOL

Quick Look

▶ **The AOL Download Center**   **page 232**

AOL's Download Center offers literally thousands of free files you can download, including software programs, *graphics* (pictures), games, movies, music, and more. This section shows you how to browse AOL's Download Center to find some downloadable files.

▶ **Making Your Downloads Faster**   **page 237**

Downloading files from the Internet can sap your PC's resources, but there are a few simple things that you can do to make the downloading process faster — so you can have more time to use the files you've downloaded. This section gives you tips on downloading files more efficiently.

▶ **Automatic Downloads**   **page 240**

Software usually takes a while to download. You can make downloading more efficient by using Automatic AOL to schedule downloads for when you aren't using the computer, such as late at night.

Chapter 17

Downloading Software from AOL

By now, you have used many different kinds of software on your PC. You've used programs such as AOL and Microsoft Windows, and you have probably used other programs to type letters, draw pictures, listen to music, and play games. But did you know there are still thousands of other programs out there for you to try? Some programs can be purchased at a computer store, but an easier way to get new software (as well as graphics and other files) is to download it from AOL. AOL's Download Center stores thousands of files and programs, and by downloading them you copy them from the Download Center to your own PC. You'll see how to make downloads quicker, and how you can have AOL download large programs for you when you aren't using your PC.

Getting to Know the AOL Download Center

Software and files are easy to find online because AOL organizes downloadable files into a single location called the

Download Center. You can access the Download Center from the AOL Services menu on the AOL toolbar. Just follow these steps:

1. Start AOL and sign on.
2. Click AOL Services on the AOL toolbar and choose Download Center from the menu.

The Download Center, shown in Figure 17-1, can help you find software and files in a variety of ways. You can browse categories, view lists of the most popular downloads, or conduct a search using words such as **flight simulator** or **butterflies**.

Find It Online

You can access the Download Center by visiting AOL Keyword: **Download Center**.

Fun & Games category

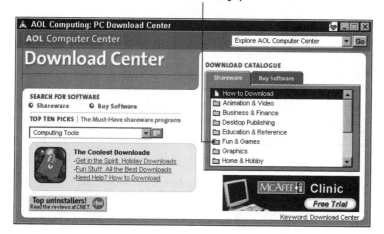

Figure 17-1. The Download Center is your portal to thousands of great software downloads.

Locating Files and Software to Download

The easiest way to find files and software in the Download Center is to browse categories in the Download Catalogue. If you're not sure what you want to download, browse the lists. For example, you can browse the Fun & Games category (refer to Figure 17-1) to find out what's available there. From the main Download Center, follow these steps:

1. Double-click Fun & Games from the list on the Shareware tab on the right side of the window.

Tip

Some programs say that you need *unzipping* or *decompression* software. Don't worry; AOL 6.0 has this type of software built in.

Downloadable Software: Free or Not?

Software in the AOL Download Center is divided into two basic categories: *shareware* and *buy software*. Buy software is software that you must purchase to use. The Buy Software tab in the Download Center contains antivirus software, Windows upgrades, the hottest games, and more.

The Shareware tab contains software that you can download and use without paying. Does this mean that shareware is free? Not necessarily. Some shareware *is* free, and you can use it as long as you want without paying. This software is often called *freeware*.

But most shareware isn't entirely free. Some shareware programs have a trial period that you can use to test a program for free before you buy, and some lack features of the full version, for which you must pay.

Shareware registration costs vary widely. Always read the description of any software you plan to download, and be sure that you agree to any terms and conditions set forth by the publisher.

Troubleshooting

Looking for advice or a secret shortcut for your favorite game? Check out the Cheats, Editors, Hints & Fixes category in Fun & Games.

2. A Fun & Games window appears, as shown in Figure 17-2. Double-click a category on the left. You may need to scroll down to see all the categories. I chose Cursors.

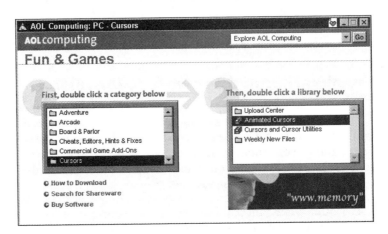

Figure 17-2. Double-click a category on the left and then double-click a library on the right.

3. After you double-click a category on the left, a list of *libraries* (groups of similar files) in that category appears on the right. Double-click a library to open it. I chose Animated Cursors. A list of items in the library appears, as shown in Figure 17-3.

4. Review the list. You'll probably need to scroll down to see the whole list. See the following section, "Getting Information About the File or Software," to learn how to get information about an item you see in the list.

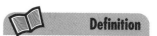

Definition

Animated cursors change the look of the mouse pointer (also called the *cursor*) on your screen.

Tip

If the list seems short, click the List More Files button to expand the list of files that you can download.

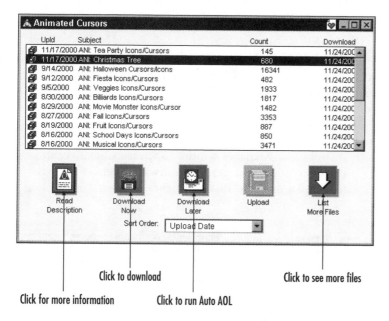

Click for more information   Click to download   Click to run Auto AOL   Click to see more files

Figure 17-3. Choose files to download here. I've chosen software that will change my mouse pointer into a Christmas tree, complete with blinking lights.

Getting Information About the File or Software

Before you download any files there are some key pieces of information that you should collect. They include:

▶ How long will the download take?

▶ What are the system requirements for the software? Does my PC meet those requirements?

▶ How should the software be installed?

To obtain information about the files you want to download:

1. Click the item to select it (refer to Figure 17-3).

2. Click Read Description. A window opens containing important information about the file. Read everything in the window and make a note of any installation instructions. If all your questions are not answered satisfactorily, you probably shouldn't download the file.

3. When you are done reading the description, click the Close button in the upper right corner of the description window.

Downloading Files and Software

Note

You can download only one file at a time unless you choose to use Automatic AOL.

After you decide which file you want to download, the downloading process is easy:

1. In the download list click Download Now (refer to Figure 17-3).

2. A Download Manager window appears. Click Save in the Download Manager. The software begins to download and a progress meter appears, as shown in Figure 17-4.

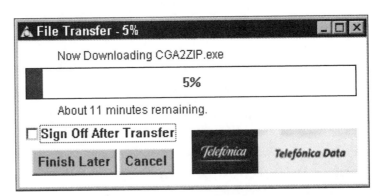

Figure 17-4. The File Transfer window shows you the progress of your download and gives an estimate of how much longer the download will take.

Cross-Reference

Downloadable files and software can contain computer viruses. See Chapter 20 for more on protecting your PC from viruses.

3. When the download is complete, a message asks if you want to locate the file. Click Yes.

4. A window opens. Usually you will see a list of files, but sometimes you'll only see a folder. If you only see a folder, double-click it to open it.

5. Use your antivirus software to scan your hard drive for viruses, as described in Chapter 20.

6. In the window containing the file or files you just downloaded, look for a file called README. The README file gives general information about the software, as well as installation instructions. Double-click the README file and read it thoroughly.

Note

By default, files you download from the Download Center are stored in the folder `C:\America Online 6.0\download`.

Speeding Up Your Downloads

When you click the Read Description button for a program you want to download, one piece of information you'll find is an estimate of download time. The estimate usually looks something like this:

```
Estimated Download Time (28800 baud):
< 30 minutes
```

To make sense of this estimate, you need to know how fast your connection to AOL is as explained in the following section.

Cross-Reference

For more information on installing software on your PC, review Chapter 16.

Assessing Your Connection Speed

Everyone connects to AOL at a different speed. That speed is measured in *bits per second* (bps), also called *baud*. A bit is a single piece of computer data, and a 56Kbps connection can transfer up to 56,000 bits of data per second. How fast is your connection to AOL? You can't just rely on the speed of your modem because other factors (like Internet traffic and the quality of your phone line) can affect the connection. To check the speed of your connection

1. Right-click the AOL icon in the Windows system tray (that's the area in the lower-right corner of the screen next to the clock) and choose System Information from the menu that appears. The AOL System Information window appears.

2. Click the Status tab to bring it to the front, as shown in Figure 17-5.

3. Make a note of the speed shown in the Session Speed box. This is how fast your modem connects to AOL.

4. Click Close when you are done checking your connection speed.

Tip

Phone line static can reduce the speed of your connection. If your actual connection speed is far less than what your modem is capable of, contact your phone company to see if the connection can be improved.

You can use simple math to figure out approximately how long a download will take. For instance, suppose your connection speed is 56000 bps. That's almost twice as fast as 28800 bps, so a download that takes 30 minutes at 28800 bps will probably take about 15 minutes at 56000 bps.

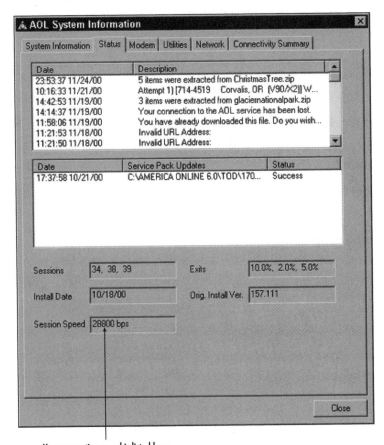

Your connection speed is listed here

Figure 17-5. The Status tab of the AOL System Information window tells you how fast your connection to AOL is.

Find It Online

If you really want to speed up your downloads, consider high speed access from AOL. Visit AOL Keyword: **AOL PLUS**.

Downloading Efficiently

The best way to make your downloads faster is to sign up for high speed access to AOL. Besides that, there are a few simple things you can do to speed up downloads:

▶ **Schedule your downloads so they occur when fewer people are using AOL.** The best times are usually late at night and early in the morning.

▶ **Schedule your downloads for when *you* aren't using AOL.** If you're browsing AOL's channels or chatting with buddies while a download is taking place, the download will be slower.

▶ **Improve the quality of your connection.** If your current connection seems unusually slow, try signing off AOL and then re-connecting.

Automating Downloads from AOL

One of AOL's best features is the ability to schedule downloads to take place automatically, so downloading the files you want doesn't get in the way of other things you want to do on AOL — and with your PC. Late night downloads can also free up your telephone during the day and evening, which is nice if you use your only phone line to connect to AOL.

Automating downloads is a two-step process: First you choose what you want to download, as shown in "Downloading Files and Software," earlier in this chapter, and then you schedule the download using Automatic AOL. You can also use Automatic AOL to automatically download e-mail and e-mail attachments, as well.

Choosing Software to Download

To automate the download process, follow these steps:

1. Locate software that you want to download as described in "Downloading Files and Software."

2. Select the software and click Download Later instead of Download Now. A message appears telling you that the software has been added to your Download Manager.

3. If you want to download more than one file, repeat steps 1 and 2.

4. Choose File⇨Download Manager. The Download Manager appears, as shown in Figure 17-6.

5. Review the files you want to download. If you change your mind about a file, click the file and then click Remove Item.

6. Click the Close button to close the Download Manager.

You can sign off AOL without scheduling a download. The list of files you want to download remains in your Download Manager.

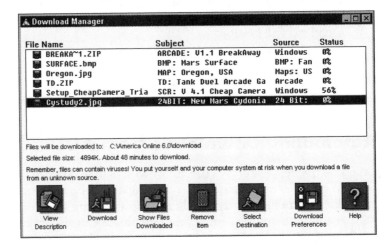

Figure 17-6. The Download Manager helps you schedule downloads to take place automatically.

Scheduling Downloads with Automatic AOL

You do not have to be signed on to AOL to set up Automatic AOL.

After you select software to download, you can schedule the actual download using Automatic AOL. Here's how to set up Automatic AOL the first time you use it:

1. Click Mail on the AOL toolbar and choose Automatic AOL from the menu.

2. A Welcome Screen appears. Click Continue in the Welcome Screen.

3. Answer the series of yes or no questions to decide if you want Automatic AOL to automatically download mail for you, send mail you wrote offline, and download files in your Download Manager.

4. Select the screen names for which you want Automatic AOL to run and click Continue.

5. When you are asked if you want to run Automatic AOL on a regular basis, click Yes to set up a schedule.

6. Choose the days of the week and how many times a day you want Automatic AOL to run.

7. Choose a starting time. If you want Automatic AOL to run once per day, set the time for when you won't be using your PC, such as late at night.

8. Click OK in the final screen.

You must leave the AOL program window open on your PC for Automatic AOL to run, although you can sign off your AOL account. When the scheduled time for Automatic AOL to take place arrives, Automatic AOL automatically logs on, downloads the files you specified, and then automatically logs off.

You can always change your Automatic AOL settings by choosing Mail⇨Automatic AOL. A window with check boxes next to each of the tasks you want Automatic AOL to perform appears. To change the schedule, click Schedule Automatic AOL. A scheduling window appears, as shown in Figure 17-7.

Note

The starting time in the Automatic AOL scheduler uses a military-style 24-hour clock. This means that 3:00 p.m. is shown as 15:00.

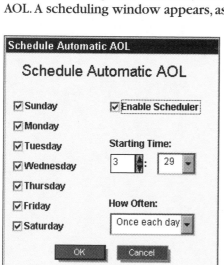

Figure 17-7. Schedule Automatic AOL to download software while you are away.

Summary

Downloading software from AOL is a fun way to add to the programs you already have on your PC. Many files are available, and they're easy to find. This chapter showed you how to download those files, as well as how to speed up the download process. You also saw how to automate AOL downloads while you are away. In the next part, you can find out about keeping your PC in tip-top condition, as well as learn how to upgrade it and get help from AOL.

P A R T

V

MAINTAINING AND ENHANCING YOUR PC

Quick Look

Chapter 18

Optimizing and Maintaining Your PC

The best way to ensure that your PC performs properly is to keep it well maintained. A well-maintained computer runs efficiently and is less likely to have problems, which will take a load off your mind if you're worried about having your system crash. This chapter helps you discover how you can protect your investment on an ongoing basis; you can prevent future problems by automatically scheduling and running the Windows Maintenance Wizard, keeping software up-to-date, and following my advice to keep your computer in good shape all the way around. If worst comes to worst and your system does become unstable, Chapter 19 shows you what to do if your PC crashes.

Optimizing Your Hard Drive

Your PC's hard drive stores all of your programs and document files. Keeping your hard drive in good shape helps ensure that your PC can read those files quickly and reliably. Fortunately, Microsoft Windows comes with some programs that help you keep your hard drive in good condition. The following sections show you how to check for and fix problems on your hard drive. The section "Scheduling Regular PC Maintenance" shows you how you can set up Windows to perform these tasks automatically.

Understanding ScanDisk

ScanDisk is a Microsoft Windows program that checks your hard drive for errors. If ScanDisk finds errors, it attempts to correct them and prevent future problems. Hard drive errors arise from general PC use and won't cause any harm as long as you maintain your PC. ScanDisk is one of the programs that you can schedule with the Maintenance Wizard, which I discuss in the following section, but you can also run ScanDisk yourself at any time.

To check your hard drive for errors, close any programs and follow these steps:

1. Open ScanDisk by choosing Start⇨Programs⇨ Accessories⇨System Tools⇨ScanDisk.

2. In the ScanDisk window, select the drive that you want to check. Make sure the Automatically Fix Errors check box is selected so that any errors are corrected without asking you to confirm the corrections. Unless you are experiencing a lot of disk error messages, leave the Standard Test option selected. The Thorough Test option takes far longer to run and is generally not necessary.

3. Click the Start button to begin. If you see a message that reports results when ScanDisk finishes, click OK to close the message. You can use your PC as usual as soon as ScanDisk closes.

Defragmenting Your Hard Drive

Disk Defragmenter is a Microsoft Windows program that re-arranges the files on your hard drive so that your PC can open those files more quickly. (This process is sometimes called

Troubleshooting

If your computer seems to be having a lot of trouble opening files, select the Thorough Test option in ScanDisk to check for physical errors on your hard drive.

defragmenting or *defragging*.) You need to run Disk Defragmenter on a regular basis; otherwise, your computer's performance will slow over time. You can run Disk Defragmenter whenever your PC seems to be running slower, or you can simply allow Disk Defragmenter to run when the Maintenance Wizard runs it automatically (if you choose to use the Maintenance Wizard).

To defragment your hard drive, follow these steps:

1. Open Disk Defragmenter by choosing Start⇨ Programs⇨Accessories⇨System Tools⇨Disk Defragmenter.

2. Select the drive that you want to defragment. In most cases, select the C: drive.

3. Click OK to begin. Running Disk Defragmenter may take some time to complete if you haven't run it recently.

Cleaning Up Your Hard Drive

Disk Cleanup is a program that deletes unneeded files from your hard drive. Over time, your hard drive accumulates hundreds of files — files you never open or use — that can safely be removed to free up disk space. For example, when you sign on to the Internet with AOL and visit Web sites, you may pick up what are called *temporary Internet files,* files that are only useful when you're visiting the Web site, but which don't automatically disappear when you log off.

To delete the unneeded files, follow these steps:

1. Open Disk Cleanup by choosing Start⇨Programs⇨ Accessories⇨System Tools⇨Disk Cleanup.

2. On the Disk Cleanup tab, select the files you want to delete (see Figure 18-1). Generally speaking, selecting any of the file types shown in this dialog box is probably safe.

3. Click OK and then click Yes to delete the files.

Avoid having other programs, including screen savers, running while Disk Defragmenter is working. Otherwise, Disk Defragmenter may continually restart.

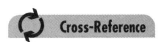

See Chapter 21 for information on adding more storage capacity to your PC.

The Description box at the bottom of the Disk Cleanup window explains the characteristics of each kind of file that can be deleted. You can even see the files you're deleting by clicking View Files.

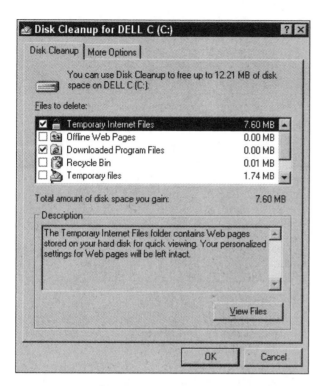

Figure 18-1. Use Disk Cleanup to remove files that are wasting disk space.

Scheduling Regular PC Maintenance

Your PC needs regular maintenance, but you don't have to handle all the maintenance tasks yourself. You can set up Microsoft Windows to automatically handle maintenance tasks — even when you aren't using your PC. These tasks include things like checking your hard disk for errors, rearranging files for more efficient access, and removing old files that no longer serve a useful purpose.

Setting Up the Maintenance Wizard

The Maintenance Wizard is a tool that automatically schedules several important system maintenance tasks. You answer a few simple questions, and the Maintenance Wizard does the rest.

As you use the Maintenance Wizard to schedule your PC's routine maintenance, you have the option of choosing Express

Troubleshooting

This Wizard is unavailable to Windows 95 users. Check out "Optimizing Your Hard Drive" for more information on running maintenance tasks on your own.

setup or Custom setup. The only real difference between the two options is that you have slightly more control over the specific times that the tasks are performed if you choose Custom setup. However, this additional control comes at a price. You have to wade through a whole series of somewhat confusing screens. The Express setup makes these choices for you.

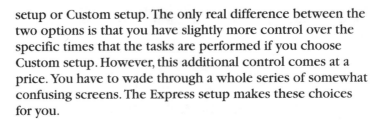

To use the Maintenance Wizard, follow these steps:

1. Choose Start⇨Programs⇨Accessories⇨System Tools⇨ Maintenance Wizard. The Maintenance Wizard starts and presents you with the choice of Express or Custom setup.

2. Select the Express setting (the default) and then click Next to continue.

3. Choose the best time to run the maintenance tasks and click Next. Choose a time when you won't be using your PC, and remember to leave your PC on during the scheduled time. You can find out how to save power while your PC is on in the following section, "Conserving Power with Your PC."

4. Review the settings (see Figure 18-2) and click Finish. In this case, the Maintenance Wizard has set up Disk Defragmenter to periodically rearrange the files on your hard drive, ScanDisk to check for errors, and Disk Cleanup to remove unnecessary files. You can activate the check box near the bottom of the dialog box if you want to run the three tasks immediately, but if you simply allow the tasks to run at their scheduled time, you won't tie up your PC immediately.

If you need to change the times at which the Maintenance Wizard performs its maintenance tasks, you can at any time. See the following section for more information.

Making Changes to the Maintenance Wizard Setup

The Maintenance Wizard gives you options for setting up routine maintenance tasks to run automatically. After you set up a maintenance schedule using the wizard, you can add tasks to the schedule or modify the existing schedule if necessary. For example, if you have a backup program that can run without your presence, you can schedule backups to run nightly.

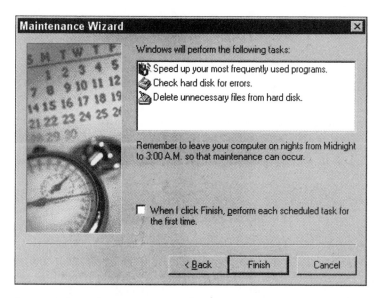

Figure 18-2. Use the Maintenance Wizard to maintain your system automatically.

To add to or modify the Maintenance Wizard's schedule, follow these steps:

1. Open the Scheduled Tasks folder by choosing Start⇨ Programs⇨Accessories⇨System Tools⇨Scheduled Tasks. Figure 18-3 shows the Scheduled Tasks folder.

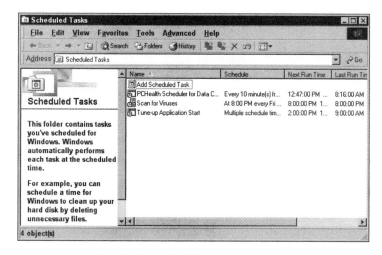

Figure 18-3. Use the Scheduled Tasks folder to adjust the task schedule.

For more Windows help, check out AOL Keyword: **Windows.**

2. If you want to add a new task to the schedule, double-click the Add Scheduled Task icon. The Scheduled Task Wizard opens. You can choose a program to run and then set up a schedule for the task.

3. Double-click an existing task to modify its schedule. A dialog box where you can choose the dates, times, and program options for the selected task appears. When you modify a scheduled task, make sure that you don't change any settings that you don't understand. You could accidentally change the settings so that tasks cannot be completed.

Keeping Your Software Up-to-Date

You need to keep your PC's software up-to-date so you can make certain that you have the latest available features. Another reason to update your software is because *bugs* (errors) are always being discovered, reported, corrected, and re-released. The newer the version of software is, the more likely it is to be bug-free. Fortunately, most software updates that you need for Microsoft Windows or for your AOL software not only are free, but are also very easy to add to your PC.

Updating Microsoft Windows

To keep your version of Microsoft Windows updated, you need to follow these steps:

1. Choose Start⊏⟩Windows Update, which is near the top of the menu. Your PC then logs on to the Internet and opens the Windows Update Web site. If necessary, confirm that you want to connect to the Internet.

2. Click the Product Updates link and wait for the list of available updates to appear. You may need to confirm that you want to download the Microsoft update software.

3. Select the updates you want to install and then click the Download button.

4. Read the installation instructions and click the Start Download button to begin the download. Most updates are installed automatically, but you need to read the directions to know for certain.

Print out a copy of the installation instructions before you begin the download — that way you can follow them as you go through the process.

Many updates require that you restart your PC before they take effect. Make sure that you save your work and close any programs before you download updates.

Downloading AOL Updates

You should keep your AOL software up-to-date so that you can enjoy all the latest features. You update AOL by signing on to AOL and then visiting the AOL Upgrade Center. If an update is available, simply follow the on-screen directions for downloading and installing the update.

Some updates can take a long time to download. You may want to download the update when you won't need to use your PC for an hour or more — depending on the size of the update.

Sometimes, AOL automatically updates its software as you're signing off. The AOL update doesn't require anything of you, but AOL will keep you online for a few more seconds while it optimizes your files. You're not billed for any extra time you're online.

 Find It Online

To find out if an AOL update is available, check out AOL Keyword: **Upgrade**. Also, AOL automatically sends you an e-mail message to inform you when an update is available.

18

Optimizing and Maintaining Your PC

Conserving Power with Your PC

Your PC itself uses very little power, but some of the peripherals can waste power when you aren't using them. You can minimize wasted power and still have your PC turned on and ready for use by adjusting your power options. The options that are available vary depending on the capabilities of your PC. Some of them include:

▶ **Turn off monitor:** Turns off your monitor after a specified period of time. The monitor turns back on when you wiggle the mouse or start typing.

▶ **System stand by:** Places your system in stand-by mode. Various devices are turned off, but your system quickly wakes up if you press a key on the keyboard or wiggle the mouse.

▶ **System hibernates:** Saves everything in memory in a special file on your hard drive and turns off the power. This option enables you to quickly return to the same set of open programs and windows, but your PC can't run scheduled tasks if it is hibernating.

 Tip

Your monitor uses more power than your PC. Set the monitor to turn off if the PC isn't used for 15 minutes to balance power savings and convenience.

Note

Laser printers also take a lot of power to run, but they can usually be placed into a power-conservation mode automatically after a set period of inactivity. Consult your owner's manual to find out if your printer has this option.

To take advantage of your PC's power-saving options, follow these easy steps:

1. Choose Start⇨Settings⇨Control Panel.

2. Double-click the Power Options (called Power Management in Windows 98) icon to open the dialog box shown in Figure 18-4.

3. Select the settings you prefer and click OK. The most important setting to choose is the Turn Off Monitor setting. The remaining options save far less power than turning off the monitor.

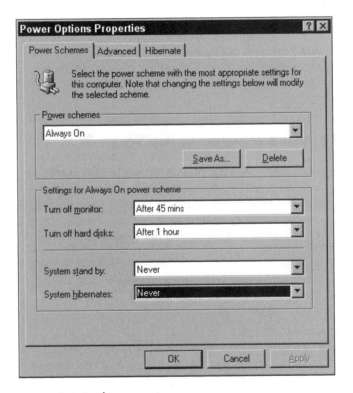

Figure 18-4. Use the power options to conserve power.

Protecting Your PC from Power Surges and Other Problems

Power surges can be very dangerous to your PC. They can damage your computer or corrupt data with no warning. You can easily protect your PC from power surges by plugging your PC into a good surge protector (which typically costs less than $20) and following some fundamental safety precautions. Note that most power strips do not provide surge protection unless this is specifically mentioned on the package. Also, even if you have a good surge protector, unplugging your PC when a lightning storm is in your immediate area is a good idea.

The following sections tell you what else you can do to keep your PC healthy.

 Cross-Reference

See Chapter 13 for information on battery backup units that protect your PC from power outages *and* power surges.

Cooling Your PC

The components that make up your PC generate a lot of heat. Your PC has one or more fans that blow air through the system and over the hottest components to prevent your computer from overheating.

In most cases, the fans are sufficient for keeping your computer cool — if you let them do their job. In fact, your PC can easily be left on all the time without overheating as long as you don't do anything that prevents your PC from keeping its cool. Here are some precautions for protecting your computer from overheating:

▶ Keep the vents clear so that you don't block the airflow from your PC.

▶ Avoid placing your PC in direct sunlight or where heat from your home's heating system will blow directly on your computer.

▶ Don't operate the PC without the case on. Operating the PC without the case disrupts the airflow patterns inside the PC and can cause components to overheat.

If you accidentally spill liquid onto your keyboard, shut down your computer and try to dry the keyboard using the lowest heat setting on your hairdryer. Don't allow the keyboard to get too hot — you may cause permanent damage.

To find fresh supplies to keep your printer in top shape, check out Shop@AOL's Printers, Software & Accessories department (AOL Keyword: **Printer Store**).

You don't have to worry about turning your printer off to save power unless you know you won't be using it for long periods of time.

Cleaning Your Keyboard and Mouse

Because you use your keyboard and mouse every time you use your PC, they will inevitably get dirty. You can clean them if you are careful and use the proper procedures. Here are some cleaning pointers:

- ▶ Turn off your PC before you do any cleaning.
- ▶ Never use harsh solvents or strong cleaning products. A slightly damp cloth is all you need in most cases.
- ▶ Use a vacuum with a soft brush attachment to clean lint from your keyboard.
- ▶ Turn your mouse over to see if the cover over the ball is removable. If it is, gently open the cover and wipe the ball clean with a damp cloth. Vacuum any dust or lint out before you replace the ball and cover.

Maintaining Your Printer

Properly maintaining your printer helps you avoid printing problems. Here are a few pointers for keeping your printer in good shape:

- ▶ Use the recommended ink cartridges. Less expensive replacements may contain poor quality ink that can clog the print heads.
- ▶ Regularly vacuum out any dust in the printer. Carefully stick the nozzle of the vacuum into any place where you see dust buildup, but don't jam the nozzle in so hard that you damage anything.
- ▶ Use high-quality paper. Poorer quality paper can cause paper jams that can damage your printer.
- ▶ Use printer cleaning sheets often. These special sheets of paper clean the paper path and reduce smudging.
- ▶ Use your inkjet printer fairly often to keep the print heads from becoming clogged with dried ink.

Summary

Buying and owning a PC can be a very rewarding experience, especially after you begin to understand how it works. But protecting your investment by taking good care of your PC is also essential. In this chapter, you found out how to keep your PC in top operating condition. You learned how to schedule maintenance checks that run automatically, and got your hands dirty using Microsoft Windows' tools to keep your hard drive working properly. Another way to keep your PC in peak shape is to keep your important software up-to-date. In addition, you found out how conserving power, protecting your PC from power surges, and keeping the system cool can prolong your PC's life, and how keeping your keyboard, mouse, and printer clean can also keep them functioning well. In the following chapter, find out how to diagnose and fix problems with your PC.

Quick Look

Chapter 19

Diagnosing and Repairing Computer Problems

Sometimes PCs don't work the way we expect them to, no matter how careful we are. With the right attitude and the proper approach, you can minimize the effects of any problems that occur and solve those problems with as little inconvenience as possible.

In this chapter, I show you how to approach computer problems correctly so that you can get your PC back into operation as soon as possible. You will see that most problems are actually fairly easy to correct and that you can prevent many problems from coming back in the future.

Documenting Problems with Your PC

If your PC *crashes* (or stops responding to the keyboard or mouse), you need to take a calm, logical approach to solving the problem. If you do, you'll find that most problems aren't as bad as they seem at first glance. In the following sections, I show you how to approach crashes to get your PC back up and running as quickly as possible — often within a few minutes.

The most important step in correctly identifying a problem with your PC so that it can be solved is taking the time to actually read (and write down) the exact text of any error messages you see. You don't expect your doctor to correctly diagnose an aliment if you call and simply say, "I'm sick." Similarly, the more specific you are about a PC problem, the more helpful a PC professional can be if you have a problem.

You may be able to print a copy of an error message by pressing the Print Scrn key (or Print Screen, depending on your keyboard) while the message is displayed. Then, open Paint and choose Edit⇨Paste to paste the message. Choose File⇨Print to print the message that you pasted.

What to Do If the System Crashes

One of the most frustrating problems you may encounter with your computer is when it simply stops responding. Your system has *frozen*, or *crashed*. When your PC freezes, it usually does so because a program has run into a problem that is making your entire system act strangely. Or maybe you've got more than one program running and entered several commands all at once. Here are a few signs that your PC has frozen:

▶ You move your mouse, and it remains locked in one position on-screen.

▶ You try to type, but nothing seems to happen.

▶ You try to close a window or dialog box but get no response.

You may discover over time that a single program crashes, but the rest of your PC seems to be working okay. If you encounter a program that freezes up but won't come back to life, you may be able to close the program that has crashed without affecting any other program that's open. Then you can save your work in the other programs so that you don't lose the work that you haven't saved yet. Be sure to restart the computer to help the system recover from the problems it has encountered.

In many instances, you can walk away from your computer and let it sort itself out — but first, try to save any work you've been doing. When you come back to your desk, you may be able to resume your work with no problems. If, however, the system is still frozen, you may need to follow the steps in this section to bring your system back to life again.

If a program crashes, or if the whole system has frozen, follow these steps to solve the problem:

Troubleshooting

If one program has crashed, your whole system is taxed and moving slowly. If you don't get an immediate response the first time you press Ctrl+Alt+Del, wait several seconds, even a minute or two, before you make any more moves.

Troubleshooting

If the whole system has frozen, select and close all open programs that don't have any unsaved work. The idea is not to tax your PC's resources so that your PC can correct its problems.

1. Simultaneously press the Ctrl, Alt, and Del keys. The Ctrl and Alt keys are in the lower-left corner of most standard keyboards. The Del key (which may appear as Delete on some keyboards) is in the upper-right corner of most standard keyboards. Even if nothing happens immediately, resist the urge to press these keys again — doing so will shut down and restart your PC. You don't want to restart your PC if you have open files and unsaved work, because you could lose those files and your work.

2. The Close Program dialog box appears (see Figure 19-1). Click the program that is not responding to highlight it and then click the End Task button. You may need to scroll through the list of open programs.

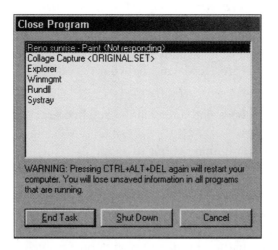

Figure 19-1. Use the Close Program dialog box to close programs that aren't responding.

3. Wait about 20 seconds to see if a message appears telling you that the program is still not responding. If this message appears, click the End Task button in that message box. If no message appears after about 20 seconds or so, continue to the next step.

4. Do not attempt to close other programs or shut down your system until the crashed program is closed. Then, close all other open programs after you have saved any open files. If you still don't see a message on-screen, try closing other programs.

5. If you've successfully closed the programs and un-frozen your PC, you can restart your computer by choosing Start⇨Shut Down and choosing the Restart the Computer radio button. Your PC should run fine again now. If, however, your PC is still frozen and has open files, you can shut down your PC by pressing Ctrl+Alt+Del again.

6. Your PC restarts. Before Windows opens, you may see a message on-screen that indicates that your system was shut down improperly. Your system checks itself out to make sure no problems exist.

7. If you had to shut down your system with files still open, there is a possibility that you lost some or all of them. However, if you saved the files at any point before your system froze, you may be able to recover them. Open the program you were working in before the crash. The recovered document may appear.

If your PC is still unstable, or if you're having a hard time getting Windows to restart, see the following section, "What to Do if the PC Is Too Unstable to Restart."

What to Do If the PC Is Too Unstable to Restart

If your system has crashed, you can often restart your PC and continue working, as explained in the previous section, "What to Do If the System Crashes." You may lose some work, but nothing more severe happens. Sometimes, however, a crash may be so severe that you cannot restart Windows normally. If Windows has shut down and won't stay running, review the following sections to help you determine the cause of the problem — and the best solution.

Find It Online

For more information on dealing with PC problems, check out AOL Keyword: **Get Help Now**.

Troubleshooting

You should always manually save documents and files by pressing Ctrl+S or choosing File⇨Save — even if the program has an AutoSave or AutoRecover feature. Save your work manually every 15 to 30 minutes, especially if you have more than one program running.

Diagnosing the Cause of a PC Crash

If you have a problem with your computer, you need to re-member that you probably aren't the first person who's had the same problem. With a little careful observation, you can identify the cause of your PC's crash; and knowing the cause may help you prevent the same problem from happening again. Go back to the days and minutes before the crash and ask yourself these questions:

Cross-Reference

See Chapter 18 for informa-tion on protecting your PC from a variety of problems, including heat and power surges. Check out Chapter 13 for information on battery backup for your PC.

Cross-Reference

See Chapter 16 for informa-tion on installing and unin-stalling software. See Chapter 20 for information on protecting your PC from viruses.

▶ Did the lights in your home flicker at about the same time that your PC crashed? If so, your PC probably lost power or was hit by a power surge.

▶ Was the weather unusually hot when your PC stopped responding? If so, your computer may have overheated.

▶ Did you install new software in the days or hours be-fore the crash? If so, the new software could be con-flicting with your PC.

▶ Has it been awhile since you updated your antivirus software? Do you open a lot of file attachments? If your PC began to display odd or rude messages just before it crashed and you suddenly couldn't locate important files, then your computer may have crashed because it was infected with a virus.

▶ Has it been awhile since you last used your computer, or have you been moving things around lately? If your computer, monitor, or printer won't turn on, you may have a loose power cord, a switch that is turned off, or a circuit breaker that is tripped. In this case, your PC hasn't crashed at all.

The better you can answer these questions, the more likely you are to have good luck when you try to troubleshoot the problem.

Starting Windows in Safe Mode

Sometimes a system is so unstable that it crashes immediately when Windows starts. You may need to start Windows in *safe mode* so that you have a chance to fix the problem. Safe mode is a special way to run Windows without loading programs or *drivers* (the files that allow your printer and other devices to run). Safe mode can be a great thing for two reasons. First, lim-iting the resources that your unstable PC can use can mini-mize the risk that more problems will arise. Second, the programs and drivers may be causing the problem.

Identifying Memory Problems

If your PC displays a blue screen with a message telling you that your system has halted due to a *memory parity error*, this means that your system has detected a problem with your computer's *RAM* — random access memory. If this message appears, restart your system to see if you see the message again.

- If the memory error message does not reappear, continue using your PC but be careful to save your work often. The problem may have been a random occurrence rather than a real problem.

- If the message continues to appear, your PC will need service to replace a bad memory module.

If your PC is unable to start up normally, call a PC-savvy friend who can help you troubleshoot the problem, and then follow these steps:

1. Restart the system to see if the problem goes away. If your computer is unable to start Windows, a menu may appear on-screen.

2. If you don't see a menu on-screen when you try to start your PC, and your PC is still having problems, you can bring the menu up manually by holding down either the Ctrl key or the F8 key as your PC is starting. Which key to use depends on what kind of PC you have, so try both options. See the section, "Using Windows System Restore," later in this chapter, for information on restoring your PC to working condition.

3. Choose safe mode from the menu that appears. (You'll need to use the keyboard for this.)

4. After Windows starts in safe mode, a Help and Support screen appears. Click Troubleshooter to try to find and correct the problem.

5. Follow the on-screen prompts to tell the Troubleshooter what has happened so that it can suggest possible solutions.

19

Diagnosing and Repairing
Computer Problems

 Find It Online

You may also want to go to AOL Keyword: **Win** and check out the Frequently Asked Questions.

Creating a Windows Startup Disk

If your PC won't start at all, it may be having a problem reading its hard drive; if this is the case, you may not even be able to start Windows in Safe mode. It's time to resort to using a *startup disk*. The startup disk is a diskette (or floppy disk — depending on what you prefer calling it) that contains a number of diagnostic programs you use to fix the problem. Although you probably won't ever encounter this problem, it's good to be prepared in case your PC ever does just sit there doing nothing when you try to start it. Of course, if this does happen, it's probably a good time to call for help as discussed in "What to Do If You Don't Know What to Do" later in this chapter.

Now that your system is set up, you need to be able to access it, even if there's a problem with your hard drive. You need to create a startup disk. You create a startup disk by following these steps:

1. Choose Start⇨Settings⇨Control Panel.
2. Double-click the Add/Remove Programs icon.
3. Click the Startup Disk tab (see Figure 19-2).
4. Place a blank disk in drive A and click the Create Disk button.
5. Label the disk as the Windows startup disk and keep it in a safe place.

If you ever come to a point when you think you may need to use your startup disk to start your PC, call a friend who is tech-savvy to help walk you through the process.

Make certain you store your startup disk in a safe place where you can easily find it in an emergency.

Repairing the PC's Software

Many computer problems are really software problems. Your PC may be perfectly fine. In the following sections, I show you what to do about software problems.

Updating Programs

Problems with a program may appear after the program is released and thousands of people have it. Although software manufacturers test their software, real-world experience has no substitute.

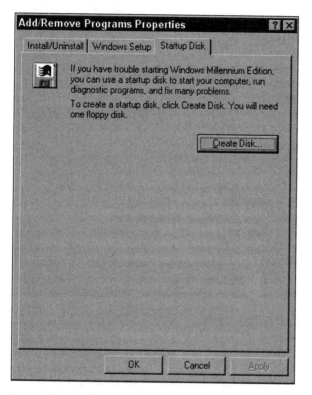

Figure 19-2. Make certain you create a startup disk before you need it.

Most software manufacturers now make program updates available on their Web sites. Usually the easiest way to visit a manufacturer's Web site is to click the Help menu in the program and look for a menu item that mentions the Web. Click that item and after the Web site appears, look for a link to the manufacturer's online support.

Identifying and Fixing Corrupted Files

If a program that has been working fine suddenly stops working, some corrupted files that the program needs may be causing the problem. A power outage, random disk error, or new software that's interfering with the program may be the cause of the problem.

Tip

You can use AOL Search (AOL Keyword: **Search**) to find the Web sites for most software manufacturers. Just type the name of the manufacturer into the AOL search box.

19

Diagnosing and Repairing
Computer Problems

Note

If you're positive that the cause of your system problems is related either to Windows or AOL, reinstalling the software may resolve the problems. Before you reinstall *any* software because you think it's affecting your PC, talk to a professional or friend who knows a lot about PCs.

Tip

Always create a new restore point just before you install new software so that you can correct any problems that result from the installation immediately.

Note

System Restore automatically creates a series of restore points that you may be able to use if you neglected to create your own restore point.

If one of your programs stops working, follow these steps to correct the problem:

1. First, look on the program's Help menu for a Detect and Repair choice. If this option is available, choose it and follow the onscreen directions.

2. If you cannot correct the problem using the Detect and Repair option, removing and then reinstalling the program is best. Choose Start⊅Settings⊅Control Panel. Double-click Add/Remove Programs so that you can remove and then later reinstall the program.

Using Windows System Restore

System Restore is a tool in Windows Me that you use to return your PC to a previous state if you find that installing something new has caused problems. To use System Restore, follow these steps:

1. Choose Start⊅Programs⊅Accessories⊅System Tools⊅System Restore. The System Restore window appears.

2. System Restore gives you two options, as shown in Figure 19-3. If you haven't installed the new program yet, choose Create a Restore Point. Choosing this option allows you to restore your computer to its original state if the new program causes problems after you install it. If you have already installed a new program that is creating problems with your PC, choose Restore My Computer to an Earlier Time to have your computer revert to a restore point that you created earlier or that your system created automatically. After you pick the appropriate option, click Next.

3. Follow the on-screen prompts for the option you select.

Repairing the PC's Hardware

In addition to software problems, you may encounter an occasional hardware problem. Mechanical devices can fail, and you need to be ready to deal with those problems as well.

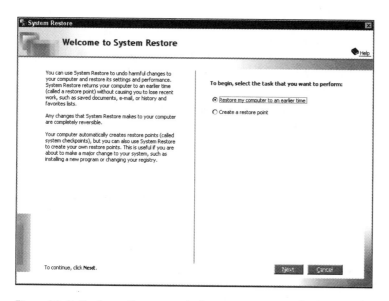

Figure 19-3. Use System Restore to undo changes to your system that have caused problems.

Reviewing the Warranty

If you suspect a hardware problem — perhaps because you saw smoke coming out of your monitor or because your printer won't turn on — the first thing you should always do is locate the manufacturer's warranty for the hardware that is giving you problems. Many PC peripherals have warranties that cover the hardware for one to three years. If your hardware is still under warranty, simply follow the steps in the warranty to have the unit repaired or replaced.

Caution

Unauthorized repair attempts can void a warranty. If your PC hardware is still under warranty, don't try to fix it yourself.

19

Diagnosing and Repairing Computer Problems

Evaluating Troublesome Disks

If your PC reports that it cannot read information from a disk, you need to isolate the problem in order to find your best course of action. Here are some considerations:

▶ If your PC cannot read data from a CD-ROM, try using a different CD-ROM in the drive. If the new disc doesn't have any problems, the disc that can't be read may be defective, and you probably just need to replace it. If no discs can be read successfully, your CD-ROM drive may need to be repaired or replaced.

▶ If your PC is having problems reading disks in drive A, try a different disk using the same procedure you use to check your CD-ROM drive. If a disk is bad, throw the disk away — don't try to reuse disks that are developing problems.

▶ If your PC is having problems with your hard drive, close all programs and try to correct the problems by running ScanDisk.

What to Do If You Don't Know What to Do

If you find that your PC has a problem that requires more knowledge than you have, you probably need to find someone to help you. Seeking help is a good idea if you find yourself in one of the following situations:

▶ Your hard drive is so unstable that it doesn't start or starts and immediately crashes.

▶ You think you may have lost data from your hard drive because of a software problem or a virus.

▶ Some hardware isn't working but you can't determine why.

▶ Fixing the problem probably requires opening your PC's case.

Whom should you call? Well, here are some ideas:

▶ Call a trusted PC-savvy friend.

▶ Call your PC manufacturer's tech support hotline. (Look in your owner's manual to find the correct phone number.)

▶ Call a PC retailer that provides repair service. (That tech-savvy friend may even be able to suggest some reputable retailers.)

Above all, don't panic. Just about every problem you encounter with your PC can probably be fixed quickly and without a lot of pain. Just remember to write down what's going on (be as detailed as possible about what messages that appear on screen say) and give whomever you call for help as much information as possible. Chances are, your PC will be up and running again in no time.

Summary

In this chapter, you saw how to diagnose and solve many common PC problems. You learned how to solve system problems, and you saw how keeping a cool head can make all the difference when you need to fix software problems. You learned a bit about assessing hardware problems and found out how to assess whether you need to call someone with more PC experience to help handle a problem. I hope the most important thing you took from this chapter is that the best cure for any PC problem is prevention. Be sure to find out how you can keep your system in good shape in Chapter 18. Also find out about antivirus software in Chapter 14 and about installing software in Chapter 16.

20

PROTECTING YOUR COMPUTER FROM VIRUSES

Quick Look

▶ **Virus Prevention**   **page 275**

You can avoid computer viruses by taking a few common-sense steps, the first of which is getting good antivirus software. This section shows you how.

▶ **Virus Hoaxes**   **page 276**

The more friends you make online, the more likely you are to receive a variety of virus warnings via e-mail. Although some of these warnings are valid, a majority of them are probably hoaxes. Find out how to tell the difference between a real virus warning and a hoax.

▶ **Scanning Your PC for Viruses**   **page 279**

To ensure that your PC is clean and free of viruses, you must *scan* (check) it using special software called antivirus software. This section shows you how to scan your PC.

▶ **Disabling Antivirus Software**   **page 280**

When you install new programs on your PC, the installation instructions often tell you to temporarily disable your antivirus software. This chapter shows you how to disable the software and get it up and running again.

Chapter 20

Protecting Your Computer from Viruses

I f you've listened to the news over the last couple of years, you've no doubt heard of viruses with names like *Melissa* and *I Love You.* Hundreds of new viruses appear every week, and most of them don't make the news. Most viruses don't cause serious damage, but they can inconvenience you or attempt to violate your privacy.

You can avoid viruses by taking a few common-sense precautions. First, use some good antivirus software like the programs described in this chapter. Also be aware of how viruses can infect your PC. Usually they can infect your PC only if you open an infected file. This chapter helps you recognize viruses and protect your PC against them.

Understanding Computer Viruses

Computer viruses are programs that hide inside other files, and like biological viruses, many of them replicate themselves and cause your files and PC to act abnormally. Viruses can lie dormant for days or even months before becoming active. Your PC can be infected with a virus three basic ways:

- ▶ **Files attached to e-mails could be infected.** Simply downloading a file from your Online Mailbox won't infect your computer, but if you open an infected file, your PC could become exposed. E-mail has become the most common route to infection. You can do numerous things to avoid receiving virus-infected files, but one thing you can do right now is decide to *never* open a file attachment sent from a stranger.

- ▶ **Software or file downloads may be infected.** Installing software or opening files you downloaded online could expose your PC to a virus. Always scan downloaded files before opening or installing them on your PC. Be sure you know and trust the source of any files you download.

- ▶ **Software you purchase may have viruses.** When you install new software from a CD-ROM, it is possible that a virus could hide on the disk. This type of infection is rare because it means even the manufacturer didn't detect the virus.

Now that you know the ways viruses can get on your PC, read the following sections to find out what you can do to keep them away.

Safeguarding Your PC from Viruses

Fortunately, protecting your PC from viruses is pretty simple. Here are several basic precautions you should take:

- ▶ **Buy and use a good antivirus program.** See section, "Understanding Antivirus Software," later in this chapter for more information on what to look for in a program.

- ▶ **Keep your antivirus program up-to-date.** Virtually all producers of antivirus programs offer free online updates to ensure that you are protected from new viruses. Many antivirus programs offer daily updates.

 Find It Online

Your best online resource for virus information is AOL Keyword: **Virus**. You can find virus alerts and much more.

 Caution

AOL staff will never ask you for your password in an e-mail message, on the phone, or in a chat room. If you receive an e-mail message or phone call asking for this information, do not provide it.

Caution

If you use another kind of program, such as Microsoft Outlook, simply opening e-mail can infect your PC. Never open e-mail from strangers.

▶ **Don't open an e-mail attachment unless you are certain who it came from and what the attachment is.** Even if you know everyone who sends you mail, always use your antivirus program to scan *every* attachment before opening it. If you use other e-mail programs, such as Outlook, be wary of opening e-mail messages from anyone you don't know.

▶ **Teach your children about virus safety.** If your kids use AOL, teach them how to scan attachments for viruses, or set up Parental Controls so that they cannot send or receive attachments.

▶ **Always scan for viruses.** Scan every piece of software you download or buy before you install it.

Avoiding Virus Hoaxes

Find It Online

An excellent site that chronicles virus hoaxes is www.vmyths.com. Another good source is www. datafellows.com/ news/hoax.

Virus hoaxes are almost as common as the actual viruses themselves. How could a hoax be almost as common as the real thing? Say you receive one e-mail message from a well-meaning friend that warns you of impending PC doom because of the latest new virus. If your friend sent this same message to everyone she knows and even half of those people sent the message to half the people they know, you can see how quickly the panic can become widespread.

Virus hoaxes almost always come via e-mail, and they have these other characteristics in common:

▶ They often warn you not to open an e-mail message with a certain subject heading.

▶ They almost always include assurances that AOL, Microsoft, and Bill Gates himself are cowering in fear at the mere thought of this virus.

▶ The hallmark of nearly all virus hoaxes is the insistence that you send the warning to as many people as possible in an effort to help spread the word.

Find It Online

To find out about online safety and viruses, visit AOL Keyword: **Neighborhood Watch.** Click the Computer Safety link. To find out about scams and hoaxes, click E-Mail Safety.

If you ever receive a message warning you about a new virus, check the facts before you take action. Several online services offer up-to-the-minute virus information, including:

▶ AOL Keyword: **Virus**

▶ www.mcafee.com

▶ www.ciac.org

▶ www.symantec.com

Understanding Antivirus Software

The most effective way to protect your PC from viruses is to have and use antivirus software. Antivirus software is designed to run on your PC at all times. Choose antivirus software capable of performing the following functions:

- ▶ When you first boot up, the antivirus software checks to make sure that start-up files aren't infected.
- ▶ When the PC is running, antivirus software works in the background and continuously monitors your PC for possible virus activity.
- ▶ If you have some files or a disk that you want to check for viruses, the antivirus software can perform a detailed scan to make sure that the files or disks aren't infected.
- ▶ If a virus is identified, the antivirus software immediately notifies you and takes steps to disinfect your PC and repair any damage that was caused.

Little Timmy Needs Your E-Mail

A cousin of the virus hoax is the e-mail chain letter telling the sad tale of a sick youth whose dying wish is to see his e-mail message forwarded to 10,000,000 people. The story is usually heart wrenching, but is seldom, if ever, based in reality. Naturally, you are warned not to break the chain and urged to send this e-mail to everyone you know.

Many other kinds of hoaxes exist. A popular hoax warns of a bill in the U.S. Congress that would require you to buy postage stamps to send e-mail messages. And then there are the ones that promise to give you money or free soft drinks for simply forwarding the e-mail to others. Whatever a message says, be suspicious of any message that asks to be forwarded to other people.

▶ When you shut down your PC, antivirus software scans system memory and your floppy (A:) drive for viruses that become active during the shutdown process.

Many good antivirus programs are available. Before choosing a specific program, look for these additional characteristics:

▶ **Online updates.** You should be able to update the virus definition file quickly and easily online, and the updates should be free for at least a year. Some programs offer free lifetime updates.

▶ **Operating system support.** Make sure that the antivirus program you choose supports the exact version of Windows that you have. If you have Windows Me, don't assume that an antivirus program designed for Windows 98 will work on your system.

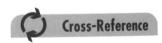
Note

Most antivirus programs have a built-in list of viruses called a *virus definition file*. The virus definition file needs to be updated regularly to ensure that the antivirus software knows how to identify new viruses that appear.

Cross-Reference

Don't remember how to install software? See Chapter 16 for more information.

Getting and Using Antivirus Software

Your best defense against computer viruses is a good antivirus program. An antivirus program scans your PC for viruses, disinfects it, and continues to guard against new infections.

If you have Windows 95 or 98, you can download free versions of antivirus programs at AOL Keyword: **Virus**. You can also buy antivirus software at your local computer or office supply store.

Here are some antivirus programs you may be interested in checking out:

▶ Norton AntiVirus, from Symantec (www.symantec.com).

▶ Dr. Solomon's Anti-Virus and VirusScan, both from McAfee (www.mcafee.com).

Some antivirus programs are becoming online applications. This means that rather than installing a lot of software on your PC, they simply install a small program that acts as a guard against viruses on your system. If you want to access features of an online application, you simply visit the Web page for the program.

Scanning Your PC for Viruses

One of the most important features of any antivirus program is to scan your PC for possible infections. Follow these general steps:

1. Click the antivirus program's icon in the Windows system tray next to the clock.

2. From the menu that appears, choose Scan Now or a similar option.

3. From the window that appears, choose the disk drives you want to scan. If you want to scan everything (that's the safest bet), choose All Local Drives or a similar option.

4. Be sure to scan all files, and make sure to also scan subfolders.

5. Click Scan.

The scanning process takes a few minutes, during which time not much appears to happen. Be patient. When the scan is complete, a report is generated in an information box stating that the scan is complete and how many viruses (if any) were found. If the program finds a virus, it is identified and removed automatically, and any damage the virus caused is identified and repaired.

Updating Your Antivirus Software

Hundreds of new viruses appear every week. For this reason, software engineers that produce antivirus software work around the clock to keep antivirus programs up-to-date. But if you don't keep your antivirus software updated, you may not be protected against new virus threats.

All antivirus programs can be quickly updated online. To find out how, just visit the Web page for the company that made your antivirus program, or locate an update at AOL Keyword: **Virus**.

Disabling Antivirus Software

Often when you buy or download new software, the instructions say to disable your antivirus program. Is this safe? Yes, and it is usually necessary. Many installation programs mimic virus activity, so keeping your antivirus program running could prevent new software from installing properly. Here's what you do to disable your antivirus software:

1. Scan the installation disk or the download file for viruses, as described earlier in the section, "Scanning Your PC for Viruses."

2. Disable your antivirus program. Right-click the antivirus icon in the Windows system tray and choose Disable (or a similar option) from the menu that appears.

Nearly all antivirus programs place an icon on the system tray, so just right-click on that icon and look for a menu option that says Close, Exit, or Disable.

Tip

Don't forget to re-enable your antivirus software after you install the new software! To do so, simply restart Windows.

Summary

Computer viruses must be taken seriously, but by taking a few simple precautionary measures, you can protect your PC from most of them. In this chapter, you found out how viruses can infect your computer, and how to use antivirus software to protect and disinfect your PC. In the next chapter, you'll learn about expanding your PC's capabilities by upgrading it.

Quick Look

Chapter 21

Upgrading Your PC

You have probably heard people say that computer technology moves so fast that the PC you buy today will be obsolete tomorrow. Fortunately, this doesn't always have to be the case. You can do many things to extend the useful life of your computer, ensuring that it will still be as useful to you next year as it is now. Your PC can be upgraded with new features, improved speed and power, and better versions of your software (such as Windows).

Deciding Whether to Upgrade

Some people get the same kind of enjoyment out of upgrading their PC that a hot-rod enthusiast gets from souping-up his car. But whether you enjoy hot-rodding your own PC or not, you want to consider any upgrades carefully. Here are a few good reasons to upgrade your PC:

> ▶ **Your PC doesn't meet the system requirements for a new program.** If your computer doesn't meet the minimum requirements of some new software you want to use — for example, you don't have enough

free hard drive space or you need some special hardware — you may need to consider whether you need to upgrade your computer. Or, you may decide you don't really need the software.

▶ **Your PC isn't as fast as you would like it to be.** The "need for speed" drives many improvements in computer technology. A faster CPU (central processing unit) or additional RAM (random access memory) can really speed-up your PC.

▶ **Downloading files and other activities doesn't go as quickly as you'd like.** If you'd like to connect to AOL and the Internet faster, consider upgrading to a high-speed connection. Visit AOL Keyword: **AOL PLUS** to learn about AOL's high-speed service.

▶ **You need more storage space.** If you have many files and programs on your PC (especially graphics and music files, which take up more space than word processing documents), you may benefit from a bigger hard drive. More storage can greatly improve your computing experience because you won't have to constantly delete old files to make room for new ones.

▶ **Your PC crashes frequently.** If your PC is always freezing up, you may need to upgrade your software programs, as well as the Windows operating system.

▶ **You want to add a new feature to your PC.** You can make your computer more useful by adding new hardware, such as a digital camera or CD-RW drive (which lets you record your own CDs).

Troubleshooting

Sometimes the best way to improve the performance of your PC is to upgrade to a newer version of Microsoft Windows.

Find It Online

Would you like to shop for upgrades online? Visit AOL Keyword: **Computing** to find a great deal.

Upgrading Windows

Microsoft is always working to improve Windows, which means that the version of Windows installed on your computer may not be the latest and greatest. Incremental improvements are always being made, and sometimes Microsoft releases a whole new edition of Windows.

Choosing between Windows Me and Windows 2000

If you have an older version of Windows, such as Windows 95 or 98, you may want to upgrade to the latest version. Newer versions of Windows support new kinds of hardware, as well as offer some new features.

Currently, Windows is offered in two versions: Windows Me and Windows 2000. Table 21-1 compares the two.

Find It Online

The prices listed in Table 21-1 are official list prices. You can usually find better deals online at AOL Keyword: **Computing**.

Table 21-1. Windows Me versus Windows 2000

Features	Windows Me	Windows 2000
Reliability	Reasonably stable, but does crash occasionally	Very stable; seldom, if ever, crashes
Networking	Home Networking Wizard makes networking with other Windows computers easy	Professional-quality networking; can network with Mac and Linux-based computers
Hardware compatibility	Most hardware is easy to install and configure	Supports less hardware; configuring often takes more work
Extras	Windows Movie Maker, which lets you create and edit movies	Doesn't have Movie Maker, but does have robust networking tools
Price (upgrade from Windows 98)	$109	$219

Each version of Windows has advantages and disadvantages. But unless you're a professional and have advanced networking needs, Windows Me is probably a better deal for you (especially considering the price difference).

Finding and Installing Free Windows Upgrades

Microsoft will never stop improving and upgrading Windows; in fact, Microsoft frequently offers free upgrades online. Some of these upgrades repair flaws (called *bugs*) in Windows, while others add new capabilities. These upgrades are easy to find; here's how:

1. Close any open programs and choose Start⇨Windows Update. Your computer automatically connects to AOL. Note that Internet Explorer, Microsoft's Web browser, launches.

2. On the Windows taskbar (that's the strip along the bottom of the screen), click the Internet Explorer button to bring it to the front. The Windows Update page loads, as shown in Figure 21-1.

Find It Online

You can also visit the Windows Update site by visiting `windowsupdate.microsoft.com`.

Click to view Windows updates

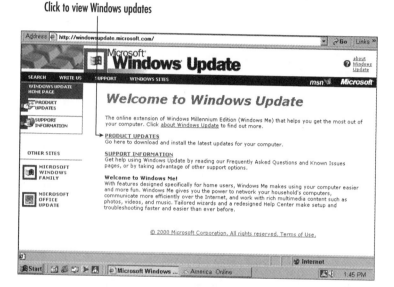

Figure 21-1. Use Windows Update to upgrade Windows on your PC.

3. Click the Product Updates link on the Windows Update Web site.

4. When you see a security warning asking if you want to install and run Microsoft Active Setup, click Yes. Active Setup checks your system and determines which upgrades, if any, you may need.

5. When Active Setup is complete, the Select Software page (shown in Figure 21-2) appears. Review the available upgrades that are listed on this page. You may need to scroll down a bit to see everything that is listed.

6. The list contains critical updates for Windows, as well as components that add new features to Windows. Place a check mark next to each component you want to download. Packages in the Critical Updates section are the most important.

Troubleshooting

If you have previously run Microsoft Active Setup, you may not see a security warning.

Select items you want to download   Check estimated download time   Click to begin download

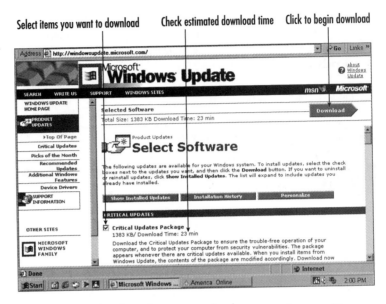

Figure 21-2. On the Select Software page, select the components you want to download and install.

To keep Windows in tip-top condition, visit the Windows Update page at least once a month. You may even want to add this monthly visit to your AOL Calendar!

7. After you select the components you want to download, click the Download button at the top of the page.

8. On the next page, review the Download Checklist and click View Instructions to view specific instructions for each component or upgrade you have chosen to download. When you're ready, click Start Download.

The download begins, and most components are installed automatically. You'll probably have to restart your computer when the installation is complete. Again, make sure that you follow any instructions you were given when you clicked View Instructions.

Speeding Up Your PC

Be sure to double-check the warranty information for your PC before performing any upgrades. This way, you ensure that upgrades are authorized.

Making some hardware upgrades is a lot easier than you may think, but other hardware upgrades require a certain level of technical expertise. Most computer stores offer professional hardware installation, and if you're new to PCs, you may find that the $30 or so that these stores charge for hardware installation is cheap insurance.

If you want your computer to be faster, you can do two things—upgrade to a faster CPU or install more RAM. Here's a closer look at each option.

Upgrading Your CPU

Upgrading the CPU in your computer is difficult and often not possible. You must obtain a CPU that is compatible with the motherboard in your computer, and often the motherboard doesn't support a CPU that is faster than the one you already have. Usually it is best to replace the CPU and the motherboard at that same time to ensure they match; and, of course, the motherboard must match the rest of the components in your PC.

If you really want to upgrade to a faster CPU, you have two options:

▶ Purchase a CPU upgrade kit, such as one offered by Evergreen Technologies. Each kit is matched specifically to the make and model of your PC, and comes complete with all the tools and instructions needed to perform the upgrade. Upgrade kits typically cost between $75 and $400, depending on the upgrade.

▶ Consult a PC professional or get help from a friend who has a lot of PC hardware experience. He or she can help you determine if an upgrade is possible on your PC, as well as help you with the actual upgrade.

Often, you may find that it is easier to buy a new PC. Compare the price of a new motherboard and CPU (and don't forget to count the labor costs to have them installed) with the price of a new PC before you decide to upgrade.

Adding More RAM

RAM (random access memory) is easier to add to your computer than a new CPU, and it can speed up your PC by helping the CPU and all the other components work more efficiently. RAM comes in easy-to-install modules, and to add more RAM to your PC, all you have to do is add another module. Two types of RAM modules are used in modern PCs:

▶ **SIMM:** A *single in-line memory module* is approximately 4.25 inches long. SIMMs must be installed in matched pairs, meaning that if you want to add 32MB

Find It Online

Evergreen Technologies sells CPU upgrade kits for many computers. Visit its site at www.evertech.com.

Cross-Reference

If you want details about how RAM works, see Chapter 9. Figure 9-2 shows you what a memory module looks like, and Figure 9-1 illustrates the memory slot on a motherboard.

Troubleshooting

SIMMs and DIMMs are not the same size. This means that you can only put a SIMM in a SIMM slot, and a DIMM will only fit in a DIMM slot.

Note

Before you buy more RAM, make sure that your computer has an open DIMM slot or open SIMM slots.

Troubleshooting

When you ground yourself by touching bare metal, you discharge any static electricity that is built-up in your body. A tiny amount of static electricity can damage PC components.

worth of SIMMs to your PC, you must buy two 16MB modules rather than a single 32MB module. *Note:* SIMMs are being phased-out in new PCs.

▶ **DIMM:** A *dual in-line memory module* is approximately 5.5 inches long and has 168 pins. Most newer PCs only have DIMM slots. DIMMs may be installed individually.

Most computer stores that sell memory modules offer free or low-cost ($30 or less) installation, although you can install new memory modules yourself. If this is your first time upgrading PC hardware, you should get some help from a friend or professional. Here's how to install a new memory module:

1. Shut down the PC's power and position the PC's case to ensure that you don't bump the power button back on while you perform the upgrade.

2. Open the computer's case. Check your PC's documentation for instructions on opening the case and a list of tools that are required (usually you just need a screwdriver). Ground yourself by touching a piece of bare metal on the PC's case.

3. Carefully remove the memory module from the antistatic bag that it came in and gently insert it into an appropriate memory slot. Adjust the module so that it is seated completely down in the slot and listen for the locking mechanism on each end of the module to engage.

4. Close the case and power up your PC to make sure everything works properly.

Adding Storage Capacity

Note

If you replace your main hard drive with a new one, you'll have to reinstall Windows, AOL, and all of your other software.

Two options for adding storage capacity to your PC are to add a second hard drive or to replace your old one with a newer, bigger drive. More storage space allows you to install more programs and gives you additional storage space for documents, pictures, and digital video. Hard drives are pretty affordable today; you can buy a huge, 40GB (gigabyte) drive for less than $150. However, adding a new hard drive to the inside of your PC is relatively complicated, so consult a professional or friend who has a lot of PC hardware experience.

Fortunately, there are easier ways to add storage capacity to your PC:

> **Add an external hard drive.** External hard drives are easier to add than internal hard drives because all you have to do is connect an appropriate cable between the drive and a port on the back of your PC. External hard drives usually use either a USB or FireWire port. (See Appendix C to determine if your computer has either of these port types available.) After it's installed, an external hard drive works like a second hard drive on your PC, and you can access it through My Computer just like any other drive.

> **Add a removable disk drive.** You can add a removable disk drive by simply connecting it to the appropriate port on the back of your PC. With removable disk drives, storage capacity is limited only by the number of blank disks you can afford. Popular types of removable disk drives include Zip drives and recordable CD drives.

Definition

The term *removable drive* usually refers to a drive where only the disk is removable, not the whole drive. Floppy drives and CD-ROM drives are removable drives.

Upgrading Sound and Video

If you use your PC to play games, watch videos, or listen to music, you may eventually want to upgrade your PC's audio and video capabilities. You can improve audio in one of two ways:

> **Upgrading speakers.** You can find good computer speakers for less than $100. Speakers are easy to install because all you have to do is unplug the old ones from the back of your computer and plug in the new ones.

> **Installing a new sound card.** When choosing a new sound card, *bits* are good. A 32-bit sound card is better than a 16-bit card. Sound cards usually use either an ISA or PCI expansion slot on the motherboard. See the following section for details on installing an expansion card.

Upgrading video usually means installing a new video card. Modern video cards use either PCI or AGP expansion slots, with AGP being the preferred type. Video cards work best with lots of built-in RAM—the more the better. For decent video, avoid cards with less than 8MB of video RAM. To install a new video card, see the next section.

Cross-Reference

See Appendix C for more on identifying expansion slots in your PC.

New Hope for Old Hard Drives

When you upgrade from your old hard drive to a newer one with a higher storage capacity, you inevitably end up with a leftover drive that you don't need or want. Rather than throw away that old drive, why not turn it into an external drive? External drive kits can turn almost any old hard drive into an external drive that connects to a USB or FireWire port. You can use the old drive for backing up important files or as extra storage space on your PC.

To find a kit that will turn your old drive into an external hard drive, visit your local computer store or go to AOL Keyword: **Computing**.

Installing New Expansion Cards

Expansion cards — also called *adapter* cards — slide into slots in the motherboard and provide many important functions for your PC. Sound cards, video cards, FireWire adapters, and modems are all common adapter cards installed in PCs. Three types of adapter slots are used in modern PCs: PCI, ISA, and AGP. Before you buy any new adapter card, make sure that your motherboard has an open expansion slot that's the right type for that adapter card.

Expansion cards are relatively simple to install, but if you haven't handled PC hardware before, you should consult a professional or get help from someone who has worked with PC hardware. To install a new adapter card, follow these steps:

1. Shut down your PC and open the case. See the documentation that came with your PC for instructions on how to open the case, as well as a list of necessary tools. Also review the documentation that came with the expansion card to see if it contains any special instructions or procedures you should follow.

2. Before removing the new card from its antistatic bag, touch a bare-metal spot on the case to ground yourself. Grounding yourself discharges static electricity from your body. Static electricity can damage the expansion card when you handle it.

3. Identify the slot you plan to use, and remove the blank-off plate on the back of the case in front of that slot. Set the blank-off plate to the side, but keep the screw that held it in place handy.

4. Test-fit the card in its place to ensure that nothing on the card or motherboard will cause an obstruction.

5. Carefully press the card into its expansion slot. You may need to gently wiggle it back and forth a bit to get it fully seated.

6. Use the screw that you removed in Step 3 to secure the expansion card in the case.

7. Reassemble the case and complete installation according to the instructions that came with the card.

After you install the expansion card in your PC and power up Windows, you'll probably have to install some software to make it work properly. The software is probably on a CD-ROM or floppy disk that came with the card. Check the instructions that came with the expansion card to see what software needs to be installed.

Caution

When you insert the expansion card, avoid pressing down hard. Too much pressure could damage your PC's components.

Summary

Updating software and hardware is just as important as cleaning and repairing your hard drive with Windows maintenance tools or running antivirus scans regularly. Upgrading your PC can lengthen its life, keep it running smoothly, and enable you to accomplish more with your computer as new technologies are developed. In this chapter, you considered some reasons why you would want to upgrade your computer. You also found out how to upgrade Windows, as well as how to make your PC faster, increase storage capacity, and add new features.

Quick Look

Chapter 22

Getting Help from AOL

IN THIS CHAPTER

Evaluating your support needs

Finding online help at AOL

Getting support from AOL on the telephone

Getting help if you forget your password

Everyone who uses a computer has questions now and then. Let's face it: We're not born knowing how to use these things, and learning the ins and outs of a PC takes some time. And no matter how long you've been using your PC and how knowledgeable you've become, there are always new questions that you can't answer on your own.

Thankfully, AOL has a team of experts ready and willing to help you with your PC questions. Whether you're having trouble getting your PC started, you forgot your AOL password, or you just can't remember how to schedule automatic downloads, AOL has a variety of tools to help you out.

Deciding What Kind of Help You Need

America Online offers many different kinds of help. Before you decide which help services you want to take advantage of, answer several important questions:

▶ **Do you need information about your AOL account?** If you have a question about your account or billing, choose Help⇨Accounts and Billing from the AOL menu bar.

▶ **Are you having difficulty signing on to AOL?** First, make sure that the phone line that your PC uses to connect to AOL is working properly. Also, try restarting your computer; and if you have an external modem make sure the modem's power is turned on. If all else fails, call AOL Technical Support at 1-800-827-3338.

▶ **Are you having trouble with your PC hardware or software?** Search AOL's online help (Help⇨AOL Help). You can also contact AOL Customer Service via e-mail or telephone. See AOL Keyword: **Customer Service** for details.

▶ **Do you want to learn how to use new features and programs?** Visit one of AOL's online tutorials and classes at AOL Keyword: **Get Help Now**.

In the following sections, you find out about some of AOL's help services in more detail.

Getting AOL Help

AOL's online help resources are so extensive that you probably won't be able to come up with a question that hasn't already been asked and answered. Online help can be accessed in many ways. After you launch AOL and sign on, you can access online help in one of the following ways:

▶ Press the F1 key on your keyboard. F1 is in the upper-left corner of most keyboards, near the Esc key.

▶ Visit AOL Keyword: **Help**.

▶ Choose AOL Help from the Help menu on the AOL menu bar.

▶ Choose AOL Help from AOL Services on the AOL toolbar.

Each of these methods gets you to the main AOL Help window, shown in Figure 22-1. From this window, you can find a variety of resources, including information about

Find It Online

You can also access billing information at AOL Keyword: **Billing**.

Cross-Reference

See Appendix B to find out more about troubleshooting your AOL connection.

22

Getting Help from AOL

▶ Using and customizing e-mail

▶ Setting up a Buddy List and chatting in real time

▶ Setting up Parental Controls and finding more information about online privacy

▶ Conducting fast, efficient online searches

▶ Handling your personal finance online and making investments

▶ Getting around on the Internet

▶ Downloading files and attachments

▶ Customizing your AOL experience with Favorite Places, the AOL Anywhere service, and other features

▶ Using AOL's multimedia features, including AOL's Media Player

▶ Installing updated versions of AOL

Tip

The main AOL Help window also gives you quick access to Accounts and Billing, a new member orientation, and important contact information and help with the AOL Address Book. If you want to conduct a search, just type the word or phrase you want help on into the text box and click Search.

Figure 22-1. AOL Help is your gateway to AOL's many help services.

Using AOL Keyword: Get Help Now

Besides giving you additional resources to help you understand e-mail, chat, Parental Controls, and much more, AOL Computing's Get Help Now (AOL Keyword: **Get Help Now**), shown in Figure 22-2, gives you many PC-specific resources. From the Get Help Now window, you can get answers to FAQs (frequently asked questions), find AOL Help resources similar to those found at the main AOL Help window, and step-by-step how-to information. Just click a tab and scroll through the list of topics until you find the topic you want to know more about.

You can find many more resources at Get Help Now. The following sections tell you how to get technical terms defined instantly, how to get live online support and other online resources, and help you keep on top of important preventative maintenance.

Accessing AOL's PC Dictionary

The computer world is filled with many strange and unfamiliar words and acronyms. Terms such as SCSI, AGP, Ethernet, chipset, and FireWire add to the veritable alphabet soup of PC jargon. Fortunately, AOL's online dictionary can help you make sense of unfamiliar words you encounter as you use your PC. To access the PC dictionary, follow these steps:

1. Visit AOL Keyword: **Get Help Now** if you aren't there already.

2. Type a word, such as **DSL,** in the Dictionary text box (refer to Figure 22-2).

3. Click Search. In a few seconds the AOL Computing Webopaedia appears with a definition for your term.

Note

Listings in the AOL Computing Webopaedia usually contain links to related Web sites.

Tip

To explore the Computer Center, choose an item from the drop-down list at the top of the Get Help Now window and then click Go.

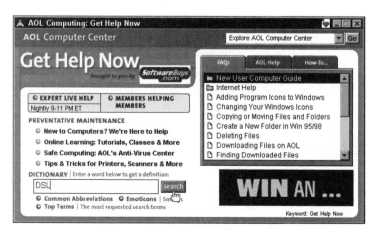

Figure 22-2. AOL Keyword: **Get Help Now** provides a variety of help resources, including online tutorials and a dictionary.

Find It Online

You can also access online forums and classes directly by visiting AOL Keyword: **Online Learning**.

Using Online Support Forums

AOL Keyword: **Get Help Now** is your gateway to a huge selection of online support from AOL. One of the coolest things you'll find there are online tutorials, classes, and support classrooms. To visit these resources, click the link next to "Online Learning" in the Get Help Now window. The Online Learning window appears, as shown in Figure 22-3.

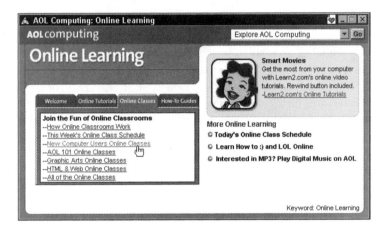

Figure 22-3. Online Learning from AOL gives you access to interactive support.

To attend an online class for new computer users:

Note

Times for all online classes in AOL's schedule are listed for the Eastern time zone.

1. Go to the Online Learning window in AOL and click the Online Classes tab.

2. Click the New Computer Users Online Classes link. After a few seconds, a schedule of classes appears.

3. Locate a class in today's schedule that you'd like to attend. If you're not sure which one to pick, choose New Member Classes. The New Member Classes window (AOL Keyword: **Help Classes**) appears, as shown in Figure 22-4.

4. In the Class Schedule locate the next occurrence of the class you want to attend. Make a note of the classroom (A, B, or C) where the class will be held.

5. To enter a classroom, click the appropriate room link on the right side of the Class Schedule window.

6. When the classroom is free, you can enter and interact with the class host, as shown in Figure 22-5. If the classroom is closed at the moment, a message appears on screen telling you so.

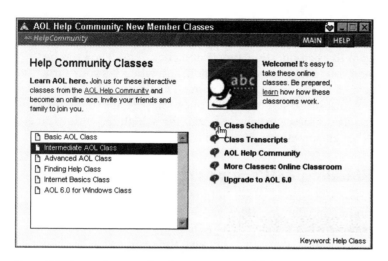

Figure 22-4. Use AOL Keyword: **Help Community** and click New Member Classes to view a schedule of AOL's online classes.

Online classes work like chat rooms. The dialog in the classroom is separated into two halves so that you can easily see who the expert is. The top portion, the *Stage Chat Area*, shows text from the experts, hosts, and teachers, and the bottom portion, the *Audience Chat Area*, shows questions asked by class participants.

Type your question here

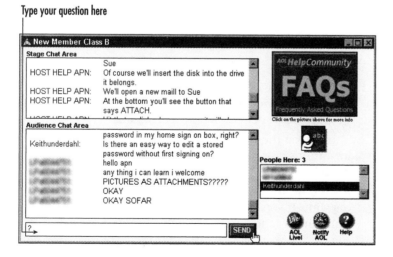

Figure 22-5. Online classes are a great way to ask questions of the experts.

Tip

As with chats, if you observe inappropriate behavior in a classroom click Notify AOL.

Cross-Reference

If you've never used a chat room before, see Chapter 8 to learn more about live chat.

Note

Remember, AOL staff will never ask you for your password or billing information in e-mail or a chat room.

All the normal protocols for chat rooms apply for online classes — except you can't speak until it's your turn. If you want to ask a question, type **?** and click Send. The class host puts you in line to ask a question, and when it's your turn, the host calls on you by screen name. Then you can ask your question. Just make sure that your question pertains to the topic of the class. Classes usually last until the scheduled ending time, although sometimes they end early if there are no questions.

E-Mailing AOL's Support Staff

Another great way to get help from AOL's experts is by sending in your questions via e-mail. E-mail support is handy because when a member of AOL's support staff responds to your question, you can easily save the response in the Filing Cabinet for future reference.

When you send an e-mail to AOL's support staff

▶ **Be as specific as possible.** Specific questions yield more relevant responses. If you are asking about an error message, try to provide AOL with the exact text of the message, as well as what you were doing when the message appeared.

▶ **Provide information about your PC.** Be sure to include which version of Windows you have, which version of AOL you're using, and, if possible, the brand and type of PC.

To contact AOL customer service and support personnel via e-mail:

1. Visit AOL Keyword: **Customer Service**. In the Customer Service window that appears, click the Contact Customer Service by E-mail link.

2. The box on the right side of the window displays links for various customer service inquiries, including technical, billing, and general. Click an appropriate link.

3. A window appears, as shown in Figure 22-6. Type your question. If you see menus asking questions on the right, answer them to the best of your knowledge.

4. Click Send. You will receive a response in your e-mail box within 72 hours.

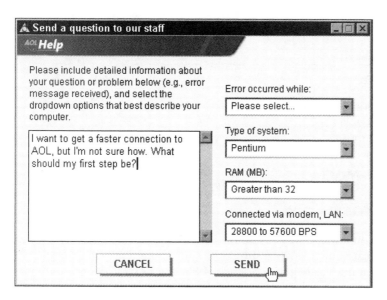

Figure 22-6. E-mailing your questions to AOL staff is easy, and you can keep a copy of the response for future reference.

Using AOL's Phone Support

Sometimes, you may be so frustrated with your PC that the last thing you want to do is go online to ask questions. In that case, you can call an AOL representative on the telephone. Before you do, collect as much information about your problem as possible. Table 22-1 lists important AOL phone numbers. AOL has representatives available 24 hours per day.

Tip

If you're traveling outside the United States or Canada, you can call for technical support all around the world. Dial 703-264-1184.

Table 22-1. AOL Telephone Numbers

Service	Number
Technical Support	888-346-3704
TTY Service	800-759-3323
Password and Screen Name Support	888-265-8004
Local Access Numbers	888-265-8005
Billing	888-265-8003

(continued)

Table 22-1. *(continued)*

Service	Number
Orders	888-265-8002
Account Cancellation	888-265-8008
Online Safety Information	888-209-6656

Getting Help with a Forgotten Password

Tip

If you must write down your password, make sure you write it down in a place that is secure and not easily accessible to others.

You know that you should keep your password secret, and that your password should be something that other people cannot easily guess (such as the name of your pet or your favorite football team). You should also change your password fairly frequently. Unfortunately, doing all of these things can lead you to forget your password. What do you do when you can't log on to AOL because you've forgotten your password?

Call AOL. You can call toll-free at 888-346-3704. An AOL representative will reset your old password and give you a new, temporary password. Then, immediately sign on to AOL and visit AOL Keyword: **Password** to change your password to something else.

Summary

Everyone needs help sometimes. Luckily, AOL offers a variety of support services that can help you get around AOL. AOL can also help you understand your PC. In this chapter, you got a snapshot of a few of the resources available to you when you need a helping hand. You found out how to determine your help needs, and you learned how to access AOL's online support resources. This chapter included information about using AOL's telephone support and how to deal with a forgotten password.

AGP

Accelerated Graphics Port. A video card that provides advanced graphics to your PC and requires a special slot on your PC's motherboard. See also: *video card.*

antivirus program

A software program that protects your PC from computer viruses. See also: *virus.*

AOL keyword

A word that acts as a shortcut to a Web site, place, or feature on AOL. To visit a keyword, just type it in the Address box on the navigation bar and click Go.

application

A program that allows you to perform useful tasks. AOL version 6.0, Microsoft Word, and Solitaire are all applications.

bit

The smallest unit of data in a computer. See also: *byte.*

byte

In computer systems, a single piece of data (such as a letter, numeral, or dot of color in a picture) that is eight binary digits (bits) long. See also: *bit, gigabyte, kilobyte, megabyte.*

CD-R

Compact Disc-Recordable. A recordable CD-ROM. CD-R discs can only be recorded on once. See also: *CD-ROM, CD-RW.*

CD-ROM

Compact Disc-Read Only Memory. A read-only disc used to hold data. All modern PCs have CD-ROM drives. A CD-ROM disc is shiny on one side, 5¼ inches in diameter, and looks just like a music CD. See also: *removable disk, read only.*

CD-RW

Compact Disc-Recordable/Rewritable. A disc similar to a CD-ROM that can have data recorded on it. CD-RW discs can also be erased and re-recorded on several times. See also: *CD-R, CD-ROM.*

CPU

central processing unit. Your PC's brain; part of the motherboard. Popular CPU models include the Intel Pentium III and the AMD Athlon.

cursor

A blinking line in a document that indicates the location of the next character that will be added. When you type on the keyboard, the cursor indicates where the letters will appear. The mouse pointer is also sometimes referred to as the cursor.

desktop

In Windows, the main screen you see when you first turn on your computer and Windows starts up. The Windows desktop includes icons called My Computer, My Documents, Recycle Bin, and others. See also: *icon, Start button, Windows.*

desktop PC

A computer designed to be used at a desk is sometimes called a desktop PC (as opposed to a laptop PC, which you can easily carry with you when you're on the go). See also: *laptop.*

dialog box

A window or box that appears on-screen and allows you to add data and choose options.

digital camera

A camera that stores pictures electronically on a disk, as opposed to storing pictures chemically on film, as traditional cameras do. Digital images from the camera can then be easily transferred to your PC.

directory

Another word for a folder on a disk drive (such as your hard drive). See also: *folder.*

disk drive

A storage device for computer data, files, and programs. Hard drives, floppy drives, and CD-ROM drives are all disk drives. See also: *removable disk, storage.*

document

A file you create when you use an application, such as Microsoft Paint or Microsoft Word. Document files are stored on disk drives. See also: *disk drive, file.*

domain

A company or organization that provides an online home for you. AOL is the world's largest Internet domain. See also: *Internet.*

DSL

Digital Subscriber Line. A special modem that provides high-speed access (also called broadband access) to AOL and the Internet, up to ten times faster than a traditional modem. See AOL Keyword: **AOL Plus**. See also: *modem.*

DVD-ROM

Digital Video Disc-Read Only Memory. A disc that looks just like a CD-ROM disc but holds much more data. If your PC has a DVD-ROM drive, you can use it to watch DVD movies. See also: *CD-ROM, removable disk.*

e-mail

The exchange of computer-stored messages by using an Internet connection. The e-mail message arrives in a mailbox, where the person can read it at his or her leisure. E-mail messages can also contain pictures.

expansion card

An adapter that allows you to add capabilities to your PC. The card slides into an expansion slot on the motherboard. Sound cards, video cards, network cards, and internal modems are common types of expansion cards. See also: *motherboard.*

file

A collection of data stored on your PC that's given a unique filename. Document files hold work that you've done, and program files make your programs run. See also: *document, folder.*

FireWire

A type of high-speed connection that can be used to connect a digital camcorder to your computer. Other FireWire devices are available, including external hard drives and printers. Also called *IEEE-1394.* See also: *port.*

floppy disk

A removable disk that is 3½ inches square and has a rigid plastic housing (it isn't actually *floppy*). These disks store files of data that can easily be transported to and used on another PC. Floppy disk drives are identified by the letter *A* (A:) on modern PCs. See also: *disk drive, removable disk.*

folder

A collection of related files. A disk can have many folders, including folders within folders. In Windows, a folder is identified by an icon that looks like a manila folder. See also: *file, subfolder.*

gigabyte

A unit of measurement used to determine the storage capacity of a hard drive. One thousand megabytes equals 1 gigabyte (GB). See also: *byte, megabyte.*

hard drive

A disk drive that is permanently mounted inside a PC. Most PCs have only one hard drive, identified by the letter *C* (C:). Data stored on a hard drive remains there even after the PC's power is turned off. See also: *disk drive, storage.*

hardware

The physical components of a PC. Hardware includes the keyboard, monitor, printer, CPU case, speakers, and expansion cards. See also: *software.*

hub

A central device to which several PCs are connected by cables. All the PCs connected to the hub make a network. The hub directs data that travels between computers over the network cables. See also: *network.*

hyperlink

A word or picture on a Web page or AOL area that a user can click to visit a different page. Hyperlinks are usually (but not always) underlined and colored blue. See also: *World Wide Web.*

icon

Files and programs are represented as icons in Windows. The actual icon is a picture that usually tells you what kind of file or program it is. Double-click an icon to open the file or program it represents. For instance, double-click the AOL icon to launch AOL.

instant message

On AOL, you can chat with someone else using instant messages. Instant messages go back and forth instantaneously, meaning that although you are typing words on your computer, you can carry on a conversation as if you were talking on a telephone. To send someone an instant message, he or she must be online. See also: *e-mail.*

Internet

The world's largest network of computers. The Internet includes the World Wide Web, e-mail services, newsgroups, and more. AOL is your connection to the Internet. See also: *network.*

kilobyte

A unit of measurement used to determine the size of a file. One kilobyte (KB) equals 1,024 bytes. See also: *byte, megabyte.*

laptop PC

A PC that you can easily carry with you when you travel. Laptops usually can be opened and closed like a briefcase, with the monitor on the top half and the keyboard and disk drives on the bottom.

Macintosh

A line of popular computers that was first introduced by Apple in 1984. Macintosh computers use different programs than PCs, although they can often share document files. Many software programs, such as AOL, have versions for both Macs and PCs. See also: *PC, Windows.*

megabyte

A unit of measurement used to determine the size of a large file. One thousand kilobytes equals 1 megabyte (MB). See also: *byte, kilobyte.*

memory

The short-term storage (often called *RAM*) used by a PC; memory stores the data that the central processing unit needs to function efficiently, and this data is erased when the PC's power is turned off. See also: *CPU, RAM, storage.*

modem

The component of your PC that connects a PC to the Internet. Dial-up modems and DSL modems connect to a telephone line, and cable modems connect to both a telephone line and a coaxial television cable.

monitor

The part of a PC that displays text, graphics, and other data. See also: *video card.*

motherboard

A circuit board inside a PC that contains and connects the central processing unit, memory, and expansion cards. Hard drives usually connect to the motherboard, as well. See also: *hardware.*

mouse

A small pointing device that has two or three buttons on it. It's used to move a pointer on the screen. Clicking the buttons executes commands (such as opening files). See also: *pointing device.*

My Computer

An icon on the Windows desktop that represents your computer's storage areas. My Computer lets you explore all the disk drives on your computer.

network

Two or more PCs connected together via cables and a hub. A network can be used to share files or even a single connection to AOL. See also: *hub.*

operating system

The software that manages all other programs on a PC. An operating system enables a PC's hardware and software to work together. Microsoft Windows is the world's most popular operating system. Other operating systems include the Mac OS, Linux, and UNIX. See also: *PC, software.*

parallel port

A port on the back of your computer that is often used to connect a printer. See also: *ports.*

PC

personal computer. An abbreviation often used to differentiate the variety of computers built by several manufacturers from computers built by the Apple Corporation. Most PCs use the Windows operating system, but they can also run Linux, UNIX, or one of a variety of other operating systems. See also: *Macintosh, operating system, Windows.*

peripheral

A piece of hardware that attaches to a computer via a cable. Common peripherals include printers, digital cameras, scanners, and external disk drives. See also: *hardware*.

pointing device

Any device with buttons that is used to control the on-screen pointer and to input commands by clicking. A mouse is the most common pointing device, but you can also use a trackball. Laptops often have a touchpad or pointing stick in place of a mouse. See also: *mouse*.

port

The plug on the back of a PC into which cables connect peripheral devices, such as printers, scanners, and digital cameras. Appendix C lists the different types of ports found on PCs.

program

Synonymous with *software,* a list of code created to allow users to execute tasks. Programs are designed to perform specific functions. AOL and Microsoft Word are examples of programs. See also *application, software.*

RAM

random access memory. A PC's short-term memory. RAM allows the PC's central processing unit to execute tasks quickly and efficiently. The more RAM a PC has, the faster the CPU can run, and the more programs that can be run simultaneously. Data stored in RAM disappears as soon as the PC's power is turned off. See also: *CPU, memory, storage.*

read only

A type of storage that cannot be erased and on which new files can't be saved. Programs can access and read files in read-only storage, but those files cannot be edited and re-saved. CD-ROM discs are a type of read-only storage. See also: *CD-ROM, storage.*

removable disk

A type of disk that can be removed from its disk drive (for example, a floppy disk). Some removable disks, such as CD-ROMs, are *read only,* meaning that they can be used to transfer information to a PC but can't have new data saved to them. See also: *disk drive, storage.*

rewritable

A type of storage that can be erased and reused many times. Files can be saved in rewritable storage, edited, and then resaved. Common types of rewritable storage include hard drives, floppy drives, and CD-RW drives. See also: *disk drive, read only, storage.*

scanner

A peripheral device that takes a digital image of an object and turns it into a file that is compatible for use on PCs. A scanner usually has a glass surface area similar to a photocopier. See also: *digital camera, hardware, peripheral device.*

screen name

An online identity. On AOL, an e-mail address consists of your screen name. You can create up to seven screen names on one AOL account.

serial port

A type of port on the back of a PC to which peripheral devices, such as a mouse or other pointing device, may be connected. See also: *parallel port, peripheral, port.*

software

Synonymous with *program,* a list of code that makes it possible for a PC to execute tasks. Software includes applications, document files, and the operating system. See also: *hardware.*

sound card

A type of adapter that, when plugged into the correct expansion slot, enables a PC to produce audio. A PC's speakers and microphone plug into ports on the sound card.

Start button

The button labeled Start in the lower-left corner of the Windows operating system screen. Click the Start button to access programs and other PC features. See also: *taskbar.*

storage

The holding of files of data on removable disks and hard drives. Storage saves data even after the PC's power is turned off. See also: *disk drive, memory.*

subfolder

A folder within a folder on a disk drive. A folder can have many subfolders, and subfolders can have subfolders of their own as well.

system tray

The area on the Windows screen in the lower-right corner. The system tray includes a clock and other small icons. See also: *taskbar.*

taskbar

The strip along the bottom of the Windows screen. The Start button and the system tray are part of the taskbar. Programs that are currently active on a PC also have buttons on the taskbar.

toolbar

A row of related buttons along the top of a screen. Each button allows the user to execute a task in the given program. Some programs have several different toolbars, each created to enable the user to do specific tasks by pointing and clicking the buttons. Some programs allow users to create their own special toolbars to simplify projects.

URL

Uniform Resource Locator. The technical term for addresses on the Internet. Examples of URLs include e-mail addresses (billy@aol.com) and Web addresses (www.hungryminds.com). See also: *Internet, World Wide Web.*

USB

Universal Serial Bus. A type of port found on most modern PCs that connects to various peripheral devices. USB devices are easier to use than serial or parallel port devices. Common devices that connect to USB ports include digital cameras, printers, and portable MP3 players.

video card

A type of adapter that, when plugged into the correct expansion slot, enables a PC to produce video images. The PC's monitor is usually connected to the video card. See also: *AGP, expansion card.*

virus

A program that can replicate itself and secretly infect other files and programs on a PC. Viruses may be benign, or they could destroy files. Opening an infected file can infect a PC, so use an antivirus program to protect your PC.

Windows

A popular operating system developed by the Microsoft Corporation. Like the Macintosh operating system, Windows makes PCs easier to use because computer resources are represented graphically, allowing users to point and click options and simplifying the execution of tasks. See also: *PC, operating system, software.*

World Wide Web

A network of graphics and text pages on the Internet. Users can move from Web page to Web page by clicking hyperlinks. AOL gives you access to the World Wide Web. See also: *hyperlink, Internet.*

Zip disk

A popular type of removable disk developed by Iomega. Zip disks usually hold either 100MB or 250MB of data, and to use them, a PC must have a Zip drive installed. See also: *disk drive, removable disk, storage.*

Have you been having trouble getting signed on to AOL? This appendix can help you troubleshoot the most common causes of an AOL connection problem.

Check Your Phone Line

The most common cause of a disruption of service is a problem with the phone line. If your PC connects to AOL using a phone line, the first thing you should do is make sure the line has a dial tone. If there is a dial tone, try connecting again. If not, check the wire connecting your PC to your phone system and, if necessary, contact your phone company. Also, make sure that someone else in your household didn't pick up a receiver on the same phone line that your modem uses, which can disrupt your connection to AOL.

Also consider whether call waiting could have disrupted your connection. If the phone line has call waiting, the call-waiting tone may have disrupted your connection to AOL unless you temporarily disabled it when you connected to AOL. To prevent further interruption from callers when you're online, call your local phone company to find out what you can do to temporarily disable call waiting. The operator will tell you a code number. When you have the correct code number, follow these steps to have your call waiting temporarily disabled when you sign on to AOL:

If you connect to AOL using a
cable modem, make sure that
your cable service is functioning properly by checking
your TV.

If callers call when call waiting is disabled, they hear a
busy signal or are automatically connected with your
voice mail (if you have it).

1. On the AOL Sign On screen, click Setup and then click
   Expert Setup.
2. In the Connection Setup box that appears, click Expert
   Add and enter the appropriate code (provided by your
   phone company) to disable call waiting.
3. Click OK and Close to close the dialog boxes. From this
   point on, every time you sign on to AOL, your modem
   dials the code. When the modem hangs up (after you
   sign off), call waiting becomes operational again.

Check Your Modem

After you confirm that the phone line is ready and has a
proper dial tone, check the modem for your computer:

▶ Make sure the phone line is connected to the correct
  jack. Most modems have two phone jacks, labeled
  Phone and Telco. The line from the wall should be connected to the Telco jack.

▶ Restart Windows using the Start⇨Shutdown command.
  (Make sure you choose Restart in the dialog box that
  appears.) This action often fixes a stuck modem.

▶ Ensure that another program on your PC isn't using the
  modem. If you see an icon on the Windows system tray
  (that's the area in the lower right corner of your screen
  next to the clock) that looks like the one in Figure B-1,
  a program other than AOL is using your modem.
  Double-click the icon and choose Disconnect in the
  window that appears.

If you have an external modem, make sure its power
cord is plugged in and that
the modem's power switch is
turned on.

▶ Make sure your modem is installed properly. Click
  Setup in the AOL sign-on screen and choose Add
  Modem. Follow the instructions on the screen to re-
  detect your modem.

Connection icon

Figure B-1. If you see this icon in the system tray, a program other than AOL is using
your modem.

Check Your AOL Sign On Information

If you have confirmed that your phone line and modem are working properly but you still can't sign on to AOL, make sure that your computer is signing on to AOL correctly:

▶ Try picking a different access number. Click Setup in the AOL Sign On screen and then click Edit Numbers to modify your AOL access numbers.

▶ Make sure that your screen name and password are correct if you had to enter them.

If you have exhausted your options and still can't connect, try calling AOL technical support at 888-346-3704. Outside the USA and Canada call 703-264-1184 and for TTY service call 800-759-3323. If you have questions about your Mac, dial 888-265-8007.

Caution

Remember, when you select an AOL access number, choose one that will not cause you to incur long-distance phone charges.

Find It Online

To manage your AOL password, visit AOL Keyword: **Password**.

When you're new to a topic, it can be hard to know what your questions are until they arise. That's why I've assembled this Appendix, which you can use to answer hardware questions quickly — when you need to know the answers. I know from experience that questions come up at pivotal moments, such as when you're about to upgrade your PC with some new hardware, or when you're thinking about installing new software. How do I know if my computer has the kind of connector that is needed for a new external device I want to buy? How can I tell if I have an open expansion slot? Do I have enough free hard drive space? Is my computer fast enough?

Even if you plan to have a professional perform the upgrade, it's still a good idea to know what you can and can't add to your computer. This appendix helps you take inventory of your PC so that you can answer these questions.

Getting Information about Your System

Windows includes some useful tools to help you get information about your system. If you are ever asked what kind of CPU your PC has, how much RAM is installed, what kind of display adapter you have, or almost anything else about your PC, where do you look to find the answers?

One of the most useful tools found in Windows 98 and later versions is the System Information utility. You can launch it by

Tip

If you still use Windows 95, it's a good idea to upgrade to Windows Millennium Edition before you think about upgrading your hardware. Windows Me has built-in support for newer hardware.

choosing Start⇨Programs⇨Accessories⇨System Tools⇨System Information. Figure C-1 shows what system information looks like in Windows Me (Millennium Edition).

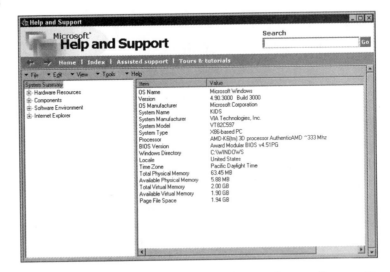

Figure C-1. The Windows System Information utility collects information about your PC.

Important information you can collect here includes:

▶ **Version:** You may be asked to provide the exact version number for Windows. Because new updates happen often, there may be slight differences between the version of Windows Me you bought at a retailer and the version your sister bought. The more accurate you can be about the revision number for your version of Windows, the better off you may be.

▶ **Processor:** You may be asked about the type and speed of the CPU in your system. Processor is just an abbreviated term for CPU.

▶ **Total Physical Memory:** If you're ever asked about your PC's *physical memory,* you may not realize that you're being asked how much RAM (*random access memory*) is installed in your PC. Many programs have a minimum RAM requirement.

The System Information utility offers information about most other components installed on your computer as well. Click the plus sign (+) next to Components and choose a category to get further information about a specific device.

Using the Windows Device Manager

Another way to get information about your PC is with the Device Manager. Every version of Microsoft Windows since Windows 95 has this tool, which is part of the System Properties dialog box. You can access the System Properties dialog box using one of two methods:

▶ Right-click on My Computer and choose Properties.

▶ Choose Start⇨Settings⇨Control Panel, and then open the System icon.

After the System Properties dialog box is open, click the Device Manager tab. A list of all the device categories is shown. Click a plus sign (+) next to any category to see a listing for a specific part of your computer. As you can see in Figure C-2, the Device Manager usually lists the brand name and model number for each device.

Tip

To get more information about a specific device, select it and click Properties.

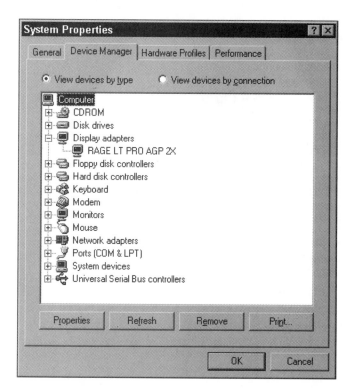

Figure C-2. The Device Manager helps you keep track of your PC's components.

Checking Available Hard Drive Space

Installing a new program on your PC requires that you have
some free space on your hard drive. Most programs list on the
packaging how much space is needed. To check for free space
on your computer, open My Computer, right-click on your
main hard drive (the C: drive), and choose Properties. A dialog
box similar to the one shown in Figure C-3 appears.

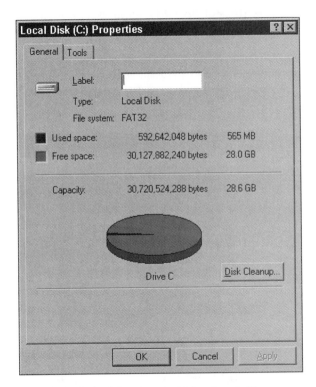

Figure C-3. This hard drive has 28.6GB (gigabytes) of free space—more than
enough for any program.

Review the amount of free space listed and click OK when
you are done. Remember, you should always maintain at least a
few hundred megabytes of free space on your C: drive. If your
C: drive becomes full, your system will run slowly and crash
often.

Performing Visual Inspections of Your PC

Although the utilities that come with Windows can tell you a lot about your computer, a visual inspection can only collect some information.

Identifying External Connection Types

Most components that you buy for your computer are designed to plug into an external connector. If you are buying a printer, digital camera, handheld PC, scanner, or any other peripheral, you should first ensure that you have a compatible connector available. Table C-1 lists the various types of external connectors you are likely to find on your PC.

Caution

Before you turn a single screw consult the warranty information for your PC to ensure that you aren't voiding the warranty.

Table C-1. PC Connectors

Illustration	Connector Name	Used For
	Parallel Port	Printer, scanner, external drive
	Serial Port	Mouse, external modem, digital camera
	Monitor Port	Monitor
	PS/2 Port	Mouse, keyboard
	USB Port	Digital camera, printer, keyboard, mouse, scanner, external drive

(continued)

Table C-1. *(continued)*

Illustration	Connector Name	Used For
	FireWire (IEEE 1394) Port	Digital camcorder, external drive
	Keyboard connector	Keyboard
	Phone line connector	Phone line for modem
	RJ-45 network connector	Network hub
	SCSI Port	External drive

Notice that some of these connectors, such as the phone line and RJ-45 connectors, look similar. Always use care when connecting a device and never force a stubborn connector. And as always, if you're not sure, consult a professional or get help from someone who has a lot of PC hardware experience.

Identifying Expansion Slots

Some PC upgrades must be installed inside your computer rather than attached to the outside. Many PC components, such as internal modems, FireWire controllers, and sound cards, come on printed circuit boards called *expansion cards*.

If you plan to upgrade your computer with an expansion card, you must first make sure that you have an open *slot* of the correct card type. Figure C-4 shows the three types of expansion slots you are likely to see in a modern PC.

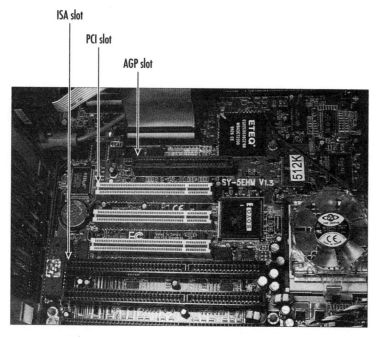

ISA slot

PCI slot

AGP slot

Figure C-4. These expansion slots are typical of those found in modern PCs.

Although ISA slots are still common, they are disappearing because they are associated with older devices. Most new expansion cards use PCI slots. AGP slots are only used for AGP video cards.

Index

L

Notes

Notes

Notes

Notes

Notes

Notes

Notes

Notes

Notes

Notes

Learn Microsoft Office Programs
The Easy, Interactive Way!

- *Work faster and more efficiently with expert tools at your command*
- *Save hundreds, even thousands of dollars by teaching yourself!*
- *Learn at your own pace*
- *Increase your job skills*

Word
Excel
Access
Outlook
Windows
PowerPoint

6 CD-Roms for one low price!

Six interactive training CD-ROMs covering each major module in the Microsoft Office 2000 suite. It's like having your own private tutor! LearnKey Experts are master trainers and know how to demonstrate and explain the many powerful features of this software. Our Experts will teach you the fundamentals you need to increase your productivity.

System Requirements
Windows 95, 98, 2000 or NT 4
66 Mhz Pentium Processor
5 MB hard drive space
8 MB RAM

Order Today!   1-888-299-0329

AOL's Office 2000 Training
$49.95 (s&h $5.95)   **#0019986N00012905**

Please allow 1-3 weeks for delivery. Prices and availability are subject to change without notice.

AMERICA
Online
So easy to use,
no wonder it's #1

Just Say It And Send It!

- **Send Instant Messages Faster!**

- **Write E-mails by Simply Using Your Voice**

- **Create Word Documents at the Speed of Your Voice**

Use your voice to type!

AOL's Point & Speak lets you talk naturally and as you talk, your words are transcribed like magic onto your computer screen. It's fast, easy and fun - not to mention a snap to learn! It can handle up to 160 words per minute with a 99% accuracy rate, and will learn your speaking style-including dialects and accents.

- Uses same technology as award winning Dragon NaturallySpeaking!
- Works with AOL and Windows applications!
- Contains 30,000-word active vocabulary and 230,000-word total vocabulary.
- Great for creating reports, letters, documents, school projects and more!
- Comes with high quality microphone!

System Requirements
Windows 95, 98, 2000 Millenium,or Windows NT 4.0 (with SP-6 or greater)
266 Mhz Processor
150 MB free drive space
64 MB RAM
CD-ROM installation
Speakers
Noise-canceling headset (included)

Order Today!   1-888-299-0329

$39.95 (s&h $5.95)   #0019987N00013013

Please allow 1-3 weeks for delivery. Prices and availability are subject to change without notice.

AMERICA
Online
So easy to use,
no wonder it's #1

The Fast, Easy Way to Share Your Photos Online!

America Online's

PhotoCam plus

LCD DIGITAL CAMERA

Download Your Pictures Directly To Your PC!

PhotoCam Plus is a high-quality yet affordable digital camera that allows you to create, edit, share and send photos to friends and family. It comes with an easy to follow manual and custom editing software. There's no film, no developing, and no waiting!

- Easy to follow step-by-step manual with a Quick Start section to help you get started fast.
- MGI's PhotoSuite III SE included. This powerful software packed with exciting features will help you enhance your photos as well as create fun projects.
- 8MB of of built-in memory enables you to store up to 128 photos.
- Automatic 3-way flash helps to produce clearer photos.

Order Today! 1-888-299-0329

$199.95 (s&h $8.95)   #0019988N00012828

Please allow 1-3 weeks for delivery. Prices and availability are subject to change without notice.

AMERICA
Online.

So easy to use,
no wonder it's #1

Smart Scanning Made Simple!

The Visioneer® OneTouch™ technology is changing the way people think about and use scanners, thanks to its revolutionary integration of hardware and software. An incredibly powerful way to scan – it's the faster, smarter, easier way to fax, copy, e-mail, or publish documents. With its dedicated function buttons and powerful software integration, it's the office tool you have been waiting for!

• **600 x 1200 dpi Color Scanner**

System Requirements
Pentium processor or equivalent
Windows 95/98 or NT 4.0
32MB RAM
70MB of available Hard Drive Space
CD-ROM drive (for installing software on your PC)
Color Monitor
Parallel or USB Port
Windows 98 required for USB

 Scan
Scan photos, business documents, articles, even 3-D objects directly into Visioneer's award-winning PaperPort software.

 Copy
Create clean, crisp digital copies by sending scans to your color or black-and-white printer.

 Fax
Transmit your scan directly to your fax software. Simply fill in the fax number on-screen and you are done!

 OCR
Scan text-based documents directly into your word processor with the touch of a button! OCR has never been easier.

 E-Mail
It takes 14 steps to scan and e-mail a photo with other scanners. The OneTouch 8600 does all 14 steps with a press of the e-mail button.

 Custom
Configure this button to send your scanned page to the application or device of your choice – a second printer, your favorite word processing software, or your image editing application.

 Stop/Cancel
Instantly cancel any scan in progress.

Welcome to AOL Press and Software - resources to help AOL members enjoy a fun, easy and rewarding online experience. AOL is committed to developing quality products that are easy to use and affordable - and serve every aspect of your online life. We hope you enjoy the AOL Press titles and we welcome your feedback at AOL Keyword: **Contact Shop Direct**

Sharing Your Photos Online Has Never Been Easier!

America Online's
Pictures Online

This easy to follow guide shows you how to get your pictures online and share them with family and friends. Loaded with expert advice on everything from taking better pictures to selecting the right hardware.

America Online's
Digital Imaging Made Easy™

- Learn about digital imaging in minutes with multimedia videos
- Receive, view and personalize your photos online with "You've Got Pictures"™
- Share your online pictures in email, web pages, photo albums and other online projects

Create Your Own Web Page In Just Minutes!

America Online's
Creating Cool® Web Pages

This easy-to-understand guide explains how to use the AOL Web design tools – and shows you step-by-step how to put together a great-looking page with all the bells and whistles. And, once your page is done, you'll get the scoop on setting up a Web address in *AOL Hometown* – and spreading the word about your page.

America Online's
Web Pages Made Easy™

- Complete package offers step-by-step instructions for preparing, designing, jazzing up and publishing your web site.
- Create and publish your own personal or small business web site in minutes.
- Learn the simple "secrets" of good web page design, and find out how easy it is to make your web page exciting and original.

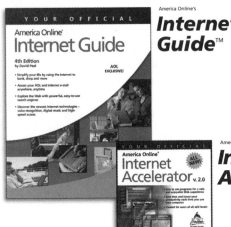

Home PC Upgrade Kit

Enhance your computing experience with the latest accessories from Logitech!

- **Upgraded Internet Keyboard** – with cool buttons to launch your favorite sites online and your desktop software with just a click of a button.

- **Internet/Multimedia S4 Speakers** – for getting the most out of your PC, games and listening to your favorite music.

- **Revolutionary Optical Wheel Mouse** – for scrolling through AOL, the Internet or your favorite software – saves time and work. It's optical too so you have a smother feel and better control.

System Requirements
Pentium PC
Win95/98
16MB RAM
80MB Hard Drive Space
CD-ROM
Sound Card
PS/2 Port

Order Today! **1-888-299-0329**

$69.95 (s&h $8.95)   **#0019991N00013295**

Please allow 1-3 weeks for delivery. Prices and availability are subject to change without notice.

AMERICA
Online®
So easy to use,
no wonder it's #1